The Secret Power of MUSIC

A study of the influence of music on man and society, from the time
of the ancient civilizations to the present.

The Secret Power of MUSIC

by

DAVID TAME

Destiny Books
Rochester, Vermont

Destiny Books
One Park Street
Rochester, VT 05767

U.K. edition published by Turnstone Press, Ltd.
Denington Estate, Wellingborough
Northamptonshire, NN8 2RQ England

LIBRARY OF CONGRESS CATALOGING IN PUBLICATION DATA

Tame, David.
    The secret power of music.

        Bibliography: p.
        1. Music-Philosophy and aesthetics.   2. Music and
        society.   I. Title.
ML3845.T28   1984   780'.1   83-24073
ISBN 0-89281-056-4

Printed and bound in the United States of America

Destiny Books is a division of Inner Traditions International, Ltd.

Distributed to the book trade in the United States by
Harper & Row Publishers, Inc.

Distributed to the book trade in Canada by
Book Center, Inc., Montreal, Quebec

to the seventh angel
to the two olive trees
and to all who will sing the new song

The good is one thing; the sensuously pleasant another. These two, differing in their ends, both prompt to action. Blessed are they that choose the good; they that choose the sensuously pleasant miss the goal.

Both the good and the pleasant present themselves to men. The wise, having examined both, distinguish the one from the other. The wise prefer the good to the pleasant; the foolish, driven by fleshly desires, prefer the pleasant to the good.

— *Katha Upanishad*

Contents

Grand Unified Field Theory of Physics — *the* ascent *of the Word;* Astrology as the Music of the Spheres — *the validity of astrology;* The Planets Suite — *Bode's Law* — *planetary conjunctions as chords;* Infrasonics, Ultrasonics and Acoustic Oddities — *the Northern Lights* — *the Big Hum;* Conclusion.

Acknowledgements

The author acknowledges with gratitude the permission of George Allen & Unwin (Publishers) Ltd to quote from *Twentieth Century Music* by Peter Yates; of the Aquarian Press to quote from *Music, Its Secret Influence Throughout the Ages* by Cyril Scott; of Macmillan Publishers Ltd to reproduce the two tables, 'The Eight Traditional Classes of Chinese Musical Instruments' and 'The Five Notes and Their Symbolic Correspondences' from the 1954 edition of *Grove's Dictionary of Music and Musicians*, edited by Eric Blom; and of Elizabeth Clare Prophet to use extracts from *The Chela and the Path* and *The Science of the Spoken Word*, both published by Summit University Press.

Also my deepest thanks to Fidelio for the many helpful suggestions and for the anchorage.

Overture:
Music and its Power

Our subject is not music as an abstract art, but music as a force which affects all who hear it. Music – not as entertainment only, but as a literal *power.*

Whenever we are within audible range of music, its influence is playing upon us constantly – speeding or slowing, regularizing or irregularizing our heartbeat; relaxing or jarring the nerves; affecting the blood pressure, the digestion and the rate of respiration. Its effect upon the emotions and desires of man is believed to be vast, and the extent of its influence over even the purely intellectual, mental processes is only just beginning to be suspected by researchers.

Moreover, to affect the character of the individual is to alter that basic atom or unit – the person – from which all of society is constructed. In other words, music may also play a far more important role in determining the character and direction of civilization than most people have until now been willing to believe. The powers of music are multi-faceted, sometimes uncannily potent, and by no means, as yet, entirely understood. They can be used or misused. We forsake the conscious, constructive use of these powers to our own loss. We ignore these powers at our peril.

Though little thought is given today as to the meaning or function of music within society, the civilizations of former times were usually very conscious of music's power. This was especially true of the pre-Christian era. In fact, the further back in time we look, the more people are found to have been aware of the inherent powers locked within the heart of all music and all sound.

It has been easy for modern man, born and raised within a society permeated with the philosophy of materialism and reductionism, to fall into the trap of regarding music to be a non-essential and even peripheral aspect of human life. And yet such a viewpoint would have been regarded by the philosophers of antiquity to be not only irrational, *but also, ultimately, suicidal.* For from ancient China to Egypt, from India to the golden age of Greece we find the same: the belief that there is something immensely fundamental about music; something which, they believed, gave it the power to sublimely evolve or to utterly degrade the individual psyche – and thereby to make or break entire civilizations.

Something immensely fundamental about music ...

It was exactly this that Pythagoras was driving at in his research through which he discovered that all of music could be reduced to numbers and mathematical ratios – and that the entire universe and all phenomena therein could also be explained in these same terms of the *same* particular numbers and mathematical ratios which were found in music.

Pythagoras' understanding of music was far more than a merely materialistic, academic one, and such an understanding is lamentably rare today. Yet we discover something of this timeless flame of ageless wisdom preserved in that small minority of musicians who still today have combined academic knowledge and the practical experience of music with a genuine and earnest inner spiritual development.

Few would disagree that such a person is the much-beloved musical personality, Yehudi Menuhin. And we find a deep and truly Pythagorean flash of insight in the opening sentences of his book, *Theme and Variations.*[1] Here, this great contemporary violinist has expressed the inner meaning of the tonal arts in terms so pointedly true, and yet so all-embracing in their truth, that they are food for a great deal of careful thought:

> Music creates order out of chaos; for rhythm imposes unanimity upon the divergent, melody imposes continuity upon the disjointed, and harmony imposes compatibility upon the incongruous.
>
> Thus a confusion surrenders to order and noise to music, and as we through music attain that greater universal order which rests upon fundamental relationships of geometrical and mathematical proportion, direction is supplied to mere repetitious time, power to the multiplication of elements, and purpose to random association.

We could stop right there. We almost need to go no further. These words of Yehudi Menuhin render a core explanation of the entire ancient-world conception of the power of music; of why and how the ancients believed that music could affect man and civilization. The ancients were convinced that music could become internalized by the individual; the music influencing, as it were, the rhythm of man's thoughts, the melody of man's emotions, and the harmony of his bodily health and manner of movement. In all these ways, music was thought to determine the manner of our thoughts and actions.

As in music, so in life – this one timeless axiom contains the central concept upon which entire civilizations once founded almost every aspect of their society. And upon this same seed concept generations of kings, priests and philosophers based the whole work of the long span of their lives.

As in music, so in life.

An axiom which declares that consciousness and all of civilization is shaped and moulded according to the existing style or styles of music. A shattering concept indeed! When one ponders upon its implications: that music magnetizes society into conformity with itself ...

Could it actually be true that music tends to mould us, in our thoughts and our behaviour patterns, into conformity with its own innate patterns of rhythm, melody, morality and mood? Immediately, one's mind turns towards specific examples: styles of music of which we know, and the society or sub-culture which is to be found around them. What of the music of today? The society of today? Clearly the above axiom, should it prove to be valid, is one fraught with significance for modern civilization.

MUSIC AS A MOULD FOR SOCIETY

Whenever, at any time during the course of his life, modern man has listened to music, has he *really* known the meaning and the implications of what he was doing? Certainly not according to the ancient philosophers. We may take ancient China for example:

Each year, in the second month, Emperor Shun could be found journeying eastward in order to check upon his kingdom, and to ensure that everything was in order throughout the vast land. Yet he did not do so by auditing the account books of the different regions. Neither by observing the state of life of the populace, or by receiving petitions from them. Nor by interviewing the regional officials in authority. No, by none of these methods. For in ancient China there was considered to be a much more revealing, accurate and scientific method of checking on the state of the nation. According to the ancient Chinese text, *Shu King,* the Emperor Shun went about through the different territories and ...*tested the exact pitches of their notes of music.*

Back in his palace, if the Emperor wished to monitor the efficiency of his central government, what did he do? Get expert advice on policy making? Review the economy, or the state of popular opinion?

The Emperor was not ignorant of any of the above methods, and at times may have taken recourse to all of them. But most important of all, he believed, was to listen to, and check, the five notes of the ancient Chinese musical scale. He had the eight kinds of Chinese musical instruments brought before him and played by musicians. Then he listened to the local folk songs, and also to the tunes which were sung in the court itself, checking that all this music was in perfect correspondence with the five tones.

Primitive superstition? Certainly Emperor Shun did not believe so. According to the philosophy of the ancient Chinese, music was the basis of *everything*. In particular they believed that all civilizations are shaped and moulded according to the kind of music performed within them. Was a civilization's music wistful, romantic? Then the people themselves would be romantic. Was it strong and military? Then the nation's neighbours had better beware. Furthermore, a civilization remained stable and unchanged as long as its music remain unchanged. But to change the style of music which people listened to would inevitably lead to a change in the very way of life itself.

If Emperor Shun, on his travels about the kingdom, had discovered that the instruments of the different territories were all differently tuned from each other, then he would have considered it a foregone conclusion that the territories themselves would begin to (if they did not already) differ from each other. They might even lose their unity and begin to squabble among themselves unless the tuning was at once corrected and made uniform from one place to another. And if the music he heard performed in the villages had begun to become vulgar and immoral, then the Emperor would have expected immorality itself to sweep the nation unless something was done to correct the music.

A graphic account has come down to us from the time of Confucius which shows the very real and practical importance the wise men of China placed upon music. A gift of female musicians was sent by the people of Ts'e to the kingdom of Loo. Confucius himself protested to Ke Huan, the ruler of Loo, that these foreign musicians should not be received, lest their alien, and possibly sensual, music influenced the native musicians of the kingdom. Confucius believed that if the music of the kingdom was altered, then the society itself would alter, and probably not for the better. Unfortunately we do not know today entirely how the episode ended, and what effect the foreign music did have on the kingdom. But what we do know is that despite the protestations of the legendary moral philosopher, Ke Huan did receive the females, and no court was held for three days while the Emperor and his government availed themselves of the sight and sound of the exotic foreign performers. So much for the government's sense of responsibility to the kingdom! But Confucius? The famous philosopher was absolutely uncompromising on the issue. The same level of importance which politicians today would attach to *military* or *economic* matters, Confucius attached to the issue of the kingdom's *music*. He was certain and firm in his moral convictions, and was prepared to back them up to the hilt. Refusing to listen to the music, he stormed out of the court in protest. He had heard the alien music, and he had seen the writing on the wall. He *knew*.

And just what was it that he knew? Along with all of the other great philosophers of his land, Confucius believed there to be a hidden significance to music which made it one of the most important things in life, possessing potentially tremendous power for good or evil. And we discover the same basic beliefs regarding music in virtually every advanced civilization of antiquity. It was the same in Mesopotamia. The same again in cultures as far apart as India and Greece. These various peoples of the past were in agreement in their viewpoints upon music to a most striking degree. Music was not conceived by any of them, as it is conceived today, as being merely an intangible art form of little practical significance.

Rather, they affirmed music to be a tangible *force* which could be applied in order to create change, for better or worse, within the character of individual man; and, what was more important, within society as a whole. In fact, though today we still can hear people speaking of the 'magic of music', the ancients used the phrase far more literally, for music was even believed by them to be capable of effecting change upon matter itself.

SOUND, MUSIC AND THE WISDOM OF THE ANCIENTS

A famous example of tonal magic is the story of Joshua's destruction of the walls of Jericho. According to the biblical account,[2] Jericho, a city rampant with evil, had closed its gates and prepared to withstand the seige of righteous Joshua and his forces. But when Joshua had arrived near to the city he met a strange man, who called himself the captain of the hosts of the Lord, and who told Joshua how to destroy the mighty walls of Jericho through the use of sound produced in sequences of seven. Following the instructions, Joshua's legions marched around the city, headed by seven priests blowing seven trumpets of rams' horns. The rest of his men Joshua commanded to remain absolutely silent, uttering not a word. Once, they went around the city. And again on the next day. And the same for a total of seven days. But on the seventh day they circled the city seven times, and on this occasion Joshua told his people to shout along with the sound of the trumpets. This they did – and the walls of Jericho, according to the account, fell down flat, the city then being stormed and taken.

Of course, as our modern materially-minded friends can tell us, the story must be only superstition; a mere legend.

— Except that the ruins of ancient Jericho have been unearthed, and it has been found that the walls apparently did at some stage collapse, falling *outward.*

But still, the modern scholar tells us, there must obviously be some perfectly natural explanation.

— Yes, we reply, a *natural* explanation. Certainly it must have been *natural.* And yet – in order to fully understand the account, perhaps we need to wait a little longer, for science to progress a little further in the field of acoustics ....

While the people of ancient times certainly did believe that sound was capable of such spectacular feats, they were nevertheless equally concerned with the more usual effects of sound and music – upon the human psyche and upon society. If a civilization's music was in the hands of the evil or ignorant, the ancients believed, it could lead the civilization only to an inevitable doom. But in the hands of the illumined, music was a tool of beauty and power which could lead the way for an entire race into a golden age of peace, prosperity and brotherhood.

To the major civilizations of antiquity, intelligently-organized sound constituted the highest of all the arts. And more, for they also believed music – the intelligent production of sound through musical instruments and the vocal cords – to be the most important of the sciences, the most powerful path of religious enlightenment, and the very basis of stable, harmonious government. More than anything else, however, the great thinkers of antiquity emphasized the powerful effect of music upon the character of man. Since music seemed to hold such sway in determining the morality of people, it was a subject which none of the great moral philosophers could ignore. Aristotle, for one, wrote that:

> ... emotions of any kind are produced by melody and rhythm; therefore by music a man becomes accustomed to feeling the right emotions; music has thus power to form character, and the various kinds of music based on the various modes, may be distinguished by their effects on character – one, for example, working in the direction of melancholy, another of effeminacy; one encouraging abandonment, another self-control, another enthusiasm, and so on through the series.[3]

Both Plato and Aristotle discuss the moral effects of music in several of their major works.

Music and morality. Is there a connection in reality? Certainly the idea that music exerts an influence – and a powerful one – over the character of man persisted on a widespread scale beyond the time of Christ, through the Middle Ages and the Renaissance, and into the last century. The concept that music affects character was the one great inspiring force behind the creative lives of the great classical and romantic composers. It is clear from what we know of their characters that each of them, motivated by an earnest desire to serve and spiritualize humanity, saw their music as one of the most powerful means possible of influencing the consciousness and direction of the human race. Wars and politicians come and go, but music abides indefinitely, never failing to affect the minds and hearts of all who hear it.

As Andrew Fletcher, the writer and orator, stated in the Scottish Parliament of 1704: 'I knew a very wise man who believed that if a man were permitted to make all the ballads, he need not care who should make the laws of a nation'.

It can easily be seen, then, that the subject of music and its possible psychological and societary influences is anything but an abstract, theoretical one. If music can be used to exert powerful influences of either a negative or a beneficial nature over us, then we had better know about it! What damage might certain kinds of music have already imposed upon our personalities without our realizing it? What opportunities might there be for us to take the correct kind of music and use it from now onwards in order to accelerate our own mental and spiritual evolution? Clearly, these questions are of importance to each and every one of us. Virtually everybody listens to music in one form or another. When we speak of 'man' or of 'the listener' in the pages ahead – that also means you and me! Few could claim to be free from any possible influence which music may exert, directly or indirectly.

... Perhaps *none* could, if we are to accept the ancients' viewpoint. For in addition to music's more direct effects upon man – the psychological effects of its audible melodies and rhythms – there was also to be taken into account music's second, yet more extensive and more potent, power. A mystic power this, a force inaudible and invisible, and a force only understandable in terms of the ancient philosophy and its distinctly non-materialist basis.

THE HIDDEN SIDE OF MUSIC

One evening in London I attended a concert of Bach's Brandenburg Concertos. Seating myself, I exchanged some words with my companion, and took pleasure in glancing around at the marvellous Royal Festival Hall as it began to fill up. It was only as the players came out and took their bow, and as they tuned up, that I dimly began to feel it. *Something very different and unique* was lurking about. It could not be seen or heard, but I could feel its presence, and it seemed to be approaching!

And then, as the players prepared to begin and as the audience hushed, this unknown *something* saturated the air with a crackling, pregnant potential of which none other seemed to be aware.

Then, *literally from the first note,* the timeless moment was upon me. Yet I was already far beyond the ability to reflect consciously upon it, for the experience was totally engulfing and all-encompassing. It left no scope whatever for any other mental activity other than to *be* the perceptions to which my mind now seemed to have been opened.

My body seemed to come alive with light; my heart was a fire which flared forth to consume the dross of my soul. My perceptions were opened as though they had always before been firmly closed. Never had I heard music in that way! What previously I had often listened to as abstract sounds were now *Sound* – a tangible, living filigree lattice-work of mathematical precision which I could almost reach out and touch, and which I could virtually see as it flowed from the leading violin. Every note hung suspended in the air, timeless and immaculate beyond all powers of verbal description. My body froze into a coma-like rigidity as I hung my consciousness upon each next chord. For several long minutes I lost all awareness of myself. The sheer beauty of it all was quite indescribable. From the first bar, silent tears ran from my staring, unblinking eyes.

The Fifth Brandenburg Concerto had opened the evening, and

just as the sublime vision seemed about to wane, there began the concerto's unique harpsichord solo. Again I was whisked quite beyond myself, and saw the music in a way never perceived before. The long, fugal arpeggios trilled through the air like visible, emanating waves of divine essence, one behind the other, filling all the hall and passing beyond its walls into the city. I cannot say that I *saw* the music-waves, for the process did not involve my eyes; yet nevertheless I somehow *did* see them. *I saw the music!*

As the other instruments came in once more with indescribable loveliness, this impression of emanating waves of a tangible *goodness* became reinforced still further. It felt as though the music possessed a definite and very real *energy,* and that this was radiating out beyond the hall in all directions. My consciousness seemed to encompass the entire city. For a few moments I felt as though I were looking down from a viewpoint which revealed to me the entire urban spread; and not only the visible, physical city, but also the underlying, causative forces which shaped and moulded it. The understanding came that this music, as it radiated forth, was somehow acting as a sustaining, invigorating force for the whole surrounding area.

As the awareness of my body returned, sitting in its seat in the Royal Festival Hall, the impression was left with me that the concert was in some way a glowing light amid a great, chaotic sea of darkness. The darkness threatened to encroach upon the flame and extinguish it forever. I shall never forget this sensation: one not of fear, but of the deepest, gravest concern; of the vast importance of the music which I was hearing, of the deepest gratitude for the opportunity of experiencing it, and that it should at all costs be preserved for the humanity of the future.

Mystical experiences have been a subject of debate for centuries among philosophers. Up to the present day no general consensus of opinion has been arrived at as to the reality of such experiences. Are they less real, equally real, or more real than our usual experience of everyday life? Each must judge for himself. But it is interesting that visionary and mystical experiences are known to have provided the initial inspiration behind many of the world's greatest inventions and scientific breakthroughs; even those of such giants of the mind as Albert Einstein and Nikola Tesla.

It can be noticed from others' accounts of such experiences that unless we are of the stature of a Ramakrishna or a St John of the Cross, they can come upon one when one least expects it — and then they are gone, seemingly impossible to recapture or call back. Fickle and fey, as though they have minds of their own; for our own imperfections do not enable us to embody such experiences on a permanent basis. Or as the mystic would word it: it is the vision of transcendent reality which is permanent and eternal, and we who insist upon being fickle and fey in our relationship to the Supreme.

Christians may be correct in speaking of divine grace. Those who are searching for truth seem frequently to be granted a kind of spiritual 'honeymoon' period. All kinds of experiences and revelations come to them in the early days of their quest, and at the time it is as though All Truth were already theirs. But then the honeymoon is over, and one comes to realize that one has been granted a vision of the goal, as though as a goad to move towards it. For a few months or a year the veil was drawn back for one, but only as a temporary act of grace, bestowed by destiny. And now it is one's duty to reclaim that vision and that knowledge through one's own unaided effort. Truth has temporarily been brought to us, but only in order that we might then be encouraged to find our own way along the long and difficult path to its permanent abode.

In retrospect, I now see that my experience of that evening was one of the key starting points which eventually led to the development of this book. Only later did I discover how closely the occurrence of that evening tied in to the ancients' conception of music and its innate power.

PRIMAL VIBRATION

In ancient times sound itself, the very basis of all music, was thought to be intimately related in some way to non-physical and sacred dimensions or planes of existence. Why was this? Because audible sound was considered to be but an earthly reflection of a vibratory activity taking place beyond the physical world. This vibration was more fundamental, and nearer to the heart of the meaning of things, than any audible sound. Inaudible to human ear, this Cosmic Vibration was the origin and basis of all the matter and energy in the universe.

In its purest, least differentiated form, this Cosmic Sound was known to the Hindus as OM. Yet just as pure white light differentiates into the colours of the rainbow, so this Primal Vibration was believed to differentiate into a number of more greatly defined superphysical vibrations. These different frequencies or Cosmic Tones were thought to be present in differing combinations throughout the universe. Not only were they present within all substances and forms, in differing vibratory combinations, but they *were* the substances and forms. According to the combination of Cosmic Tones present within any given area of space, so was the nature of the substance within that space determined.

And thus we find ourselves throwing light upon the widely-held belief that all matter is composed of one basic substance or energy. According to the great thinkers of old, this energy was Vibration. In modern times, the physical sciences are now arriving back at this original point of departure. Once again, science is beginning to suspect that matter is all composed of one fundamental something, and that the frequencies or rhythms of this something determine the specific nature of each object and atom.

The universal vibratory energies were called by the ancient Egyptians the Word or Words of their gods; to the Pythagoreans of Greece they were the Music of the Spheres; and the ancient Chinese knew them to be the celestial energies of perfect harmony. The Cosmic Tones, as differentiations of the OM, were the most powerful force in the universe according to the ancients, for these Tones *were* the universe – the very source of the Creation itself.

And herein lay the vast significance of all audible, earthly sounds, such as are produced by the performing of music or the uttering of speech. For audible sound was believed to be a 'reflection', within the world of matter, of the Cosmic Tones. Audible sound itself, which is taken so much for granted today, was in those days thought to contain within itself something of the enormous Creative, Preservative and Destructive force of the Cosmic Tones themselves. The very phenomenon of sound was regarded with great reverence. He who knew how to could release sacred energies through the use of audible sound, and thereby wield a mighty power. And, in fact, specific knowledge was not necessarily required, for something of the mighty energies of the Primal Vibration was believed to be released whenever and wherever audible sound was produced. According to the nature of the audible sound, so would its hidden effect be determined.

Hence, the role of music within civilization could not have been considered more vitally important. In the long run, the power of sound as a force which could be used for good or evil was considered to be unsurpassed. And as a specific and concentrated form of sound production, music was of ultimate importance, deriving its energy from Above for the working of change in the world below.

As Julius Portnoy, the musicologist, puts it, the common belief throughout the world in many past epochs of history was, 'that wherever gods reign, be them one or many, the physical character of music is indeed based on mechanics and explained by mathematics, but its origin is in the heavens'.[4] The remarkable fact is that almost everywhere we look throughout the ancient world (and even in some parts of the earth today) we discover this same conception: *that music is a releaser into the material world of a fundamental, superphysical energy from beyond the world of everyday experience.* In the spoken or intoned rituals of many of the world's religions there is again a similar concept: *that the voice of the priest within the realm of time and space becomes a vehicle for the energizing Voice of the Creator to manifest its forces through.*

The role of music and the role of religious intonation and liturgy was to release into the earth a form of cosmic energy which could keep civilization in harmony with the heavens. Without such activities, it was thought, all could lose its alignment with the harmony of the universe, with catastrophic consequences. Sacred sound was even thought capable of preventing natural cataclysms such as earthquakes; while on the other hand, the evil or ignorant use of sound was believed to contribute strongly *towards* such cataclysms. In its good and beneficial use, however, music was held to possess a mediating role between heaven and earth – being a 'communications channel' from man to God, from God to man, and a key for the releasing of the energies of the Supreme into the earth-plane.

MUSIC AND THE TWENTIETH CENTURY

Over the passing of the centuries the details of the ancient mysticism of music were lost or forgotten. The belief that music played a role in determining man's moral nature took on a more earth-bound rationale. But nonetheless, the basic concept, *as in music, so in life,* prevailed in one form or another even up until a hundred years ago. Only during our present century has the belief in music as a force capable of changing individual and society become almost totally forsaken and lost. This means that in the comparative lack of importance which twentieth-century man attaches to music, our civilization stands virtually alone. Whether or not this is the result of modern man's greater wisdom and progress, or whether it is the result of an over-materialistic world-view and a peculiar ignorance, remains an open question.

Not quite all men of modern times have ignored the possible relationships between music and civilization, however. I quote, for example, from the writings of Cyril Scott, himself an eminent twentieth-century composer of the impressionistic school. In a book based upon this very thesis, that music shapes consciousness and society, Scott expressed his belief that:

> ... wherever the greatest variety of musical styles has obtained, there the adherence to tradition and custom has been proportionately less marked; and where musical styles are limited, as for instance, in China, adherence to – nay, even worship of – tradition obtains to a marked degree. We are fully aware that in stating this we would seem to be lending weight to the prevalent notion that styles of music are merely the outcome and expression of civilizations and national feelings – that is to say that the civilization comes first, and its characteristic species of music afterwards. But an examination of history proves the truth to be exactly the reverse: an innovation in musical style has invariably been followed by an innovation in politics and morals. And, what is more ... the decline of music in [Egypt and Greece] was followed by the complete decline of the Egyptian and Grecian civilizations themselves.[5]

Again, one cannot help but note the possibly vital importance of this entire subject. When Cyril Scott writes, 'an innovation in musical style has invariably been followed by an innovation in politics and morals', one thinks immediately of the vast waves of moral and political change which have swept the Western world since the early 1960s. It seems virtually indisputable that these waves of change began with the appearance on the scene of a new sub-culture and lifestyle among the young – which was definitely inspired by and based upon the new forms of popular music which came forth at that time. And in this modern instance of the relationship between music and civilization it is difficult to disagree with Scott in that the music did come first, and the cultural changes afterwards; not vice-versa.

Can we, then, agree that music wields a force which affects the world around; a force with both a physical (audible) and a mystical aspect?

Certainly music is very much physical, and not at all abstract or insubstantial. The air vibrations of its sound are not only real and measurable, but capable of shattering glass. Music and other forms of sound can cause all kinds of sympathetic vibratory resonances within objects at a distance. Contemporary research into sounds of a lower frequency than is audible to the human ear suggests that certain instances of nausea or of headaches may be caused by such sounds being emitted from items of machinery at a distance. Similar effects upon human beings and animals appear to be caused by the subsonic vibrations which precede earthquakes, coming even many hours before the 'quake itself. Rhythm too can be all too real a force. Military experience has taught from centuries past that when troops marching in unison need to cross a bridge, the commanding officer should give the order for them to break step, for the effect of the marching " ri', lef', ri', lef' " rhythm has more than once led to the collapse of such constructions (and casualties even before the enemy are engaged!).

And does music emanate other, superphysical, powers? This is one of the prime questions which we must attempt to answer. Though modern opinion would answer with an unhesitating 'no', we would be unwise to accept this answer before examining the validity of the modern viewpoint itself. In this respect, it is possible to point to an enormous (and potentially dangerous) paradox: that despite the general lack of concern about the real nature and effect of music, this latter half of the twentieth century has witnessed a huge explosion and proliferation in the availability and variety of tonal art. There are vastly more musical styles for the listener to choose from today than at any other time in history. Recordings, and even live performances, are available of types of music as wide-ranging as that of Mozart and of the *gamelan* of Bali; as that of the electronic experimentalists and of Frank Sinatra; the Indian *raga* and punk rock.

Musically, then, the twentieth century is notable for its stagger-ing variety of available sounds. But more: an equally unique twentieth-century development is the ease with which the sounds of music can now be acquired. Let us not forget: a century ago it was only possible to experience a Beethoven symphony when dozens of trained musicians were gathered together to rehearse and perform it live. A constraint we can hardly conceive of today, when that same concert can be heard from cassette or radio, even if we choose to find ourselves on a trans-globe expedition across the poles. Practically the same aural experience as a live concert is now avail-able at the flick of a switch. True, somehow nothing will ever quite replace the live performance, but hi-fi and Dolby video-cassettes can come very close. And today, should we choose to listen to Beethoven's Ninth, we can pick between conductor X's 1978 performance or conductor Y's classic 1954 recording. We can even keep it repeating in the background as we go about our daily work

— a notion quite alien (and which would possibly have seemed not a little distasteful) to the audiences of the nineteenth century.

Yes — that amazing paradox! Never was music so easily available, so diverse, so continuously pumped through the city streets and across the airwaves — yet never has theorization or real, practical knowledge regarding music's nature and its effects been at a lower ebb. Acoustical researchers pride themselves, it is true, in showing off their graphs and sine-wave displays, but these tell us no more about the real nature of music than a man's age and personal details tell us about his character and outlook on life. Is it not time to at least stop and collect our thoughts for a moment? But no, there is no time! Let those who wish to theorize do so — we are too busy: there is so much *music* to listen to! A few seconds spent tuning a radio brings to our ears the music of many different nations and cultures (the radio itself being bought at a price which even a schoolchild can afford). Then, incidental music plays almost continuously in the background during a good proportion of cinematic and television productions. During television advertisements the sound-track is utilized with microscopic care and intensity in order to extract every last penny-worth of effect out of the few seconds of time paid to the television company by the advertiser.

In fact, the average Western man often 'hears' (if the word can be used) more music during the watching of television than he hears performed on its own and for its own sake. We seldom realize just to what extent music has become a part of our lives. Surveys have shown that the average American teenager listens to no less than three or four hours of rock music each day. There are few in the modern world who do not hear a number of hours of music each day. Most of it is not truly 'heard' at all; yet even background music to which our conscious minds are oblivious affects our heart-rate and emotions just the same. (A chilling thought: an entire two-hour feature film, using incidental music extensively throughout, can pass without our consciously noting the presence of a single note. And as it happens, the screen's background music is almost always of a basically jazz nature.)

For sure, we can only conclude that music is a most important sociological phenomenon. But again, we must ask ourselves: precisely, and scientifically, what *is* music? What is it, apart from a collection of organized sounds? That is, what is its function in society? What *is* its effect upon the mind and character of man? Does anybody know?

In search of answers, we peruse the literature of our modern world. And we discover that there have been twentieth-century investigations into the nature and effect of music. The problem has been approached from several different viewpoints – philosophical, sociological, psychological and acoustical/physical. However, these studies have been surprisingly limited in number. And even more surprising is how narrow in scope they have been. Moreover, whatever limited answers they have come up with can hardly be said to be known to the average performer of music or his audience, but have been contained within a narrow circle of specialized academics. Altogether, modern knowledge or theory about the nature of music is not very inspired or illumining. In short, it would be nearer to the truth to say that any thought or significant investigation into the nature and effect of music is, in modern times, conspicuous by its absence.

MUSIC AND MATERIALISM

If there be *any* modern conception of the nature of music, what can we say to describe it? Only that the tonal arts are thought to be based upon the intelligent generation of air vibrations, these air vibrations somehow serving to communicate various subjective moods or experiences. *But, if we look deeper, we realize that a society's very conception of the nature of music is itself conditioned by the entire general philosophical viewpoint upon which that society is based.* This is most important, for it calls into question from the outset the twentieth-century conception of what music is and what it does.

The modern notion (or lack of a notion) of the phenomenon of music is, in short, the inevitable result of the current materialist-reductionist world-view. In this world-view, music is inevitably described in terms of its most tangible, measurable aspect: that it consists of air vibrations. Also, according to this world-view, human beings themselves – the very performers of, and listeners to, music – are merely biological machines, evolved by luck, possessing no ultimate purpose for existence, and whose thoughts and emotions are nothing but biochemical processes automatically produced as conditioned reflexes to the world around them. To the materialist it naturally follows, therefore, that people only perform or listen to music in the first place because past experiences have 'programmed' them to do so. At his most charitable the materialist might grudgingly concede that these past experiences consisted of 'pleasure-feelings'; that the first movement of Beethoven's Ninth Symphony, in hitting this and that vibrational frequency, somehow releases certain stimulative chemicals into the listener's biomechanical brain. Putting it this bluntly, the materialist philosophy of music seems hardly sufficient. Yet the fact remains that the majority of contemporary musicians themselves do, ultimately, conceive of music in this way – as 'sound' (whatever *that* is ...) which entertains and gives pleasure to the brain of *Homo sapiens.*

The result of this materialist viewpoint upon the music of today? A multitude of musical forms – but virtually all of them the music of, at best, materialistic humanism. A century in which, to a large degree, music has lost its way (for what direction can there possibly be to take when nothing in the universe possesses any ultimate meaning or purpose in any case?).

And yet ....

For perhaps two decades now there has occurred the beginning of a new awareness abroad in the world. Not only in music, but in many areas of life, among a certain minority of people there is to be found a resurgence of committed interest in matters of the spirit. Young and not so young people are frequently to be found rejecting the materialist world-view outright. They seek instead to embrace a mystical outlook, and tend to do so with unswerving dedication. Some speak of the new age of Aquarius, in which, it is said, religion will become more scientific in the best sense, and science more religious. Whatever its cause, that there is a new movement among some towards altruism, hope, brotherhood and an interest in self-evolution is unmistakable.

Yet what I believe will become clear in the pages ahead is that, for all our rejection of the philosophy of materialism, we have nevertheless failed to reject *the music* of materialism. Almost every form of twentieth-century music is utterly devoid of genuine regenerative spiritual value. The ancients may well have been correct in the belief that music patterns affect life patterns; and if so, then for a grass-roots movement back towards spirituality to allow itself to continue to be subjected to the music of individuals who are of an entirely different frame of mind makes no logical sense. The minds of these performers are gross and coarse. To follow them, whilst aspiring upward, makes no more sense than to attempt to climb a mountain by rolling downhill.

The non-materialist world-view demands a non-materialist philosophy of music. And from such a philosophy, in its own good time, there will be born inevitably a new music of the spirit.

The alternative is too horrible to contemplate. From down the decades there comes a warning to us on the dangers of wrong types of music – from none other than Henry David Thoreau, who wrote from his log cabin:

> Even music can be intoxicating. Such apparently slight causes destroyed Greece and Rome, and will destroy England and America.

The modern man's reaction to Thoreau's warning is likely to be one of, 'Oh, but that's taking it a bit too far, isn't it?' *Yet it is precisely, absolutely at this point that twentieth-century man departs from the viewpoint held by virtually every thinking person from ancient times right up to the nineteenth century. . .*

Possibly the greatest weakness of the modern materialistic outlook upon the world is its inability to perceive the causes behind effects. If anywhere, it is here that the philosophers of ancient China, India, Egypt and Greece deserve our fullest respect, since it could be said that they *specialized* in seeing to the cause and core of things. And they most certainly would have agreed with Thoreau, that music can destroy civilization. They explained in some detail what kind of music should prevail in order to maintain the stability and welfare of the state, as well as the happiness, prosperity and spiritual advancement of each citizen. Further, they warned in similar detail what kind of music should be rigorously avoided because of its destructive, degenerative effects upon man and nation.

Because of the importance of what the ancients have to tell us, two chapters of this book are devoted fully to the subject. These are the two chapters which are classified, or sub-titled, as chapters upon 'The Ancient Wisdom'. Of the two, Chapter 1 deals with the music and the philosophy of music of ancient China, and Chapter 4 with the music of India and its mystical basis. Following each of these chapters there is placed, for contrast, a chapter on the music of our own era. Chapter 2 investigates the serious music of the twentieth-century – the 'new music' as it is often called; and Chapter 5 reveals the origin and possible effects of jazz. In addition, the book also includes two chapters which are classified or sub-titled as 'Assessment' chapters. Each attempts to assess the validity or invalidity of the notion of the power of music. *Does* music possess a power or powers which can produce objective effects in the world around? What evidence is there for this belief of the sages and philosophers of old? The distinction between the two chapters is as follows: Chapter 3, 'Music, Man and Society', assesses what evidence there is in support of music's claimed influence upon animate matter, and in particular upon man himself. Chapter 6, 'The Physics of the

OM', analyses what evidence there is in support of the idea that music exerts an influence, not only upon life, but even upon inanimate matter. Can all things be destroyed, changed, created or re-created by the power of sound?

The above, then, is a general outline of this book; and we begin with the teachings of the sages of old. It is not that it is necessary for us to accept absolutely every single notion of the ancients on the subject of music as objective fact; to keep an open mind will suffice. But in approaching the subject of the tonal mysticism of ancient times we must also do so in humility. After all, can we *possibly* afford to be haughty towards the great spiritual musicians of the past, living as we do in an age which has virtually no philosophy of music of its own; and an age which has allowed its own music to degenerate to the point of finding acceptable that which it has, including lyrics such as:

> Right now!
> Ahhhhhh!
> I am an anti-Christ
> I know what I want
> And I know how to get it
> I wanna destroy passers by
> For I wanna be – anarchy
>
> 'Anarchy in the UK' – Sex Pistols

The ancients, then, may yet have a thing or two to teach us. And since we have already dipped into the subject of the music of China, let it be to China that we first return. . .

1.
The Ancient Wisdom:
Music in China

Almost three thousand years before the birth of Christ, at a time when the music of European man may have amounted to no more than the beating of bones upon hollow logs, the people of China were already in possession of the most complex and fascinating philosophy of music of which we know today. Whence came this involved system of musical mysticism, or how it was developed, is a mystery. We can but say that the tradition of Chinese classical music is so ancient that its origins are described today only in legend, being lost beyond the mists which govern the extent of the modern historian's gaze.

MUSIC AND MORALITY
In the case of China the rule holds true that the further we go back in history, the more sacred and vital a significance we find to have been attached to the phenomenon of sound itself. In the viewpoint of the ancient Chinese, the notes of all music contained an essence of transcendent power. A piece of music was an energy-formula. Each different piece of music qualified the sacred power of sound in different ways. Each composition exerted specific influences over man, civilization and the world. The particular mystical influences of a piece of music depended upon such factors as its rhythm, its melodic patterns, and the combination of instruments used. Like other forces of nature, music itself, as a phenomenon, was not biased towards producing either beneficial or destructive effects. The Chinese understood the power within music to be a free energy, which man could use or misuse according to his own free will.

Above all it was this fact which motivated the Chinese philosophers to direct much of their attention upon the music of their nation. For if all citizens were to be free from the dangers of the misuse of music and its power, and if all were to benefit from its optimally beneficient use, then it had to be ensured that only the correct music was played. The object of music, they believed, should never be merely to entertain; the dark side of man's nature could, after all, be as readily entertained by wrong and immoral music as by correct music. Consequently, all music should convey eternal truths, and should influence man's character for the better. Indeed, the very word for music in China (*Yüo*) is represented by the same graphic symbol as that for serenity (*lo*).[6] The writings of ancient China which have survived through to our own day leave us in no doubt that music was considered to be able to direct and influence the emotional nature of man. But the powers of music were thought to extend even beyond the art's emotional influence. Music could even directly affect the health of the physical body. (To sing well, states one text, can not only spread moral influence, but also strengthen the spine.)

Yet one effect of music was considered above all others to be the most important, and this was its moral influence.

The Chinese were certain that all coarse and sensual music exerted an immoral effect upon the listener. Therefore all music was closely watched so as to ascertain whether its tendency was towards spirituality or degradation, and whether, in general, its effect was likely to be good or bad. Confucius condemned several styles which he thought to be morally dangerous. Stated he: 'The music of Cheng is lewd and corrupting, the music of Sung is soft and makes one effeminate, the music of Wei is repetitious and annoying, the music of Ch'i is harsh and makes one haughty'.

We cannot fail to note the important difference between this outlook of Confucius and the usual viewpoint of twentieth-century man. Whereas various styles of music today are also 'lewd', 'soft', 'repetitious' or 'harsh' in their *content,* there is no longer any real consideration given to the *effect* of such styles upon the character of the listener.

On the positive side, Confucius believed that good music could help to perfect man's character. He said:

The noble-minded man's music is mild and delicate, keeps a uniform mood, enlivens and moves. Such a man does not harbour pain or mourn in his heart; violent and daring movements are foreign to him.

Further than this: since individuals are the basic building blocks of society, music could also affect entire nations for better or for worse.

According to Confucius: 'If one should desire to know whether a kingdom is well governed, if its morals are good or bad, the quality of its music will furnish the answer'.

Because of the power for good or evil inherent within the tonal arts, *the moral effect of music was considered so important by the Chinese as to rank as the most important test of a music's worth.* A thought for the day, this, for so many of our own contemporary musicians and their audiences. According to the Chinese, there was scarcely a beneficial effect which good music could not bestow upon a civilization. In the ancient Chinese work, *Yo Ki* ('Memorial of Music'), we read: 'Under the effect of music, the five social duties are without admixture, the eyes and the ears are clear, the blood and the vital energies are balanced, habits are reformed, customs are improved, the empire is at complete peace.'[6]

MUSIC AND SPIRITUALITY

Numerous Chinese legends attest to greater, and even magical, possibilities of music. One, for example, tells how the music master Wen of Cheng learned to control the elements. Master Wen was following the great Master Hsiang on his travels. For three years Master Wen touched the strings of his zither, but no melody came. Then Master Hsiang said to him: 'By all means, go home.' Putting down his instrument, Master Wen sighed, and said: 'It is not that I cannot bring a melody about. What I have in my mind does not concern strings; what I aim at is not tones. Not until I have reached it in my heart can I express it on the instrument; therefore I do not dare move my hand and touch the strings. But give me a short while and then examine me.'

Some time later he returned and again approached Master Hsiang, who enquired: 'How about your playing?'

It was spring, but when Master Wen plucked the *Shang* string and accompanied it with the eighth semitone, a cool wind sprang up, and the shrubs and trees bore fruit. Now it was autumn.

Again Master Wen plucked a string, the *Chiao* string, and accompanied it with the second semitone: a languid, warm breeze appeared, and the shrubs and trees bloomed fully.

It was now summer, but he plucked the *Yü* string and had the eleventh semitone respond, upon which hoar frost and snow came down, the rivers and lakes freezing up.

When the winter had come, he plucked the *Chih* string and accompanied it with the fifth semitone: the sun blazed forth and the ice immediately melted away.

Finally, Master Wen of Cheng sounded the *Kung* string and did so in unison with the other four strings: beautiful winds murmured, clouds of good fortune came up, there fell sweet dew, and the springs of water welled up powerfully.

This particular legend is not, of course, to be taken absolutely at face value. The Chinese did believe that music could influence the phenomena of nature. But they did not believe that the tones of mortal man could be expected to literally call forth one season after another as in this legend of Master Wen of Cheng. If we look a little more closely at the story, bearing in mind the great tendency of the ancient Chinese mind to gravitate towards matters spiritual, and to express itself in symbolic terms, then a deeper meaning stands revealed to us:

The four outer strings of the zither, and the four seasons, are symbolic of the ancient conception of the four aspects of man: his abstract mind, his concrete mind, his emotions and his physical body. (These four were later to be called by the alchemists of Europe, 'Fire, Air, Water and Earth'.) Master Wen cannot satisfy his guru, Master Hsiang, because Wen has not yet mastered his own four aspects of being. Hence, as one result, he cannot perform sublime music. But he goes off, and does not return until he has attained the full flowering of the spirituality of his heart. Now Master Wen can play the four outer strings to great effect. Likewise, and much more meaningfully, he has mastered, gained total control over, and can 'play' his abstract and concrete thought processes, his emotional nature, and the physical nature.

The result of this mastery of mind and body? The vital outcome is that in playing these four outer 'strings' (his four-fold nature) in unison, he has learned also to play the central *Kung* string (corresponding to his Higher Self or spiritual nature). From the four-sided base of the pyramid of life, he has raised himself up to the very apex of perfection. He has attained full mastery of himself, and hence his inner genius now manifests from the heart. Hence, too, his music has attained the necessary levels of grandeur required by his guru.

The moral here is two-fold: firstly, we must master our four-fold nature before we can attain self-realization. And, secondly, only by doing so can we then go on to perform music which is truly worthwhile.

Another legendary account, from the *Shu King* ('Book of Odes') describes a music so sublime that it invoked the presence of the great, spiritual men of the past who had ascended to heaven. Kwei,

Emperor Shun's chief musician, said:

> when they tapped and beat the sounding stone, and struck and swept the *ch'in* and *shê*, in order to accord with the chant, then the ancestors and progenitors came down and visited. The guests of them filled the principle seat. And the host of nobles virtuously yielded [place to one another]. At the bottom of the hall were the pipes and the tambours, which were brought into unison or suddenly checked by the beaten trough and the scraped tiger, while the mouth organ and the bell indicated the interludes.[7]

Yet even in legend the use of the power of music is not always benevolent. For instance, one account tells of a music invented by demons and spirits. This music raised a tempest, destroyed the terrace of Prince Ping Kung's palace, and then caused the Prince's own illness and death.[6,8]

THE OM IN CHINA

Why the importance, the vital importance, of music within the philosophical system of ancient China? Because music was believed to embody within its tones elements of the celestial order which governed the entire universe. As did the people of other ancient civilizations, the Chinese believed that all audible sound, including music, was but one form of manifestation of a much more fundamental form of superphysical Sound. This fundamental Primal Sound was synonymous to that which the Hindus call OM. The Chinese believed that this Primal Sound was, though inaudible, present everywhere as a divine Vibration. Furthermore, it was also differentiated into twelve lesser Sounds or Tones. These twelve Cosmic Tones were each emanations of, and an aspect of, the Primal Sound, but were closer in vibration to the tangible, physical world. Each of the twelve Tones was associated with one of the twelve zodiacal regions of the heavens.

ASTROLOGY AND THE TWELVE COSMIC TONES

The twelve Tones were at the root of man's earliest recorded conception of astrology. That is, astrology was originally conceived as being based on these twelve Tones and the influences which their vibratory frequencies exerted over the earth. *In all lands, astrology began in ancient times as the study of Cosmic Tone.*

Almost everywhere in the civilized ancient world this concept prevailed. The perfect order of the heavens was thought to be governed by the twelve Tones. Therefore the ancients set out to reflect this celestial order within the earthly world. They did so in many ways, some of which have been passed down even until our own day, though their original significance is now forgotten. Two surviving examples of the mysticism attached to the number twelve are, for example, the dividing up of the year into twelve months, and of the day into twenty-four hours. But in times past these time divisions were not arbitrary. Nor were they mere superstitious homage to the heavens. Rather, to the ancients they were instances of man's wise recognition of objective, scientific facts. It was believed that the twelve Tones really did express themselves individually to a greater degree according to the month of the year, the time of day, and so forth. A particular Tone 'sounded' more prominently in a particular month, and during a particular hour of the day.

Chinese philosophy is saturated with the idea of opposites – of two opposite (though not necessarily opposing) forces which are found throughout nature. These were called *yang* (the masculine, positive force) and *yin* (the feminine, negative force). Twentieth-century science can only agree with this concept: two opposite forces are found in everything from magnetic charge and the structure of subatomic particles to all cycles of waxing and waning, of night and day, of the sexes, of life and death. In view of this *yang–yin* basis of Chinese philosophy, it should come as no surprise then that of the twelve Cosmic Tones, the Chinese believed six to be *yang* in nature, and six *yin*. Between them, the six *yang* and the six *yin* Tones were responsible for the creation and sustainment of everything in the universe.

SOUND ABOVE AND SOUND BELOW
Audible sound was conceived as being a physical-level manifestation of the twelve Tones. In other words, sound on earth was a kind of 'undertone', as it were, of the celestial vibrations. This fact was at the very heart of why the ancients attributed such tremendous importance to worldly sound. For not only were audible sounds 'undertones' of the celestial Tones, *but they were also believed to contain something of the celestial Tones' supernatural power.* Even as the Cosmic Tones maintained harmony and order in the heavens, so then should music maintain harmony and order upon earth. And so it would, provided that its composition and performance provided an adequate reflection of the order, harmony and melody of the Cosmic Tones. And whether or not earthly music did so depended

upon the quality and nature of the composition and its performance. (So what of the musician who did not understand these cosmic roots of music? Quite simply, he would not realize the necessity for his art to be attuned to the celestial regions, nor would he be able to make it so.)

This is explained in the Chinese text, *The Spring and Autumn* of Lü Bu Ve:

The origins of music lie far back in time. It arises out of proportion and is rooted in the Great One. The Great One gives rise to the two poles: the two poles give rise to the powers of darkness and light. The powers of darkness and light undergo change; the one ascends into the heights, the other sinks into the depths; heaving and surging they combine to form bodies. If they are divided they unite themselves again; if they are united they divide themselves again. That is the eternal way of heaven. Heaven and earth are engaged in a cycle. Every ending is followed by a new beginning; every extreme is followed by a return. Everything is co-ordinated with everything else. Sun, moon and stars move in part quickly, in part slowly. Sun and moon do not agree in the time which they need to complete their path. The four seasons succeed each other. They bring heat and cold, shortness and length, softness and hardness. That from which all beings arise and in which they have their origin is the Great One; that whereby they form and perfect themselves is the duality of darkness and light. As soon as the seed-germs start to stir, they coagulate into a form. The bodily shape belongs to the world of space, and everything spacial has a sound. The sound arises out of harmony. Harmony arises out of relatedness. Harmony and relatedness are the roots from which music, established by the ancient kings, arose.

When the world is at peace, when all things are at rest, when all obey their superiors through all life's changes, then music can be brought to perfection. Perfected music has its effects. When desires and emotions do not follow false paths, then music can be perfected. Perfected music has its cause. It arises out of balance. Balance arises from justice. Justice arises from the true purpose of the world. *Therefore one can speak of music only with one who has recognized the true purpose of the world.* [my italics].

The performing of music often came in conjunction with mystical ceremony. Each of the two — music and ceremony — were valued for their harmonizing elements, which attuned man to the heavens. Each helped man's being – his thoughts, feelings and physical actions – to become aligned with the rhythms and harmonies of the universe. Confucius wrote that ceremony established the correct manner of physical movement in man, while music perfected man's mind and emotions. In the ancient text, *Li chi,* the harmony and sacred proportion of heaven is viewed as entering the earth through the mediation of, respectively, music and ritual:

> Music is the harmony of heaven and earth while rites are the measurement of heaven and earth. Through harmony all things are made known; through measure all things are properly classified. Music comes from heaven; rites are shaped by earthly designs.

The goal of the musician was to manifest within the medium of audible sound a music which expressed accordance with celestial order. And to do so demanded not only an artistic proficiency, but also a very definite scientific knowledge and discipline. This was because the relationship between earthly music and the Chinese conception of universal order was such an extremely intimate one. *Nothing* in classical Chinese music was left to chance or performed arbitrarily. (How the Chinese sages would have shuddered at the sound of much that passes for music today!) According to the Chinese conception that life patterns follow musical patterns, it followed logically that random or arbitrary notes would tend to precipitate chaos and anarchy within society at large.

Ultimately, every note was ideally intended to invoke certain specific cosmic forces. In this, classical Chinese music cannot begin to be understood when approached by the normal Western method of musical analysis.

Well might the prospective Ph.D. researcher attempt to assess the rhythms of ancient Chinese music, its forms and structures. But, in fact, we can no more grasp the heart and ultimate purpose of the music in such a way than we can assimilate *War and Peace* by analysing the frequency with which each letter of the alphabet appears. As one has put it:

> What significance the structure of the waves which bear a useful object? What matters is that the object be not lost![9]

As we have said, each of the twelve celestial Tones corresponded with an astrological month of the year, during which the Tone was believed to be more prominently sounded throughout the earth. The first six months of the year expressed the six *yang* Tones; the second six months from mid-summer to winter solstice expressed the *yin* Tones. The musician performed his music in a key which was associated with the current zodiacal month. The twelve notes, or *lüi*, of the Chinese musical system each corresponded to one of the months. The note of each month was, in audible sound, the earthly reflection or 'undertone' of the month's celestial Tone. Therefore each month of the year possessed its own tonic and dominant *lüi*, with which all ceremonial music should be performed at that time.

To the Chinese mind it was self-evident and indisputable that the perfect State could only be maintained by its remaining in alignment with celestial order. Therefore the functions of State were also associated with a tone. To do so – to keep in harmonious attunement with the principles which governed the universe – brought the blessings of indefinite preservation upon the State. To lose this attunement to celestial order, however, inevitably reduced any nation to a condition of imperfection and impermanence. Celestial principles were eternal, and all attuned with them would endure. National upheaval and decline always came about because that nation was not in harmony with the universal principles of divine order. In particular, the leading officials of the nation should be similarly attuned in their personalities and spiritual understanding. They should literally be the embodiment of the cosmic Tones. The offices of Emperor, Empress, Minister, and so forth, therefore each possessed their own special tone which was attuned to a particular cosmic Tone. The key in which the music of a rite was performed was consequently also influenced by the tone of the officiating office.[6] Harmonious music became the fulfilment upon earth of the Will of the Above. By its alignment with the principles of heaven, earthly music could force by the law of sympathetic resonance the energies of heaven to embody themselves into the leaders of the State.[10]

THE MYSTICISM OF MUSIC

Yet for all this attention paid to the details of their earthly music, the Chinese did not forget the One Origin of all Cosmic Tones and of all earthly sound. The Primal, undifferentiated Cosmic Vibration was a central concept of Chinese philosophy. It was this One Vibration which, emanating from the Great One, became the two – *yang* and *yin* – upon which all Creation was based. This One Vibration, the origin of all matter, energy and being, was considered to be the enunciated Word of the Supreme. Since each of the twelve Cosmic Tones was but an aspect − a twelfth − of this One Vibration, the Chinese felt that literally every note of their music, being a reflection of one of the twelve Tones, was also an earthly manifestation of the One Great Tone. Each note of music, indeed, was performed as a conscious celebration of, an homage unto, and an invocation unto the Father-Tone.

And since *all sound whatsoever* derived from this Vibration, the sounds of music *themselves,* on their own, irrespective of their combination with other tones in this or that melodic pattern, were held in great reverence by the sage-musicians. To understand this, it is necessary for the modern Western musician or music-lover to instil into himself a very different outlook. We tend to have a somewhat ingrained Occidental attitude toward musical appreciation, but to really get to grips with the meaning which music held for the Chinese mind, we need to go back to the beginning. We need to adjust and refocus the faculties with which we listen to and appreciate music in the first place. *Today, we do not as a rule listen to the notes of music at all.*

Strange statement! And yet true. We do not tend to listen to *the notes themselves.* All that we hear and assimilate are the combinations of a number of notes in the form of a melody. Even as our eyes, in *gestalt* fashion, look at the entire form and meaning of a drawing, and rarely focus themselves exclusively upon individual lines or marks to the exclusion of all others, so have our ears become used to organizing musical notes into overall patterns and forms. Little heed is paid to the qualities of each individual sound.

Professional musicians sometimes refer to this fact by saying that it is not the notes which we listen to in music today, but only the intervals − the pitch differences between the notes. The strong tendency is to hear only the melodic stream, as a rising and falling of pitch differences. In this, the notes themselves count for nothing except as dots on the score-sheet which govern which way the line of the melody goes, up or down. The notes are therefore very much like the abstract points of mathematics or geometry. They indicate a position, but fill up no area there; even as a line in mathematics joins up points in an abstract way, yet in theory this line has no width and takes up no area.

But not so, the musical note as appreciated by the ancients of China! For to the Chinese *the individual notes themselves were real, living and vibrant.* They were not abstract points on the mathematician's blackboard, but were large, radiant dots, swollen with feeling and esoteric significance. In the modern mind and in the ancient, mystical frame of consciousness we find, then, tendencies towards two very different ways of concentrating upon and assimilating music.

It is well worth dwelling on this matter a little further. Two different approaches to the experience of tonal art: the concrete and the mystical; the objective and the subjective. In one, the listener stands back, assesses the structure of the piece (is it A-B-A-B-A or A-B-A_1-B-A_1?), and remarks upon the originality of the harmonies during the fugal finale. In the other, the tonal pilgrim plunges into the notes, attempts to reach to their Source, to *become* them. It is not that one approach is correct and the other wrong; each is valid in its own way. What we might call the concrete approach has obviously been dominant in the West for a number of centuries. Interestingly, in its rise to prominence throughout the European baroque and classical eras, it paralleled the simultaneous rise of objective science and of man's increasing mastery over the concrete world. As Western man began to classify and experiment with the phenomena of Nature, so too did there arise a music which was also a science, each component of the music being carefully analysed, each composed note carefully considered. Eventually, like the scientific formula or experimental procedure, pieces of music became totally composed beforehand, the performers not permitted to alter a single note else the entire work be subverted.

And in the East? The Eastern mind has always tended to direct its attention, not *into* the world, but *above* it. Similarly, Oriental music. Each rhythm is a prayer, each melody a contemplation. In his quest for the One, Oriental man discovered divinity and reality within the one fundamental component of all tonal art − the individual note.

Because of this importance which the ancients placed upon each note as an entity in itself, over the centuries the music of China, India, Egypt and other lands evolved a vast array of different ways in which even the same note could be played. Indeed, is this not still the one most immediately striking difference between the music of the West and that of the Orient? In our own music, a note is a note (C, C minor, etc.), and it's as simple as that. Yet in the East the musician has that unmistakable, but at first undefinable, Oriental way of striking each note, this giving to Oriental music its distinct flavour.

The tones of Western music, like the abstract points of geometry, can usually each be written as a straightforward-enough note on the score-sheet. Even on paper we can usually see exactly how the note is intended to sound: as a certain pitch performed by a particular instrument and sustained for a stated period. In the Orient, however, the individual note is heir to a far more extensive variety of possibilities. The same note, even upon the same instrument, can be played in a dazzling multitude of different ways.

In his book on the Chinese lute, R. H. van Gulik explains:

> In order to understand and appreciate this music, the ear must learn to distinguish subtle nuances: the same note, produced on a different string, has a different colour; the same string, when pulled by the forefinger or the middle finger of the right hand, has a different timbre. The technique by which these variations in timbre are effected is extremely complicated: of the vibrato alone there exist no less than twenty-six varieties. The impression made by one note is followed by another, still another. There is thus a compelling, inevitable suggestion of a mood, an atmosphere, which impresses upon the hearer the sentiment that inspired the composer.[11]

It is often pointed out that whereas Western tonal art can be said to possess four dimensions – rhythm, melody, harmony and tone colour – Oriental music is largely lacking in the third of these, the dimension of harmony. Yet a case could be made to the effect that the Orientals nevertheless enjoy a four-dimensional art: the multitudinous choice of options in which way each single note can be sounded has no parallel in the West, and deserves to be regarded as a musical dimension in its own right.

The dimension of tone colour, or timbre (i.e. different instruments and their distinctive sound) is also very developed in the East. This further adds to the variety of sounds which can be produced even from the same note. A note played on a flute is a vastly different aural experience to us than that same note played on a harp, say, or a drum! The glittering array of variegated – and often very strange-sounding – timbres is another immediately noticeable feature of Chinese and other Asiatic music.

In the case of the Chinese, however, how fascinating it is to discover that their deep and complex philosophical system, and the mystic significance which they saw in music, led the evolution of many of their musical instruments along a most unusual path...

In almost all other cultures on earth musical instruments are designed to be able to perform the flowing streams of melodic patterns inherent in virtually all music. Frequently the same instruments are able to perform entire melodies through from start to finish, so broad are the instruments' capabilities. But we find in China a fundamentally different approach. What mattered was to use earthly tone as an aid in reaching spiritually inward and upward to the Source of all tone and of all Creation. Therefore, in their music, the tendency was to express *single tones* as clear, undifferentiated manifestations of the imminent, living Cosmic Tone which pervaded the entire universe.

So what do we find? That in the Chinese orchestra a large proportion of the instruments were those such as bells, single stones and metal slabs to be struck. String instruments followed a similar principle. Western string instruments such as the violin or the guitar have frets upon which an entire melody can be played – even upon a single string. But in China the unfretted string held prominence, as in the harp, each pluck sounding a single, pure emanation of the One. Nor in the case of wind instruments did the Chinese depart from this emphasis upon single tones. Chinese wind instruments, instead of consisting of one tube with holes or some other mechanism to vary the pitch, consisted of rows of pipes joined together, each pipe emanating its own, singular differentiation of Cosmic Vibration. Usually there were twelve such pipes: one for each of the twelve celestial Tones and their audible counterparts. (The mouth organ was also used, which is obviously based on the same principle, but in miniature.)

It may seem from the above that the resultant music was stiff, stultified and unmelodious. Yet nothing could be further from the truth. As we have seen, single notes upon a string could nevertheless be rendered in all manner of ways, extended and enriched with subtle nuances. Moreover, orchestral performances displayed the wonderful skill of the performers to blend the succession of notes from different instruments into a tightly coherent and flowing melody. That is, melodies were less frequently performed by the same instruments all the way through than they were built up from the notes of different instruments. (The practice is not entirely unknown in Western music, and is called open or pierced music. Of it Beethoven spoke in relation to his supernal Op. 131 String Quartet in C Sharp Minor, when he wrote that it contained 'a new manner of voice writing'. Striking instances are also to the fore in Holst's *The Planets* Suite.) Such 'open' melodies were the rule rather than the exception in ancient China, however, and still remain to some extent in the Chinese folk music of the modern era. The effect upon the listener is most certainly one of mind-expansion. Only by broadening and sharpening the consciousness can the full melody and its beauty be assimilated. In fact, since no one instrument is able to lay claim to the possession of the melody as it flies from one instrument to another with glittering speed, it is as though the music itself becomes emancipated from the earthly instruments. An independent spirit, it hovers above and speaks through whichever instrumental medium it will.

MUSIC AND PRACTICAL MAGIC

The Chinese emperors employed surprisingly numerous musicians. The T'ang Dynasty, for example, (AD 618-907) kept no less than fourteen court orchestras, *each consisting of from five hundred to seven hundred performers.* What would the voting public say of such grandiose, 'unnecessary' use of public funds today? And yet, according to the ancients, to keep so many musicians was far from unnecessary or superfluous but was the height of wisdom. For the energy invoked by the divinely-attuned tone-patterns of these court orchestras was believed to exert a far-reaching influence into all the affairs of the nation — affairs as crucial and wide-ranging as those of the economy, the social patterns of behaviour, agriculture, and so on.

During the aforementioned T'ang Dynasty, one regular orchestra alone was formed of no less than *1346* musicians. Little wonder that it was an *outdoor* orchestra. To fit them into London's Royal Albert Hall, one would have to place the orchestra in the rows of seats and position the rather limited audience on the stage! But it is surely apparent here, too, in this huge number of performers, that the real function of the orchestra was known to be a mystical one: such numbers are quite unnecessary for any purposes of performing pieces of music for entertainment. The actual, intended function of the orchestra? That the larger the orchestra was, the greater the volume of sound produced. And the greater the sound, as well as the more minds actively involved, the greater the proportion of cosmic energy invoked and radiated forth. Thus a vast outpouring went forth with which the entire land could be invigorated and spiritually enlightened.

The Chinese historians recorded that for the solstices and other important festivals the T'ang Dynasty also brought together an orchestra reputedly numbering no less than *ten thousand.* Obviously, then, we are dealing here with an acutely different outlook upon the function of music to that with which the Westerner is familiar. In the case of many modern music halls, ten thousand performers would fill the seating capacity *for the audience* three or four times over. Compared to our own day, we can say that the emphasis in China was much more *participation* than upon passive listening. And this because, like farmers harvesting their crops or soldiers defending their homeland, musicians and their music were without reservation believed to be functional in a very practical and extra-musical way. Sound was a *power*; music an *energy*.

MUSIC AND THE T'AI CHI

All music is based upon numbers and proportions. For example, there are twelve notes to the modern chromatic scale, of which seven are major and five minor. The harmonic relationships between the notes is determined by mathematical principles. Strange as it may seem when we focus our attention upon the fact, we cannot avoid commenting, however, that to the average Western musician the numbers and ratios of music remain just that, and nothing more. He perceives no particular significance in them. Even more surprising: he does not even search for any. His consciousness being entirely caught up in the world of appearances, he truly cannot see the woods for trees. He learns at school the rudiments of the numbers and ratios inherent in music, and from that moment on never thinks to enquire: Why?

Yet the ancient Chinese mind was always more interested in the causes behind the world of outer effects than with the world itself. In China, the mathematics of music was considered to embody the sacred, cosmic proportions and principles which governed all of Creation. And of all numbers, one and two were the most fundamental of all. The number one was the number of unity and the number of the Great One. Individual notes and individual performers were always representations of the One God. The number two stood for the first differentiation of the One into the opposite polarities of *yang* and *yin*, or of the *T'ai chi*. This concept of two balanced, interacting forces is the backbone of the entire system of ancient Chinese philosophy. Everything in the universe, including all music, consisted of different combinations of these two fundamental forces. An orchestra, for example, might be considered to hold an equal balance between *yang* and *yin* if half the performers were male and half female. Then again, certain months of the year were *yang*, and some *yin*; and among the *yang* months, for example, some were more *yang* than others. Therefore music should be performed during each month in a key which shared that month's *yang–yin* balance. Individual pieces of music were themselves sometimes classed according to how *yang* or *yin* they were. The opening bars of Beethoven's Fifth Symphony would undoubtedly have been classed as very *yang* (masculine, active and positive), and the Bach/Gounod 'Ave Maria' as very *yin*.

Beethoven's Fifth must surely be ☵ . Or even ☰ . For this was how the different balances between *yang* and *yin* were written. The principle of *yang* was symbolized as an unbroken line —— and *yin* by a broken line – –. According to the cosmo-conception of the Chinese, these two opposite forces, by combining, were the origin of the Trinity. And the concept of the Trinity was far from being a vague, abstract one: rather, all three-fold phenomena and manifestations in the universe were considered to be an aspect of the Three-in-One. In music, the Trinity manifested itself wherever or whenever there occurred triplets of notes, a rhythm in three, or any number of performers which was a multiple of three.

By writing the broken and unbroken lines for *yin* and *yang* in sets of three, the Chinese were able to represent in writing the inner balance between *yin* and *yang* which prevailed within the three-fold nature of all phenomena. Altogether there are a total of eight possible signs such as ☵ and ☰ . These eight signs (known as *kua*) were believed to symbolize the eight basic permutations and combinations of existence. Hence, the number eight also assumed a mystical significance within music.

This led to another way in which the Chinese sought to mirror celestial order within their musical system. In keeping with there being eight basic manifestations of the *yang–yin* forces in the universe, musical instruments were grouped into eight classes. In the West we classify our instruments according to the method of sound production (e.g. percussion instruments, string instruments). Not so in ancient China, where instruments were grouped according to the material from which they were made. This meant that each category of instrument became automatically associated with a wide variety of extra-musical phenomena, since, like the instruments, everything else in the universe was also associated with one of the eight basic *kua*. We see that, through its common *kua*, whenever a musical instrument was sounded, it automatically invoked, by association, the spirit of a particular season, element, compass direction, and so on (see Table 1).

Table 1: The Eight Traditional Classes of Chinese Musical Instruments

No.	Kua=(symbol) Name Sign	Substance of Instrument	Example of Instrument	Compass Point	Season	Element or Phenomenon of Nature
1	*Ch'ien*	stone	sonorous stone (chime)	NW	Autumn-Winter	Heaven
2	*Tui*	metal	bell (chime)	W	Autumn	dampness
3	*Li*	silk	zither	S	Summer	fire
4	*Chên*	bamboo	panpipes	E	Spring	thunder
5	*Sun*	wood	tiger box	SE	Spring-Summer	wind
6	*K'an*	skin	drum	N	Winter	water
7	*Kên*	gourd	reed mouth-organ	NE	Winter-Spring	mountain
8	*K'un*	earth	globular flute	SW	Summer-Autumn	Earth

From *Grove's Dictionary of Music and Musicians* (1954 edition)

THE CONCEPT OF THE *LOGOS* IN CHINESE MUSIC

One all-important purpose lay behind all the strenuous efforts of the Chinese to align their music to the principles and proportions of cosmic order. This purpose was that, through the God-alignment of music, all consciousness and life could become similarly aligned to that same celestial order.

No matter how far back in the history of Chinese music we go, we find the same: *that the Chinese associated Cosmic Sound with illumined, exalted consciousness.* Cosmic Sound — the vibratory essence of all matter and energy — was in everything and everyone... and it was possible for man to raise his consciousness, to take himself closer to the Source, to attune himself more perfectly with the One. Spirituality was literally a question of vibration. He who succeeded in harmonizing the discords within his mind, emotions and body could become a more perfect embodiment of Cosmic Sound, an incarnation of the Word. He who embodied the *Logos* was inevitably exceedingly wise, moral and just; hence he was the most fitting to rule.

There are unmistakable parallels here between this Chinese concept of man embodying Cosmic Sound and the Christian acceptance of the Christ as being the Word of God. Indeed, Chinese emperors were traditionally associated with the *Logos* from the earliest times. This we can see by examining just one or two terms of the language. For example, the name given to the foundation tone of Chinese music was *huang chung;* literally translated, this means 'yellow bell'. Yet this same phrase was also used symbolically in reference to the ruler, and to divine will.

Outwardly, the tone known as 'yellow bell' set the standard pitch upon which the music of the entire nation was based; esoterically, this foundation tone was considered to be the purest and most perfect audible manifestation of Cosmic Sound possible. If we reflect upon the relationship between two tones set an octave apart, the lower tone being an undertone which can be produced by the sounding out of the higher, then this gives us some idea of how the *huang chung* was considered to be related to the *Logos.* The *Logos,* sounding in the realms of Spirit, produced the precise pitch of the *huang chung* in the physical world as its matter-plane undertone. The 'yellow bell' tone was an Octave of octaves of octaves, and more, below its Source-Tone; but nevertheless, it was its perfect lower-plane counterpart: as Hermes said, 'As Above, so below.' The 'yellow bell' tone was therefore regarded most reverently in ancient China as a genuine, audible expression of the Word itself. The cosmological purpose of the Word was to act as mediator between heaven and earth. Cosmic Sound provided a vehicle for the transference of the Supreme Will into the physical world. Those enlightened, selfless men who so perfected themselves as to become the living embodiment of the Word were likewise mediators: as the living, manifest offspring of the Great One, they were able to convey the teachings of the Great One to the humanity who were not sufficiently developed to be able to receive the teachings directly for themselves.

As we see, then, the term *huang chung* (yellow bell) referred both to the foundation tone of Chinese music and, in the symbolic sense, to divine rulership. The colour yellow was itself the Chinese imperial colour, the colour of sacred wisdom. The emperor was a kind of priest-king: even as the yellow bell established the pitch of all the Chinese notes, and therefore the divine attunement of all of their music, so too did the Emperor set the spiritual and material laws for all his subjects, and preside over the affairs of State. He did so because just as the yellow bell perfectly reflected the Tone of the *Logos,* so was the emperor the most perfected individual through whom the Consciousness of the *Logos* could best manifest itself.

With the passing of the centuries this at times became more theoretical than actual: as in the case of the succession of Roman Catholic Popes, Chinese emperors were not always, in more recent times, completely fitted for their office. Originally, however, the emperor was indeed both Lawgiver and Guru to his devoted subjects, and the earthly spokesman for the Word of God.

To embody the *Logos* was not believed to be the calling of only one person, though. All beings were its manifestation; all could aspire to that purity and illumination of consciousness whereby they became the perfect, undistorted Presence of the Word.* And thus the very *purpose* of Chinese music was towards this end: for their ritual and classical music was penultimately directed towards the raising and purifying of all performers and members of the audience.

The Chinese music of those times was quite remarkable in the attempt it made to free the listener from the chains of the physical world. It directed the inner ear back to the Supreme Source of all sound, beyond the outer, material world altogether. And how was this done? We can gain some idea from the accounts of early Western musicologists who journeyed to China before the classical tradition had been entirely lost. One reported that:

> The music of the seven-stringed zither tends constantly towards imagined sounds: a vibrato is prolonged long after all audible sound has ceased; the unplucked string, set in motion by a sudden arrested glissando, produces a sound scarcely audible even to the performer. In the hands of performers of an older generation the instrument tends to be used to suggest, rather than to produce, sounds.[12]

OF TIMES AND CYCLES; OF MUSIC AND MODES

The extent to which music was aligned to cosmic principles simply cannot be overstated. The twelve notes of the Chinese musical system were themselves each related to one of the twelve signs of the zodiac, one of the twelve moons of the year, and to one of the twelve hours of the day (one Chinese hour being exactly two of our own). It was regarded as imperative that earthly music be attuned to the celestial harmonics of these time cycles. As we have said, the predominant Cosmic Tone was believed to change with the passing from one zodiacal month to the other; and so, too, the harmonic relationship between the twelve Tones was believed to change also with the changing of the phases of the moon and the hour of the day.[6] The problem this presented is obvious: how could the Chinese keep their music in harmonious correspondence with the harmonics of the heavens if the heavenly Tones themselves kept changing in their relation to the earth?

The solution was simple in theory; certainly not so simple in practice: for each of the regular changes in Cosmic Tone, the Chinese changed the keynote, and sometimes even the mode, of their music. It is startling for us today to hear of such a practice. Imagine the modern conductor, merrily taking the London Symphony Orchestra through Beethoven's Ninth, looking at his watch, and suddenly signalling for the music to be entirely transposed! Or a rector dashing down the aisle on Sunday morning, gesticulating to the sombre church choir that they have just passed into Taurus! Yet the Chinese were entirely serious: they had the utter faith that they knew what they were doing and why. It is doubtful that they ever engaged in such absurdity as described above. In order to compose, conduct, perform or appreciate as a listener the ancient music, a good deal of esoteric, astrological and astronomical knowledge had often to be absorbed beforehand. Musicians knew exactly what to play and how to play it according to the date and time of day.

It should be realized that not only music, but even Chinese astrology itself was also, at its source, firmly based upon the concept of Cosmic Sound. Astrology *was* the science of celestial Sound. The twelve Tones which emanated from the One Word were, in their various harmonic combinations, considered to be the real cause of astrological influences over earthly events. Astrological effects were not the inexplicable, unexplained results, vaguely attributed to the stars, that they are to the astrologers of today. Rather, there was a scientific and very plausible theory in explanation of astrological influences: it was the twelve Tones of the zodiac, radiating their super-physical Vibrations onto the earth, which were believed to affect psychological states, the phenomena of Nature, and so forth. After all, does not a piece of worldly music often profoundly affect and move us? How much more then might the Harmonics of the Beyond likewise change our state of consciousness? Indeed, is not all matter composed of energy oscillating at various frequencies? Then that high-frequency energy-waves from beyond the earth could affect matter and consciousness does not seem at all an implausible or superstitious idea. According to the Chinese, the monthly changes from one sign of the zodiac to another indicated *cosmic modulations* in the pattern of celestial harmonics. With each new stellar configuration, new Tones inundated the earth, bringing with them new tendencies in thought, new moods, different behaviour-patterns and different activities in the Nature kingdom.

Most interestingly, there has survived intact since those days some indications of which actual musical notes were associated with the twelve moons of the year and the twelve hours of the day. (We should remember that the chief significance of these audible tones was that they were each worldly counterparts of one of the very Tones of Heaven.) Rendering the musical tones according to the modern Western scale (C, C #, etc.) the correspondences were:

Note	Moon	Hour
C	6	1
C #	7	3
D	8	5
D #	9	7
E	10	9
F	11	11
F #	12	1
G	1	3
G #	2	5
A	3	7
A #	4	9
B	5	11

It would be pleasing to think that, from this data, we could now carry on the tradition of transposing and otherwise altering our music according to the month and hour! However, a note of caution for would-be revivers of the lost art: the Western notes indicated above are only the approximate pitch of the Chinese notes. The *huang chung* foundation tone was roughly F, and corresponded with the eleventh moon and the eleventh hour. But, as we shall shortly see, the *huang chung* (and therefore all the notes of the scale) varied in pitch throughout the centuries.

Taking still further the alignment of their music, below, to celestial principles, Above, the musical instruments themselves were designed with often deep esoteric symbology in mind. One of the oldest and most sacred of Chinese instruments, the *sheng*, is a wind instrument the use of which was almost entirely reserved for holy seasonal convocations. It had 24 pipes – that is, one *yang* and one *yin* tonal expression for each of the twelve signs of the zodiac.[13] Moreover, we can be sure that this was considered to be not only for symbolic purposes, but for eminently practical purposes – the invocation of cosmic forces.

Another instrument, the *chuen,* possessed twelve open strings...
plus a very different thirteenth string which, unlike the others, was
stretched along a calibrated scale. Here, the twelve strings represent
the twelve zodiacal and Tonal differentiations of the *Logos,* while
the thirteenth string corresponds to the *Logos* itself. (The same
cosmological relationship is evident in the instance of the twelve
tribes of ancient Israel and the thirteenth tribe – the priesthood.
Later, this same mandala appeared in the form of the twelve
disciples and Jesus Christ.)

At times yet another variable was employed in order to infuse
music with cosmic principles: the number of musicians. For instance,
the gigantic outdoor band of the T'ang Dynasty included 48
singers, or one to correspond with each of the four elements in
relation to each of the twelve Tones (4×12). One indoor orchestra
included 120 (10×12) harpists. No doubt there would be numerous
other examples, but our knowledge today of the precise numbers
and make-up of most of the ancient orchestras is incomplete.

Every conceivable aspect of music was, then, aligned with the
Above, that nothing remained mundane. The result was a *scientific
art;* art for the sake of *practical effects.* By creating a tonal art which
was an accurate counterpart of Cosmic Sound and celestial order,
the ancients were convinced that they had provided a medium for
the entry of heavenly proportion and sacred energies into the
matter-world.

The earth had become imperfect due to the inharmonious
thoughts, words and deeds of an imperfect humanity. But all could
be restored to perfection and maintained by the giving forth of
perfect music. Thus a line of stability could be held, through the
science of sacred sound, against the further encroachment of discordant forces which, if a balance was not held, could lead to disaster.
Sacred sound was such a balance against imperfection and evil. And
more: correctly applied music was believed to be capable of
eventually re-aligning the world to its original and perfect Source.

Does not the music of the world have its highlights, its louder or
more important passages? So it was with the symphony of the stars.
Vitally important emanations of Tone were believed to inundate the
earth at certain special times of the year. The mid-points of each
season, the two solstices and two equinoxes, were periods during
which vast radiations of sacred energy were released at the spiritual
level. Music could act as the medium to aid these life-enhancing
forces to enter more fully into the material world; therefore it was at
these four times of the year that music and ritual could be used still

more effectively than at any other time. (We have already noted that for such festivals, the T'ang Dynasty is said to have brought together an 'orchestra' of ten thousand performers.) Invigorated by these four outpourings of Cosmic Sound each year, the earth received what we might call an annual four-movement 'symphony of the stars'. By scientifically invoking as much as possible of this sacred energy down into the earth-plane, the holding of four annual periods of holy ritual ensured the greatest benefit for the nation in all its affairs during the ensuing three months.

An awareness of these four vital periods is also evident throughout the spiritual and occult history of the Western world. For example, pagan and witchcraft celebrations sought to channel – and often to pervert – the energies of the solstice or equinox into levels of the mortal libido. In reply, the early Christians, being also aware of the esoteric significance of the four mid-seasonal points, established a number of celebrations and holy rituals in order once more to see the sacred energies channelled purely and altruistically. Chief among these periods were Easter and Christmas (spring equinox and winter solstice). We might also remark, in passing, that these occasions are today, for the most part, once more celebrated in pagan and hedonistic manner... (Would the spiritual atmosphere of the earth be turned around and accelerated once more if the four sacred convocations came again to be observed in the correct way, through the more general and widespread use of holy song and beautiful music?)

THE *HUANG CHUNG* AS THE FOUNDATION OF CIVILIZATION

To the sages and emperors of ancient China, the alignment of earth with heaven, and of man with the Supreme, was literally the purpose of life. An important part of this process was to consciously align the civilization with celestial principles and proportions. For example, we have seen that great attention was paid to ensure that the music of civilization was aligned with the *Logos* by means of standardizing all musical pitches according to the *huang chung*. But – what of the dimensions of the length and the width of objects? So much for the music of civilization, but what of its system of weights? Should not *all* be standardized according to the Above, and not only musical pitches? Was it not a fact that Cosmic Sound was the basis of *everything,* and that it determined the weight, size and tone of all things? Yet here there was a problem: it was relatively simple to harmonize worldly sound with Cosmic Sound –

by discovering the earthly scale of tones which corresponded with the Cosmic Tones; but how could the *non-tonal* systems of measurement also become accurate reflections of the principles of the heavens?

As in the case of their universal adherence to one foundation pitch for their music, it was a vital matter to the Chinese that all of their systems of standardization be sacred, not profane. It was a vital matter to them since, according to the ageless philosophy, that which mirrored the heavens was, like the heavens, eternal. *A civilization which mirrored the Above would never pass away, for every institution and object within it provided a medium for the containment of life-enhancing, invigorating cosmic forces.* On the other hand, the civilization which was founded upon arbitrary, mortal principles could never long endure, but was inevitably doomed to transience and decay.

And so, thousands of years ago, at a time so distant that mankind today posssesses no accurate records of it, some individual must have set about finding the solution to this problem. Perhaps after much preparatory fasting, prayer, thought and meditation, the revelation was at last received of how, from the possession of only the divine pitch of sound, all divine proportions could be derived.

In the case of music, the key to accurate alignment with Cosmic Sound was the *huang chung* foundation tone. And to produce this tone, a pipe of specific dimensions had to be blown, did it not? Then right here were the required proportions! The pitch, length and volume of the pipe were completely interrelated: change the length, for instance, and the volume automatically changed with it, as did the pitch the pipe would produce. *Only the pipe of perfect length and perfect volume could product the perfect 'yellow bell' tone.* Hence, its length became the standard Chinese length of measurement, its capacity the standard of volume, and the number of grains of rice or of millet which the pipe could contain rendered a standard weight measurement. So closely affiliated did music and the standardization of all other dimensions in China become that the Imperial Office of Music was associated with the Office of Weights and Measurement. And the sacred pipe which gave this standardization was often owned, not by the former office, but by the latter.[6,14]† As though to demonstrate for all time the ultimate degree of their idealism and scientific devotion to the Above, the Chinese theoretically succeeded in aligning their entire culture and civilization to the *huang chung,* and therefore to the *Logos.*

THE ETERNAL QUEST

The twelve notes of the Chinese musical scale each had their individual names, this being also true of the foundation tone the *huang chung*, itself, the musical note of which was called *kung*. As we have seen, this foundation note was considered to be the earthly manifestation of divine will, and a sacred, eternal principle, upon which was based the proportional systems of the entire State. This raises, then, an ultimate question: what would happen if the note taken to be the pitch of *kung* was out of tune, no longer being the perfect receptacle for divine energies?

The entire State would become out of alignment to the Above! The accuracy of the *kung* was therefore absolutely paramount. As the Chinese text, *Memorial of Music,* warns: 'If the *Kung* is disturbed, then there is disorganization, the prince is arrogant.'[6] So that if the *kung* was inaccurate, all manner of things would be likely to go wrong. Even the ruling prince might become inharmonious and a poor receptacle for divine will, imposing his own human will upon the people. The perfect *kung* was then, in short, the great key to a perfect, golden-age civilization.

Yet how, indeed, could they ever be sure that the note which they took to be *kung* was perfectly accurate? How could there be any certainty that the pitch pipe they used was absolutely true in its tone ...?

And so it was that the search for the pure, immaculate tonal reflection of the One Tone assumed supremely idealistic, mystical proportions. The instrument which could give to man the foundation tone for a musical scale which was in perfect harmony with the universe was the key to earthly paradise, and essential for the security and evolution of the race. It became a Chinese Holy Grail, the goal of the ultimate quest. One legend tells of the wonderful journey of Ling Lun, a minister of the second legendary Chinese Emperor, Huang Ti. Ling Lun was sent like an ancient Knight of King Arthur to search for a special and unique set of bamboo pipes. These pipes were so perfect that they could render the precise, standard pitches to which all other instruments throughout the land could then be tuned. Looking closely at this and other such legends, it is discovered that they are deeply symbolic: even as the perfectly tuned pitch pipes could be the standard for the tuning of all other instruments, therefore bringing earthly music into conformity with universal harmony, so too could the perfectly 'tuned' or self-realized man become the standard for all other men to follow.

What *was* the precise pitch which was actually used as the note, *kung?* Modern researchers have not been able to determine it exactly, but estimates place it at between middle C minor and the F above.[6] The final Chinese dynasty seems to have placed *kung* at around D, at a pitch of 601.5 c.p.s. according to a report by the musicologist van Aalst in 1884.[15] However, this does not mean that all the previous dynasties took the same pitch, D, as their foundation note. The Chinese did not conceive of the universe or of the heavens as being static. Even as works of earthly music progress through various different melodies, rhythms, contrasts, keys and movements, so too, according to the ancients, did the celestial music which was the Source of all earthly tones. As astrological configurations changed, so too did the universal harmonics. We have already seen that the progression from one zodiacal month to another indicated quite literally a modulation in the Music of the twelve Tones. At times this could mean that Cosmic Sound had changed so significantly that, though the *kung* had been accurately tuned to it, it was so no longer. The *kung* would therefore require modifying.

Just think what this meant: with the modification of the *kung,* the State's entire system of weights and measures, and all objects and things based upon them also had to be altered! Only in this way could the State be realigned with celestial principles. Whenever the first emperor of a new, incoming dynasty took the throne, one thing only was on his mind as the first and foremost thing to do: to seek to correct the note, *kung.* (After all, if the *kung* of the previous dynasty had been in perfect harmony with the eternal principles of the universe, how could the dynasty ever have ended...?)

RIGIDITY VS. INNOVATION: THE CRUCIAL DILEMMA

This willingness of the Chinese to alter their 'yellow bell' foundation note constituted an ingenius theoretical solution to the timeless problem in music of rigidity vs. innovation. This vital issue is one we shall be returning to in relation to the music of India. The question is: to what extent should music be regulated and controlled, and to what extent allowed freedom of expression? To what extent should the prevailing music be rigidly maintained, and to what extent permitted to alter?

Changes in the music of the nation might ultimately prove to be genuinely beneficial; the innovations might truly be for the purpose of evolving and improving the tonal arts. *Or they might not.* One realizes the immense significance which this rigidity vs. innovation dilemma held for any culture which accepted the view that music

possesses the ability to transform – improve or degrade – civilization. Virtually every major civilization of antiquity held this view.
The wise among them were therefore very much aware of the
pitfalls of either extreme in music – over-rigidity or over-innovation
– and sought to achieve a balance between the two. An unwise
degree of innovation or a condition of outright musical anarchy
could prove deadly to the State. But, on the other hand, complete
inflexibility could cause music to stagnate.

How to avoid stagnation in music, and yet steer well clear of the
treacherous rocks of absolute anarchy? In their own way, each of
the great ancient civilizations formulated its own unique variation
on the same basic solution: stagnation could be avoided, and
creativity encouraged in safety, by the adoption of a musical system
which allowed the composers or performers free expression – *within*
certain well-defined rules and regulations. The Chinese variation on
this solution was twofold. Firstly, new compositions of music were
allowed provided that they were not obviously immoral or anarchic.
All new compositions were required to conform to the standard
system of musical notes, modes, etc. and thus were aligned with the
Above. But the fact that new works of music could come forth
nevertheless provided scope for the introduction of new melodies
and beneficial moods. This helped to guarantee that the musical arts
retained sufficient fluidity so as to be able to keep pace with new
astrological conditions.

Yet even then there remained, the Chinese believed, scope for a
dangerous over-rigidity. For what if the celestial harmonics themselves changed in a major and permanent way, and yet the system of
musical rules did not? Would not this, too, place the music of the
nation into a state of perilous inharmony in relation to Cosmic
Sound? We see, therefore, the extreme value of being allowed to
modify the *kung*. According to the Chinese, a *kung* which remained
absolutely inflexible over many centuries could ultimately prove
suicidal to a civilization. This was because a static *kung* – and a
static music – could only retain its value if the universe itself was
static, which it was not. Over-rigidity in music could therefore
prove just as dangerous as too much innovation. That which did not
adjust to the new day was fated to fade away.

However much one may agree or disagree with the specifics of
the ancient Chinese musical science, its belief that it is essential to
steer a middle-way between the twin pitfalls in music of over-
rigidity and anarchy is surely a valid and timely reminder to the
peoples of any age.

THE MYSTICISM OF MUSIC AND NUMBER

'Music expresses the harmony of heaven and earth,' states the *Memorial of Music*. And in the *Record of Rites* we are told that, 'since 3 is the symbolic numeral of heaven and 2 that of the earth, sounds in the ratio 3:2 will harmonize heaven and earth'. To apply this concept in practice, the Chinese took the foundation tone, the *huang chung,* and from it produced a second note in the 3:2 ratio. For example, having constructed a musical string which, when plucked, sounded the *huang chung* (or '*kung*') note, a second note in the 3:2 ratio could be produced by pressing the string against a fret one third of the distance from its end, and by then plucking the remaining length of two thirds. (Alternatively, a second string of two thirds the length of the first could be used.) This 3:2 ratio between the two pitches is called by musicians today the perfect fifth. By taking this second note, and then continuing along similar lines, through a certain system a total of twelve notes altogether could be produced, all being related by a cycle of perfect fifths or 3:2 ratios. The result: twelve notes all derived from the sacred *huang chung*; twelve earthly counterparts of the twelve Tones.

Of the twelve notes, or *lü* as the Chinese called them, only seven were incorporated into the musical scale which was actually used. The twelve *lü* can be said to have approximately corresponded to the twelve notes of the modern chromatic scale; and the seven more important Chinese notes with the seven major notes of today's scale: *Do–Re–Mi–Fa–Sol–La–Si*. But of these seven, the Chinese very rarely made use of the two semitones, so that in practice only a five-note, or pentatonic, scale was utilized. The same was also the case in Egypt, Greece and other ancient civilizations. This pentatonic scale therefore consisted roughly of the notes we nowadays refer to as F, G, A, C and D.

Hence, the mysticism attached to the numbers 1, 2, 3, 5, 7 and 12 is discovered within music as follows:

    1 – The One Tone, or Cosmic Sound, of the Supreme.
    2 – The T'ai chi; the first differentiation of the One.
    3 – The Trinity: offspring of the T'ai chi.
    12 – The twelve Tones of the zodiac, their earthly counterparts being produced from a series of 3:2 ratios.
    5 – The five minor tones of the twelve.
    7 – The seven major tones of the twelve (of which five are whole tones and two semitones).

In the philosophical system of China the number five was particularly important, so it is of little surprise that their musical scale
should also have been pentatonic. Phenomena of a widely diverse
nature were categorized into divisions of five, each of the five divisions being associated with one of the five musical notes. The notes
of the rulers, seasons, elements, colours, directions and planets were
as shown in Table 2.

Table 2: The Five Notes and Their Symbolic Correspondences

Category	Note				
	Kung	Shang	Chiao	Chi	Yü
Political	Emperor or Prince	Ministers	Loyal Subjects	Affairs of State or Public Works	Produce or Material Things
Season	—	Autumn	Spring	Summer	Winter
Element	Earth	Metal	Wood	Fire	Water
Colour	Yellow	White	Blue	Red	Black
Direction	Centre	West	East	South	North
Planet	Saturn	Venus	Jupiter	Mars	Mercury

From *Grove's Dictionary of Music and Musicians* (1954 edition)

It is impossible not to notice the prime importance here assigned
to *kung*. Symbolically, it was related to the head of State, the earth
element, and the centre (rather than to any direction of the
compass).‡

MODE = MOOD

The five notes were also each related to one of five important virtues
– benevolence, righteousness, propriety, knowledge and faith.[5] In
this we have one of the first, fascinating recorded instances of man's
association of different psychological qualities to specific pitches.
The belief that specific musical expressions each exert their own
objective effect upon man is at the very heart of the subject of the
inner power of music. The Chinese, in addition to linking notes with
virtues, were also convinced that the various styles of combinations
of notes – that is, the different modes – also had their own definite
influences over man's emotions. According to the tonic, dominant
and other important notes within a given piece of music, and accor-

ding to their order in the melodic note-sequences, so would the
emotional and moral effect upon the listener be determined. We
might express this concept in the short formula: MODE =
MOOD.

There is good reason to suppose that the practical application of
this formula by the Chinese musicians played a central role in determining the entire course of Chinese history. During the several
thousand years of the history of China there were at least some
periods of internal conflict and of invasion from foreign lands, and
yet through it all the essential 'flavour' of the civilization – its
philosophy, its lifestyle, and even the physical appearance of its
architecture and styles of clothing – remained much the same.
Compare this to the people of Europe during the same period (3000
BC to the opening of the twentieth-century) with all the comings
and goings of races, the risings and fallings, mass exterminations
through war and plague, and the extreme cultural differences during
those five millennia, and we begin to gain some idea of the
magnitude of the Chinese accomplishment! And now, in these
trying, final decades of the twentieth century – when calamitous
extremes of chaos reign, when many can scarcely believe that
Western civilization can survive another fifty years, the world being
threatened by an overwhelming multitude of dangers including the
threats of potential nuclear war, tumultuous social upheavals and
natural cataclysms – is it not now or never that we should step
down from our frail, insubstantial platforms of cultural pride, and
take a long, cool look – with humility – at the golden age of China?
How did they maintain the same basic culture and society, largely
unaffected by all the events which threatened them, over *thousands*
of years? What was the secret? Was it one which we could apply
today? And – perhaps equally important – what, then, was it that
eventually did lead to the downfall of the ancient Chinese civilization? Is there a warning lesson for us to be gleaned from the event?

Grove's Dictionary of Music and Musicians perceptively comments
on the fact that, 'Despite the vicissitudes of time, destruction, wars,
foreign influences and independent experiment, all has been
assimilated or rejected and guided back by ... [China's] persistent
natural philosophy as by a hidden hand.'[6]

No doubt there is considerable truth in this, that the philosophical
and religious world-view of the Chinese acted throughout the
millennia as a guiding, ordering agent. Yet how, indeed, was the
philosophy itself able to abide for so long, relatively unchanged?
Grove's Dictionary is obviously correct in speaking of a 'hidden

hand' that continued to sustain a certain mould or matrix over Chinese civilization. Yet the mould may well have consisted of something more potent and vigorous in its practical effect than the natural philosophy alone. And the Chinese themselves believed that this was so: they were convinced that life patterns follow music patterns; as in music, so in life; and that a stable music ensured a stable State.

The effect of music upon a nation was conceived as being like that of a magnet held beneath a piece of paper upon which iron filings are placed: shake the filings about, drop more upon them, do what you will, but the magnet and its magnetic field will continue to sustain the same pattern and order. The pattern of iron filings can be changed only by the moving of the magnet itself, or its replacement by a differently shaped one. In exactly the same way that a magnet compells the pattern of filings into conformity with its own field, so Confucius and the other Chinese philosophers were certain that modes ruled moods, music thus influencing life.

THE LEGENDARY ORIGINS OF CHINESE CLASSICAL MUSIC

But where did this mysterious music and its entire cosmological basis *come* from? A legitimate question, especially if we are beginning to suspect that the esoteric power claimed for this music may, in at least some respects, have been a real one. Who, then, first brought forth this music and its power, and how?

According to the Chinese themselves, the origin of their music lies in the mysterious legendary period of the third millennium BC — legendary because little or no hard archaeological evidence has been discovered to attest to this era. However, it would seem likely that the civilization did indeed exist at least as early as this, even though until quite recently, modern scholars scoffed at the mention within old Chinese texts of dynasties which the texts claimed to have existed at around 1500 BC. (Probably much of the scholars' disbelief stemmed from their very inability to accept that the civilization could have extended, relatively unchanged, over such a vast period.) Then, to their embarrassment, diggings began to unearth the relics of those very dynasties. That which had been legendary became a matter of known history. It seems wise then, not to adopt a sceptical stance towards the legendary era of the third millennium BC.

The ancient texts of China itself associate the establishment of their music with five enigmatic, legendary personages who, it is said, were China's first monarchs. No ordinary monarchs, these, however. Divine in nature, these five rulers are accredited with the entire genesis of the civilization, and with the setting forth of the philosophy which would maintain the State once they themselves had departed. The first of them, Emperor Fu Hsi, is said to have been the founder of the monarchy and the 'inventor' of music. Fu Hsi is also reputed to have been the author of the *I Ching.* He is said to have reigned from around 2852 BC. Reflecting the ancients' belief in the power of music to create an invisible matrix for the precipitation of physical events and conditions, Fu Hsi's music was called *fu-lài* (to 'help to occur'), or sometimes *li-pen* (to 'establish the foundation'). Every culture has its own unique music, and by first bringing forth the style of Chinese tonal art, Fu Hsi established the foundation for the civilization.

The following four divine rulers also placed great emphasis upon music; they seem to have realized that it was in this art that the keys could be placed for the indefinite stability and maintenance of the civilization they were manifesting. The third of them, Huang Ti (from c. 2697 BC) is said to have established the *huang chung* foundation tone and the musical system of twelve *lüi.* He also formulated a particular style of musical performance which exerted magical influences and was known as *hsien-chih*, or 'all-pervading influence'.[6] But precisely who the five enigmatic divine rulers were, and whence came their wisdom, is unknown. The full story of the establishment of the Chinese cosmo-conception and its music is therefore still shrouded in quite a heavy veiling of mystery.

The work of further developing the tonal arts was carried out by later legendary emperors. These expanded the philosophy behind music, expressed specific teachings on the psychological and moral effects of the different individual sounds, and added to the sophistication of the musical arts in their practical performance. This was the golden age of Chinese music and civilization.

THE HISTORICAL ERA

Not that the musical system remained *absolutely* unchanged throughout those many centuries. From the beginning of the better-documented, historical dynasties we find that there were a number of alternative systems of *lüi* developed at least in theory. One involved not twelve *lüi* as in the traditional system, but a total of 360, no less! Such innovative ideas seem to have had little lasting practical effect upon the music of the people, however.

Several Chinese texts speak of attempts that were made to

achieve equal temperament. (That is, to develop a system of exactly equal intervals between the twelve *lüi*, rather than to use the ancient system of twelve notes related by slightly unequal but geometrically perfect 3:2 intervals.) As late as the sixteenth-century AD, Prince Tsai-Yu is said to have embarked upon the quest for equal temperament. First studying all the works he could find on the theory of music, he then would probably have fasted, in the traditional Chinese manner, in order to purge from his form all physical and psychological dross which might hinder his reception of spiritual illumination. Then he sat down and meditated deeply upon the problem. Days and nights passed. But at last, we are told, 'the light of truth was revealed to him', and he realized the precise formula for equal temperament.

Prince Tsai-Yu's contemporaries appear not to have been taken by the idea of equal temperament, however, for no Chinese instruments have ever been discovered which were tuned in such a way. Their reason for objecting probably concerned the different cosmological significances associated with the two systems of tuning: the ancients' use of unequal but geometrically perfect intervals between the notes implied infinite transcendence and contact with the heavens, while the use of tempered, equal intervals meant that a slight geometrical imperfection – and hence, a slight cosmological inharmony – resulted.

Apart from brief experiments, then, China retained the original system of twelve *lüi* based on a cycle of perfect fifths. And as recently as AD 1712 the Ch'ing Dynasty finally rejected the principle of equal temperament once and for all. (This at the very time that equal temperament was about to become accepted in the West, through the work of J. S. Bach and others, as the firm basis of virtually all Western music from then until now.) The dynasty fully reverted to the ancient system accredited to the first divine ruler, Fu Hsi, of no less than four and a half thousand years earlier.

It is important to realize that every such decision during the history of China, whenever possible alterations in the musical system were under consideration, was treated with extreme caution and conservatism. If even the slightest of changes was agreed upon, it was done in the full belief that it would result in a definite, parallel effect upon the future of the nation itself. For we must remember: the Chinese philosophy stated that innovations in the tonal arts would ultimately become *precisely* mirrored in society at large. In the case of equal temperament, for example, the sages would have expected that its adoption, to increase the melodic possibilities of earthly music, but at the expense of geometrical alignment with the heavens, would also be mirrored in an adjustment in society — possibly towards a greater development of technology and material progress, but at the expense of spiritual attunement and the mystical frame of mind. (Exactly the course of events in the West, incidentally, from around the time of the adoption of equal temperament in the eighteenth century, make of it what we will. However, one would certainly hesitate to denounce equal temperament, since it so increases music's harmonic possibilities.)

THE LOSS OF THE *LOGOS*

For four and a half millennia the music and its civilization was maintained. And then . . . *the music fell into decline.*

It happened during the Ch'ing Dynasty — the final dynasty — of AD 1644–1912. To the ancient philosophers the decline of their people's music would have been a tendency of vast and perilous significance. Yet with the decline in the music during the Ch'ing Dynasty, the civilization also deteriorated, just as the ancients would have predicted it must; and therefore the ancient wisdom itself was gradually forgotten. In other words, once a people have lost such wisdom, they are no longer wise enough to know that they have lost it — a variation on the myopic man who cannot find his glasses (because he has not got them on). This is a dangerous closed circle from which, once fallen prey to, there is little likelihood of return, as numerous historical examples testify. As the classical music of China progressively withered, so also faded the ability of the people to understand what this really meant according to the wise of former times.

But how did the compromise and dissolution of the traditional music begin in the first place? (Not merely a surface question, this. How does any civilization and its arts begin to fall below the level of their highest achievements?)

Could it have been caused by the introduction into China of a music more totally foreign than anything its people had ever known before — that of the West? Even prior to the final Ch'ing Dynasty, Roman church music had entered with the arrival of the first Western missionaries. In time, Western secular music followed. No matter how legitimate and good the Western music may have been in itself, it obviously had precious little in common with the Oriental style. Being unable to add to the traditional art, Western music could therefore only pervert or supplant it. From the point of view of maintaining the purity of China's own native music, safety might have lain in resisting an official acceptance of Western music. The music could have been officially rejected. But the Ch'ing monarchs committed what was, from the viewpoint of their ancestors, an incredibly grievous error: with the emperor's blessing, *Western instruments were introduced!* And: Westerners were accepted – *as professors of music at the imperial court!*

In our search for the culprit responsible for the decline of China's own music, the music of the West may be something of a red herring, however. Despite the official acceptance of the foreign music, those European musicians who travelled to China during the Ch'ing Dynasty reported that the music of the West was still not appreciated there. And after all, it was far from being the first time that a foreign music had 'invaded' the land. One Chinese source reveals that in AD 581 no fewer than seven foreign orchestras were being permanently maintained at the imperial court. No lack of potential tonal subversion here! Of the so-called Seven Orchestras:

> ... one had come from Kaoli, a Tungus country; another from India; a third from Buchara; a fourth from Kutcha in East Turkistan, with twenty performers of mostly Western instruments, which had been established as early as AD 384 and was so much in favour that the emperor tried to bar it. Individual musicians from Cambodia, Japan, Silla, Samarkand, Paikchei, Kachgar and Turkey mingled in them. The 'scholars', puristic defenders of the ancient music, protested; but in vain.[16]

So robust had the traditional music and its associated philosophy proved to be over the millennia, that even such an onslaught as this came to nothing. Ultimately, the ancient music had always absorbed what it could of foreign sounds, and, like a gigantic amoeba, spitting out the indigestible remains of its prey, ejected the rest. There was no particular reason to have expected any more glorious a fate for the music of the West. That it did gain a foothold, and that the traditional music did decline, may well be due less to the alien influence of the Western music than to a weakening of the hold of the ancient philosophy over the people.

Then again, at least one contemporary writer (John Michell, in *City of Revelation* published by Garnstone Press), looking at the problem of the decline from a more exalted level, has pondered whether, perhaps, the celestial harmonics which sustained the vibrational matrix of the Chinese civilization had not themselves arrived at the conclusion of their part in the symphony of the universe ...

Whatever its cause, that a decline was occurring became progressively unmistakable. At around the middle of the 1800s the classical drama, its music and its subject matter firmly rooted in the time-honoured traditions, began to be replaced by the modern style of Chinese drama, which met with greater popularity. In the field of pure music meanwhile, the great classical modes were supplanted by styles which were more popular, noisier, cheaper and imitative.[6]

The fact remains that this decline in music *was* definitely paralleled by a general decline in the civilization itself. The emperors of the final dynasty, perceiving immense danger in the progressive cheapening of the tonal arts, attempted to direct music back to its former state of idealistic conformity with the immutable principles of the cosmos.

But without result.

In 1912 the imperial house which had governed China for the incredible period of almost five thousand years at last came to an end, being replaced by a republic. Yet from its beginning, the republic was rocked by tumult and instability.

Western music had by now begun to be appreciated. Western orchestras performed in China, and increasing numbers of European music teachers settled there. The Chinese themselves learned to perform Western, rather than their own traditional, music. White crooners crooned in clubs; jazz bands blew the blues in the Hong Kong and Shanghai bars.

But, alas, where was the *hidden hand?* Where the mysterious, unseen influence to maintain stability throughout all 'the vicissitudes of time, destruction, wars, foreign influences and independent experiment'? (The ancient philosophy and its music was by now almost non-existent.) The republic survived – not another five thousand years, but less than fifty. Soon the remnants of the Nationalist forces were fleeing to the island now known as Taiwan, and Mao Tse-tung was striding into Peking, emanating the stream of red 'thinks' bubbles of his Thoughts the while.

Of music and civilization we have not yet attempted to establish definitely which of the two leads the way for the other. But, as in the case of many other past civilizations, the saga of the land of China demonstrates clearly that the link between the two is an intimate one.

THE USE OF SOUND IN MODERN CHINA

If we go in search of the tonal arts of mainland China as they exist today, we find that they are largely based on the medium of the opera. And, believe it or not, the basic story-lines of today's operas are frequently derived from the productions of former times. However, slight changes have been made since the civil war and Communist victory of the late 1940s: in unquestioned wisdom, the fathers of the revolution have seen fit to replace the traditional protagonists in the operas. The original legendary, spiritually elevated individuals have been supplanted by uniform-clad 'workers' and revolutionaries. The titles and story-lines have also been adjusted, now being concerned with one of four basic themes: (a) revolution, (b) political reform, (c) anti-Capitalism, and (d) praise of one or more prominent political figures, the particular names and faces changing with the changes in the political climate. The modern Chinese concert-goer must choose between works such as the *Sacred War Symphony, The Ming Tombs Reservoir Cantata* and ballets such as *The Red Detachment of Women.* Strange to say, faced with such an inspiring and bewildering variety of permitted subject matter, Chinese musicians are not so noted these days for their degree of creativity and inspiration.

There is also one other medium through which sound radiates forth from the nestled villages and seething cities of latter-day China, make of it what we will ....

According, again, to the current political climate, almost the entire populace – from the youngest of schoolchildren to the eldest of workers, from Peking to the smallest of villages – is 'requested' to observe a daily routine of anti-Capitalist songs *and death-chants.* In this second half of the twentieth century, while our own schoolchildren were beginning the day with morning prayers and hymns to God, Chinese children and their elders were ending theirs with repeated, rhythmic, full-throated shouts for our death and destruction.

What was going on in their minds as they did (and still do) so? What were the real and deepest motives of their rulers in orchestrating these death-chants? Was it only that they wished to indoctrinate the Chinese millions into an anti-Capitalist stance? Personally, I believe that more was involved. We may be witnessing here the surfacing on a gigantic scale of the deep-rooted, subconscious belief, present in perhaps all of us, that by vocalizing our desires we can help make them occur.

But – death-chants? Black magic on an international scale? Of course, as respectable citizens of the twentieth century we cannot admit the possibility of such things. Granted, the ancients would have been in no doubt. They would have seen the Chinese chants to be an objective, if partly unconscious, attempt on a vast scale to weaken and disintegrate the fabric of Western society through the misuse of Cosmic Sound. The ancients would have believed in the reality of the phenomenon, and that such magic could work: that the chants might materialize their effects in innumerable ways – in anything from the West's military defeat to its economic decline, from its moral decay to the dividing of its unity between nations and generations.

But of course, such notions must remain entirely unacceptable to us, living as we do in this modern era of scientific enlightenment. We know that the practice of chanting can only be propaganda, or mere superstition.

Even as we know that it was mere coincidence that, with the disappearance of China's ancient philosophy and music, the nation degenerated from the classical opera to the 'death-chant' within but a few decades.

Praise be to the glories of twentieth-century science and art! We know today that sound is nothing more than air vibrations, for now we live in a much wiser age than did the ancient Chinese.

— Or do we ...?

Notes

*The legend of Ling Lun, in describing the original pitch of the *huang chung,* conveys most poetically the *Logoic* link between perfected consciousness and the perfect foundation tone: the original tone, it is attested, matched the precise pitch of Ling Lun's voice *when he spoke without passion.*[6]

† Less down-to-earth and more esoteric aspects of Chinese life were also related to musical principles. For instance, the *I Ching* (Book of Changes) seems to have been associated at a fundamental level with the mysticism of music. Both the *I Ching* and the ancient Chinese philosophy of music share the same system of numerology, geometry and cosmology. And as those who have used the *I Ching* will know for themselves, the *kua* or line configurations which symbolize cosmic energies, and which configurations were used as symbols to indicate the eight classifications of Chinese instruments, are also basic to the *I Ching* system of divination.

‡ A similar central relationship of the one to the other four was recognized by the Christian Gnostics in respect of the five wounds of the crucified Christ: four wounds to the two hands and two feet,

and a fifth to the torso from whence emanated the heart-beat of the Word, even as the fifth string of the Chinese zither emanated the *kung*. Similar symbolism relating to the number five is found in the diverse legends and religions of many regions of the globe.

2.
The Twentieth Century: The 'New Music'

The philosophical outlook of most composers today is simply stated: the ideal is that there should be no ideals, and the rule must be that there should be no rules.

In ancient China music was based upon the loftiest of philosophical concepts. Today serious music is more devoid of idealistic foundations than at any period during the history of man. In ancient China only certain rhythms, melodies and modes were deemed to be correct and beneficial. Today, as the listener to modern music is only too painfully aware, anything goes.

From across the aeons, these two diametrically-opposed viewpoints confront each other head-on. And the question is: which is correct? Or at least, which of the two approaches more closely to the truth? Are the 'anything goes' twentieth-century composers truly correct, and were the Chinese hopelessly superstitious and irrational to have cautiously held their music within certain margins? Or were the Chinese correct in fact? *Does* music inevitably affect morality and civilization, which would place many of our current composers, in the extent of their danger to society, firmly among the ranks of the terrorists and political agitators of our day?

The dilemma of what is right and what is wrong in music is basically a moral question. We choose which direction music should take according to our moral and spiritual outlook (or lack of it). It is not the task of the present volume to attempt to prove the existence of God; neither to dive into the complexities of moral philosophy. Nevertheless, it would be helpful to outline two fundamental postulates:

1.   that religious belief stems not from superstition, but from some form of Higher Truth which lies at the core of all things, and in which is found the origin of all the world's great religions;

2. that morality, and the personal desire to improve the quality of one's character, is not illogical or pointless, but the surest way to personal fulfilment and to the greater benefit of all people.

It is worth affirming, as in these postulates, the importance of spiritual and moral ideals, for it is precisely in the abandoning of such ideals that the music of the twentieth century has, for the most part, departed from the inner direction of the music of the past.

Ours is an age in which nothing is accepted unquestioningly – either in the realms of science, or of social traditions, or of music. All past practices and beliefs are open to question. Granted too, it is indeed acceptable, and even wise, to reassess the established traditions of life, and those of music also. But what could be more foolhardy than to answer our own questions – with the wrong answers! Precisely this occurred at around the turn of the century when science, society and the arts each supplanted their nineteenth-century predecessors with a new outlook which leaned far towards the position of complete materialism.

Let us unravel the story of how, in the world of music, this came to pass.

THE IDEALISM OF PRE-TWENTIETH-CENTURY MUSIC

Prior to the opening of our present century, serious music had been almost invariably anchored upon spiritual ideals. Throughout the Middle Ages serious music in the West had been sustained as a tradition only by the Church. The Church used plainsong, organum and other forms of religious music; and it was from this purely religious background that Western classical music emerged. Irrespective of their particular religious leanings, the great composers of the classical and romantic eras were all motivated in their art by the highest of altruistic and sanctified ideals.

Liszt, for one, in his early essay 'On the Church Music of the Future' (1834), revealed the basic motivation which was to drive him throughout the remainder of his creative life. Music, he stated, contains a great power to move and inspire. Its beneficial influence can affect all of life, both within and without the church. Therefore it could be imbued with a renewed purpose and content, being composed with the objective of returning mankind to an awareness of the Spirit, and to the true worship of God. 'Come, hour of deliverance, when poets and artists will forget the public [with their demand for profane entertainment – D.T.] and will know one slogan only: man and God.'

A large minority of the music of the eighteenth and nineteenth centuries was overtly religious in nature, oratorios and masses having been composed by all the leading figures. Yet the rest of the music of these centuries, too, is scarcely befitting of the term 'secular'. Even those works which were not undisguisedly religious were nevertheless the creation of individuals whose very goal in life was solely and uncompromisingly to radiate throughout the world, by their art, the ideals of spirituality, joy and brotherhood. We find these ideals contained within every note of the string quartets, concertos, symphonies and other works of Haydn, Mozart, Beethoven and others. To point to an example – Bach's six Brandenburg Concertos, which are among the most 'secular' of his creations, are, in the opinions of most commentators, nonetheless saturated with divinity. This, not in their text or programmes (for they have none, being 'abstract' instrumental works), but even more fundamentally, in the sublime beauty of their melodies, the immaculate perfection of the mathematics of their harmonies, and in their unerring, unswerving, yet subtle rhythms, driving onward like the cosmic pulsations of the mystical motor of the universe.

Mozart, a Freemason, held firmly to the Masonic belief that art was an instrument which should be used for the elevation and freedom of humanity. Increasingly, his output of operatic works contained within their texts and story-lines the symbolic keys to the spiritual and mystic ideals of Masonry. This tendency culminated in *The Magic Flute,* which was a work of Masonic symbology through and through. Both Mozart's operas and his instrumental works also contained spiritual keys and symbols locked within the very numerology and intervallic structures of the notes themselves.

The 'secular' works of Beethoven, more than those of any other nineteenth-century composer, have frequently been noted for their fundamentally spiritual nature. His nine great symphonies contain numerous themes and tonal references pertaining to the path of self-transcendence and its challenges. Moreover, Beethoven's final five string quartets are considered by many to be the most mystical pieces of music ever created by man.

Then, from the viewpoint of the ancient wisdom (that music is a powerful force for social change and should be used only for spiritual and altruistic purposes), towards the end of the nineteenth century things began to go astray. Those very same tendencies in music which to the ancients would have signalled danger appeared to the late-nineteenth-century observer to represent the beginning of a new phase of humanistic enlightenment. The deceptive carrot of ever-greater artistic freedom had been sighted ahead.

THE REVOLUTION OF TECHNIQUE

From the retrospective viewpoints of modern commentators, the musical revolution which led from the romanticism of the nineteenth century into the 'new music' of the twentieth century was primarily a technical one.

Unlike the music of most ancient cultures, Western music has never in recent centuries possessed a definitely formulated and rigidly enforced system of codes stating what the composer could or could not do. Rather, traditional styles were maintained simply by a common consensus of what should or should not be done. It is not surprising, therefore, that over the decades and centuries innovations were indeed introduced and, at length, accepted. And fortunate are we that there were such innovations, for from them emerged the classical era itself. Clearly, then, there can be such a thing as beneficial and constructive innovation; we must not suppose that musical traditions are an inviolable law, or that all innovation is automatically wrong. (Correct innovations as they have occurred in Western music, genuinely benefiting the tonal arts, might be compared to the ancient Chinese practice of changing the *huang chung*. The Chinese, we may recall, believed that certain alterations were essential in order to keep pace with the continually self-transcending phases of Cosmic Sound: should the necessary musical evolutions be resisted, music would inevitably fall out of step with the needs and the consciousness of the age.)

J. S. Bach, Beethoven, Wagner and others did, nevertheless, encounter various forms of opposition to their new sounds; opposition ranging from initial unpopularity and incomprehension to witheringly critical audiences and reviews. Always, when these composers created more traditional kinds of music, such works met with the greater initial success. During his own lifetime, one of Beethoven's most popular works was his 'Battle Symphony', a programmatic concoction of drum rolls and blaring brass which Beethoven himself considered to be nothing more than a joke. Yet for his more advanced works a different fate was often reserved. Many consider his most avant-garde creation to be the *Grosse Fuge* movement of the Op. 130 String Quartet, but to the critics this was 'incomprehensible; a kind of Chinese puzzle', and it had to be replaced by a more acceptable alternative movement. It was only many decades afterwards that the *Grosse Fuge* came to be more fully understood, and an inspiration to a generation of musicians.

Despite initially unfavourable reactions, however, technical innovations continued. Throughout the latter half of the nineteenth century there occurred changes in all the dimensions of tonal art. Rhythm became more complex; composers took an interest in a number of new instruments and strange tone colours; new musical forms and structures appeared, such as the tone poem; new subject matter was considered. Yet the most significant series of innovations throughout the music of the eighteenth and nineteenth centuries was the gradual but continual evolution of harmony. And associated with the harmonic innovations were changes in the use of key.

The key of a piece of music is that strangely compelling 'homing instinct' by which the melody seems to revolve naturally around one particular tone. For example, observe how the tune of 'God Save the Queen' begins and ends on the same note. Often the key of a piece of classical music is stated in its actual title, such as in 'String Quartet in A major'. And in the same way that melodies seem to hang naturally upon one central note, so too does the use of harmony. The practice of basing musical harmonics upon one key note is known as *tonality*.

In the early Baroque music of the sixteenth century we find that harmonies were usually based upon the same home key from the beginning to the end of a movement. But modulation, the transposition of the music from one key to another, gradually increased. The early classical composers of the seventeenth century practised modulation *within* movements as a matter of course, but still only at certain well-defined dramatic moments. Beethoven modulated still more freely, yet nevertheless with a continued respect for the basic 'rules' of tonality. The tendency towards increased modulation reached its critical stage, however, with the arrival upon the scene of Richard Wagner. In Wagner's later works, modulation occurred so frequently that no real sense of key survived. This was a fateful challenge to all thinking musicians; one of a magnitude which cannot be overestimated. Serious Western music had always been firmly grounded upon the concept of tonality, no matter how increasingly sophisticated the actual practice of tonality had become. Yet Wagner, in *Tristan and Isolde* and other works, had questioned the infringibility and inveteracy of the entire tradition. It was an overt questioning which could not be merely forgotten or ignored by the rest of the musical world, any more than Einstein's Theory of Relativity could have been bypassed by the scientific community.

Again we find, this time in the case of Wagner, that not all questioning or transcending of past practices is necessarily wrong. Wagner's use of continuous modulation and novel harmonics is universally acknowledged to have been a major, beneficial and constructive step forward for the world of tonal art. Wagner's motives in composing his magnificent music-dramas were morally impeccable: to forge an art form which combined spiritual and deeply accomplished poetry with a music beautiful and sublime, all for the purposes of spiritually elevating the individual listener and bringing about enlightened social change. He introduced innovations into his music because he felt them to be justified in the ideal pursuance of these aims; his new, more complicated use of tonality enabled him to manifest the particular and specific musical effects and dramatic impacts which he deemed necessary for his works.

Wagner's reasons for composing in the first place, then, were entirely altruistic. Hence they were in conformity with those of Bach, Handel, Haydn, Mozart, Beethoven and Liszt (as well as with those of the musical philosophers of ancient China). Had Wagner's motives been adhered to and emulated by the succeeding generation of composers, Wagner's technical innovations would have represented the climactic entrance into a new world of music – music of perhaps equal or even greater beauty than the music of the classical and romantic eras.

To a large extent, however, the philosophy implicitly contained within the music of the turn of the century and thereafter was to be of a different order – eventually of a *very* different order. And hence the need for this chapter, that we may study just what twentieth-century music has really come to be about.

THE REVOLUTION INTO MATERIALISM

Exactly what is the manner of consciousness or the motive behind the 'new music' of our century? Perhaps it is not altogether possible to describe in one simple definition what it *is*. It remains possible, however, to define in complete certainty what it *is not* ...

As we have observed, it is usual for modern commentators to describe retrospectively the revolution which led to the 'new music' as having been primarily a technical one. That is, the revolution is thought to have revolved around all of the new ideas in harmony, rhythm, form and timbre which emerged at that time. One point, though: as trees combine to make up a wood, and as individual cells together form a complete human organism, so do technical details, on paper, go to make up a complete work of music. However, to see the wood we must broaden the scope of our vision beyond the sight of a single tree. Likewise, individual cells, alone, tell very little about the entire human being; what his personality and appearance are like. And in music, technical details rarely reveal a great deal about the essential meaning or conveyed impression of the whole work. Therefore let us ask: *was* the revolution into the 'new music' merely a revolution of technique? Does it not strike closer to the actual heart of the matter to realize that the most fundamental difference between the music of the previous centuries and the 'new music' of the twentieth century lay in the difference of their moral directions?

The stream of serious Western music had formerly followed the contours of a philosophical landscape which was at the very least genuinely altruistic, and often deeply spiritual. It was as though the musical stream itself had been unerringly impelled towards an eventual ocean of transcendent, mystical fulfilment. But after 1900, rebellious waves burst the river banks, taking off in a number of independent philosophical directions. A new breed of musicians appeared; these did not necessarily share the same artistic motives as their predecessors. The great composers of the past had composed for the sake of the spiritual upliftment of their fellow men. But the music of the new century raised its anchor from such firm moorings. The tonal arts were now art for art's sake. The listener found his attention to be focused by the 'new music' upon levels of being which were not spiritual, but merely mental, emotional, and yes, even physical.

The intellectual or mental content of music had once consisted of the sacred mathematics of Bach or the divine symbology of Mozart. Now this was replaced by mere human intellectualism. Even by a very early stage of the twentieth century, music appeared which seemed to have been composed primarily as an exposition of this or that new harmonic or rhythmic technique. In the past, composers had often experimented for the sake of improving their music; now many composed music for the sake of experimenting. The divine intellect became supplanted by mortal mentalism.

Formerly, the emotional direction of music had been vertically upward. The very purpose of the music had usually been to direct the feelings to God, or to regions of lofty, altruistic contemplation. The 'new music' directed the feelings along a merely horizontal plane: music evoked the reactions of one mortal to another, or to the material environment. Works such as many of the compositions of electronic music might at first be thought, in fact, to have no real 'emotional content' at all. But to believe so would be a mistake: *all* music affects the emotions. It is just that the kind of emotions which are stirred by cold, heartless electronic works are likewise cold and heartless.

The new movements in the world of music also directed consciousness to the physical level. There arose a new fascination with the sheer sensuousness of certain sounds, as for instance in much of the work of Debussy. It was almost as though sounds were no longer utilized for the sake of the music, but vice-versa: musical works were sometimes the glass cabinets, presented for the sake of showing off the new collection of sonorities contained within.

The essential difference in the spiritual directions of classical music and most serious twentieth-century music becomes strikingly illustrated by comparing works from the two different eras which share a certain common purpose. Take, for example, the difference between Beethoven's 'Pastoral' Symphony and the work of Edgar Varèse. Each composer attempted to render, through music, impressions of the objective world. Beethoven, however, chose that which is beautiful: the countryside; whilst Varèse, a century later, chose as his subject matter the hustle and bustle of modern urban life. Moreover, Beethoven idealized his subject matter, while Varèse emphasized the ugly and inhuman aspects of city life. But above all, the approach of Varèse towards his subject was merely 'horizontal': his music portrays only the physical side of the city. Beethoven, on the other hand, explicitly stated that his 'Pastoral' Symphony described, not a two-point, horizontal relationship between man and his environment, but *a three-point triangle* composed of Man, Nature and God (as, indeed, is so beautifully apparent to all who hear the work). The 'Pastoral' is intended not to portray Nature alone, but rather the Presence of God *within* Nature. Thus Beethoven transcended materialism: with the addition of God to the man—environment relationship, an extra and vital vertical dimension imbued the entire work with a higher meaning. Again, it is this vertical, spiritual dimension which is lacking in Debussy's portrayal of the sea in his *La Mer*. *La Mer* is nothing like as radically avant-garde as the output of Varèse, and yet still, even in Debussy's portrayal, we find the merely horizontal relationship. No matter how artfully the musical components of *La Mer* may have been welded together, the fact remains that the work is distinctly materialistic. *La Mer* describes the impressions conveyed by the sea to man — on the physical, emotional and mental, but *not* the spiritual, levels. And here we have the most fundamental difference of all between twentieth-century music and the music of classicism and romanticism; here we have the real nature of the 'revolution' in music which took place around the beginning of the present century: *that it was a 'revolution' into materialistic humanism.*

In the study of history, when we come to examine the musical histories of Greece, India and other ancient cultures, we encounter this same revolution again and again as the same basic fall into musical materialism has taken place within numerous historical periods.* We shall discover that whenever and wherever such a revolution has taken place, there has inevitably followed, within the civilization as a whole, the same descent of spirituality and morality into an unstable and brittle state devoid of permanent values.

One thing above all else characterized the great music of ancient China, India, Egypt and Greece, and later the music of Western classicism: that the fundamental purpose of music was conceived as being the transcendence of former states of consciousness. Such music always pointed the heart of man in the ↑ direction. And one thing above all else characterized the styles of music which spiritual idealists throughout the ages had viewed as being morally perilous: irrespective of whether such music was technically anarchistic, or whether it completely conformed to the technical 'rules' of the age, its moral direction was *not* upward. Such music began to make its mark in Europe during the late 1800s, when idealism (↑) began to be pushed aside by 'realism' (→), and even pessimism (↓). Let us now trace the seeds of this revolution, turning our attention to the work of specific composers.

Mussorgsky (1839-81) was one of the first 'realists' to have a significant impact. 'I want to speak to man in a language of truth,' he declared. But by 'truth', it must be noted, Mussorgsky did not mean elevated, spiritual truth. Rather, as a 'realist', he desired to express in tone form the 'real' world around himself – as he saw it. 'Life wherever it may be found, the truth *however bitter it may be* [my italics– D.T.],' he said, adding: '— that is what I aspire to, that is what I want, and I am afraid of failing.' And again: 'It is the people I want to depict, sleeping, waking, eating, drinking . . . Again and again they rise before me, huge, unvarnished, and with no tinsel trappings.'

The point is, though, that one man's 'truth' is another man's illusion – what the Hindus refer to as *maya*. Ultimately, truth is singular; yet whenever any artist has set out to portray 'the true world' his audience has inevitably finished up being served that artist's own subjective view of the world. For an artist to 'portray truth', when that truth is secular, means no more than to express his own personality. Whereas Mussorgsky spoke deridingly about 'varnish' and 'tinsel trappings' in his portrayal of men, the idealists such as Handel and Beethoven had consciously avoided depicting the imperfect, mortal nature of people. To them, it was preferable to outpicture the divine spark within all men, which they hoped and believed that their music would itself help to nurture. It is within Mussorgsky's works that serious Western music descends from the plane of idealism and divinity to the level of human personality for virtually the first time.

Mussorgsky was largely self-taught, and gave precious little heed to the established rules of harmony, etc. as practised and adhered to elsewhere during his day. A nineteenth-century musical Jack Kerouac, he composed freely according to the whims and dictates of his mental and emotional being. If a tonal phrase sounded right in his head, accurately expressing his own feelings, then he wrote it down, irrespective of any rules of key or harmony. (Rimsky-Korsakov, much shocked by this, very often 'corrected' Mussorgsky's compositions before they were performed.) Much in the Jack Kerouac, beat-poet style, since Mussorgsky's art reflected a consciousness undisciplined by such notions as artistic correctness or spiritual motive, the result was often the naked portrayal of those less desirable levels of the human mind. Frequently, Mussorgsky's tone-sequences convey emotions which are very much of a downward direction — desolation, anguish and psychological pain. Mussorgsky was also one of the earliest composers to place so much emphasis on speech patterns in music — melodic sequences similar to the sounds produced when human beings ask a question, express a doubt, shout in anger or yelp with fear.

Such techniques were employed within one of Mussorgsky's relatively well-known orchestral works, *Night on Bald Mountain*. The impressions conveyed by this piece can best be described by referring to its role within the Walt Disney cinematic production of 1940, *Fantasia*. In *Fantasia*, Disney granted his animators complete freedom to represent in animated scenes whatever the various pieces of music chosen for the film evoked in their minds. J. S. Bach's Toccata and Fugue in D minor, for instance, evoked for the Disney artists, as it surely does for us all, abstract patterns of mathematical precision and cosmological rhythm. All of this became faithfully — and spectacularly — outpictured upon the screen. Beethoven's 'Pastoral' Symphony, of course, was accompanied in the film by the magical, pastoral scenes which this music suggests. To a large extent, works of even instrumental music do tend to suggest the same thoughts and images to different people. *Fantasia*, then, made specific and raised fully to the conscious level the kind of concepts which the chosen pieces of music usually evoked in the listener.

And Mussorgsky's *Night on Bald Mountain*, then? What manner of visual display did this give rise to within the film?

Accompanying Mussorgsky's piece, and fitting the music perfectly, Chernabog, lord of evil and death, appears on the night of the witches' Sabbath. Spirits, witches and vampires dance frenziedly about. The skeletons of all those not buried in consecrated ground are raised up. Finally, tiring of them all, Chernabog condemns them all to a fiery pit. Each visual sequence faithfully parallels the eerie, sinister and monstrous soundtrack. Which brings us to the question: why should anybody need to have such music imposed upon them in the first place? Certainly *Night on Bald Mountain* could be listened to by individuals analysing how the composer had applied this or that technique in creating the work; it might always be studied by musicologists in the same way that we study prehistoric remains or the strange customs of savages. But for higher purposes this music has always been less than worthless.

Interestingly, Mussorgsky himself did become involved early in life with spiritualism and psychic phenomena. His interest in these subjects was, however, always in their more morbid aspects. Later, at college, he disavowed them and declared himself an atheist. After having been ruined financially he was forced to keep himself by taking a job as a minor clerk in the ministry of forestry and waterways. This, and the fact that his music met with little success during his lifetime, embittered him. Other composers, too, had encountered difficulties during their careers, yet had persevered in faith until their success finally arrived. Mussorgsky, however, having become an alcoholic, died poverty-stricken and alone. It is difficult not to perceive the reflection of his life and circumstances within his music of 'truth'.

A still more significant composer whose life and personal weaknesses also dictated the final stages of his music was Mussorgsky's compatriot, Tchaikovsky (1840-93). Though often lacking in subtlety, Tchaikovsky was a master of melody. Beautiful tunes came to him almost at will. These he would then skilfully weave together, employing his almost unerring penchant for applying the perfect instrumentation to each tonal phrase. (Shostakovich was later to declare that to listen to a work by Tchaikovsky was equivalent to a lesson in instrumentation.) His most successful and popular works are the last three symphonies, the first piano concerto, and the three great ballet suites, *Swan Lake* (1877), *Sleeping Beauty* (1890) and *Nutcracker* (1891).

In short, Tchaikovsky was as deserving as a man could be of the title, Born Musician. So naturally did music of deep beauty come to him that there was, on the face of it, no need for him to have ever gone astray from the idealistic artistic precepts of his classical predecessors.

Throughout the entire span of his adult life, however, Tchaikovsky was a man tormented. For he was homosexual. Inwardly horrified with himself and his tendencies, and embarrassed in the eyes of those who shared his secret, Tchaikovsky nevertheless failed to overcome his sexual inclinations. His homosexuality became the obsessive defect of his life, the tormenting demon that would allow him no peace of mind, no freedom from self-condemnation. Lacking a family of his own, and perhaps driven by the forces inherent in his moral weakness, the composer travelled relentlessly, year after year. A marriage entered into for the sake of normalizing his image in the eyes of himself and others ended disastrously: Tchaikovsky himself came to the verge of a total nervous breakdown, and the spouse of the unfulfilled match finished her life in a lunatic asylum. Always nervous and highly strung, the composer found his life to be a ceaseless struggle against moral weakness and over-emotionalism. And it was a struggle from which, ultimately, he failed to emerge as victor.

Tchaikovsky's failure to overcome his imperfect traits stamped its mark inexorably upon the last three of his six symphonies. Whilst at work upon his famous ballet suites, the subject matter of the ballets had dictated the emotional tone of the music for him; but the symphonies were a different matter. In the symphonies he had, as he said himself, the total freedom to compose whatever came naturally to him. Thus, the symphonies became the most personalized and introspective of all of his most important works. The first three of the six, while accomplished technically, are nevertheless lacking in that distinct quality of uniqueness which goes to make a piece of music eternally memorable. With the compostion of his Fourth Symphony (1877-8) at the age of 37, however, Tchaikovsky learned to fully impose his own individuality upon the symphonic medium. The work was programmatic and intensely personal. This, and the two symphonies that followed, were to be his most popular works within the genre; furthermore, they were genuinely unique in content as well as being masterfully executed technically. They exerted a real impact and influence upon the Russian and other European composers of his time, and are still frequently performed in our own day.

Unfortunately, however, these last three symphonies are fundamentally based upon overwhelming sentiments of ... pessimism and failure.

If music patterns do hold a powerful sway over life patterns, then Tchaikovsky's last three symphonies were a most inopportune manifestation for the composer to have left to posterity. There can be no doubt at all of the judgement which Confucius and his contemporaries would have passed upon these works. The basic philosophical theme of each of them is that which Tchaikovsky, in his letters and diaries, called 'Fate'. Each in their own way, the three symphonies tell the story of 'Fate' and its relationship to the individual. Yet the individual is not so much abstract 'man' as Tchaikovsky himself. And Tchaikovsky's 'Fate' is not so much of a Universal Purpose or pre-ordained destiny as it is his personal subjection to the homosexuality which so tormented his conscience. (Throughout his diaries the issue of his sexuality is always referred to in a half-veiled manner as 'my Fate' or 'XXX'.)

Of the Fourth Symphony, Tchaikovsky wrote to Nadezhda von Meck, his benefactress:

> The introduction is the *seed* of the whole symphony, beyond question the main idea. This is *Fate,* the fatal force which prevents our hopes of happiness from being realized, which watches jealously to see that our bliss and peace are not complete and unclouded, which, like the Sword of Damocles, is suspended over the head and perpetually poisons the soul. It is inescapable and it can never be overcome. One must submit to it and to futile yearnings. The gloomy, despairing feeling grows stronger and more burning...

In the next section of the symphony, Tchaikovsky relates, the soul turns from this grim reality into a world of subjective dreams of happiness — but 'Fate' awakens one harshly. 'There is no haven,' he mourned in his letter. 'Drift upon that sea until it engulfs and submerges you in its depths. That, approximately, is the programme of the first movement.'

This was the grim picture of life which Tchaikovsky painted in the Fourth Symphony. He himself thought the picture to be objective, a true depiction of the nature of reality; but many people, of his day and our own, would surely argue that life can be far more fulfilling and joyful. And yet, by attuning ourselves to the tones of such music, even without consciously knowing the programme, we automatically absorb its philosophy of submission and despair.

After the manner of Beethoven's classic Fifth Symphony, Tchaikovsky uses the word 'Fate' in reference to that which over-powers the human individual. But we must be careful here of the subtle trap, which Tchaikovsky fell prey to, of mistaking the two 'Fates' for one and the same thing. Beethoven and Tchaikovsky actually use the same word in reference to two very different – even absolutely opposing – things. 'Fate', which manifests as a theme in Beethoven's Fifth Symphony, as well as in a number of his other works, stands for that which is *greater* than the mortal individual. In Beethoven's marvellous Fifth Symphony the process is described of the confrontation between mortal and immortal, man and the Supreme. The individual soul, in this work of Beethoven, finds itself at the point where a choice must be made: to obey the Will of God, and thus evolve, or to stubbornly hold on to its own imperfect traits and indulgences. At length, the individual learns that to surrender to the Will of the Supreme is actually no loss of selfhood at all, but the doorway to a far more glorious and meaningful existence.[17] The symphony concludes on a magnificent note of triumphant victory.

Tchaikovsky's 'Fate', on the other hand, relates to that very manner of mortal imperfection which remains forever outside of the Will of the Supreme. In compensation for his personal failure to overcome his imperfections, Tchaikovsky erroneously called them 'Fate', as though to infer that their existence was divinely decreed and immutable. Yet his 'Fate' is ultimately a self-imposed one; had he been of stronger will he might have overcome his condition, either suppressing or sublimating it. Tchaikovsky's final symphonies being built organically around his concept of an inexorable, inescap-able doom, the Russian composer thereby gained the unfortunate distinction of becoming the first major musician to conclude a symphony with the overwhelming sense, not of victory, but of defeat. The occurrence boded much ill for the future of the art.

The programme of his next symphony, the fifth, Tchaikovsky would not reveal. But in one of his notebooks a rough sketch was discovered for the first movement, which gives us some idea of the meaning of the whole. His notes read:

Introduction. Complete resignation before Fate, or, which is the same, before the inscrutable predestination of Providence. Allegro. (I) Murmurs, doubts, plaints, reproaches against XXX ...

The programme of the final Sixth Symphony was again unrevealed, but the music itself leaves the general meaning of the work in no doubt. 'Fate' is now compeltely submitted to: a few tonal attempts to rise above or forget that which clouded the composer's entire life are soon brushed aside by the return of passages of utter and desolate melancholy. Though not revealing the programme, Tchaikovsky did write that the symphony 'is permeated with subjective feeling ... composing it in my mind, I wept copiously.' The final movement concludes the work with the unmistakable feeling of death. Considered his greatest symphony, it also sounds, as it were, the precise keynote of Tchaikovsky's life.

The symphony was first performed on 28 October, 1893, conducted by the composer himself. Tchaikovsky decided soon after that he would call the Sixth the 'Pathetic' Symphony – a title which, in the original Russian, refers to emotional suffering. Eight days following its first performance Tchaikovsky was dead.

The cause of the death has long been thought to have been cholera. Recent evidence, however, indicates that his death had to do with the confluence of three factors: his expanding fame, his continuing homosexuality, and the high esteem in which the Czar was increasingly, and publically, regarding him. To understand what these three factors led to, it is necessary to realize the intense patriotism and loyalty towards their Head of State which many people felt in those days. A number of Tchaikovsky's colleagues and associates, perceiving that the secret life of the composer might soon become exposed to the world, feared that this could prove disastrously embarrassing to the Czar. Forming a kangaroo court, they decided that the composer should prevent this from happening in the surest way possible: by taking his life. Tchaikovsky, totally disgraced and crushed by self-condemnation, did so. Following this, his friends rather amateurishly engaged in a cover-up to protect the composer's own reputation, giving the death the appearance of having been natural.

As he had written of the theme of the Fourth Symphony fifteen years earlier, Tchaikovsky had drifted upon the sea of his 'inescapable Fate' until it had engulfed and submerged him to its depths.

Many earlier composers had displayed imperfect traits of one kind or another, yet they had nevertheless striven ceaselessly to perfect themselves. In their music they had portrayed only that which is divine and beautiful in life; only that which the consciousness of man should always endeavour to move towards. In Tchaikovsky's last three symphonies, however, we are called to move in another, and less enlightened, direction. What can, at least, be said of them is that they offer a most instructive lesson: that rarely, if ever, can the work of an artist rise above the main direction of his own consciousness. It is doubtful that a masterful music can ever result where the heart and mind of the musician are not themselves, for the main part, so mastered. Tchaikovsky the man was torn apart by the contradictions within himself: the spirit sought to soar; the flesh was fallow for the fall. Thus, while in music Tchaikovsky often brought forth beauty, he never attained the heights of true spirituality, and eventually, in his last symphonies, he became the instrument of the music of despair such as has proved to be the deadliest of plagues to numerous civilizations before our own.

All of which brings us to what happened next. ...

DEBUSSY POINTS THE – OR A – WAY

Less than seven years after the death of Tchaikovsky, the world found itself at 31 December, 1899. Already, a substantial number of radical composers were preparing themselves to mark the new century with the onset of a new music.

The modern composer: no more shackles of tradition to hold him back! No Confucius to whisper annoying words of warning in his ear or to storm out of the court in protest! One minute to midnight, 31 December, 1899: the old era, with its superstitious spiritual standards, was about to become a memory of the past. So many rules now cried out to be broken! So many sounds there were which had not yet been sounded! So many moods which the composers of the past had refrained from expressing! And now it could be done. Now it could *all* be done! Now *anything* could be done!

One minute past midnight, 1 January, 1900: and the new musicians charged forth into the new century like rioting students into the streets. With cries for artistic 'freedom', they overturned those 'naive' beliefs which had persisted from ancient times even into the nineteenth century – that music affects morality, that certain chords should never be sounded. The notion was derided that, according to its form and content, tonal art could be responsible for the disintegration of a civilization. Wherever the idea surfaced it was set afire; 'absolutely lacking in any scientific basis!' came the shouts of outrage. Virtually all discussion of the effects of music upon the being of man disappeared from the textbooks.

The creative years of Claude Debussy (1862-1918) were spread precisely over this period of the onset of the revolution, as the old century gave way to the new. On the alternatives of tradition or of unlimited artistic licence Debussy made his opinions plain. 'I always try to free music from the barren traditions which stifle it. I am for liberty,' he declared. And, added the Frenchman: 'Music by its very nature is free. Every sound you hear around you can be reproduced. Everything that the keen ear perceives in the rhythms of the surrounding world can be represented musically.' Debussy's interest was never in the ↑ direction, but in the → direction: his music always told of the physical, emotional and mental conditions of the world around and within himself, no matter how talented and unique his portrayal of these realms may have been.

The central characteristic of Debussy's music, even as he progressed through several different stages of his art, remained an almost tangible sensuousness. And, interestingly, it was a trait far from lacking in the man himself. All biographies tell of his profoundly feline nature. Debussy walked and moved about like a cat; during the course of his life he kept scores of cats as pets; he bought feline ornaments (and this, even when he was penniless and hungry, and the ornaments cost whatever little money he had just earned); he made a point of frequenting the Parisian rendezvous, Le Chat Noir; and the composer even conspired to be born a Leo. That the cat is also traditionally an animal of eerie mystery, being, for example, the usual familiar of witches, may also have had some relevance within Debussy's enigmatic psyche.

Such points as the exceptionally sensuous nature of Debussy are not without their significance. As we trace, in this book, the relationships between music and human life, it becomes progressively clear that the style of a piece of music depends to a large degree upon the character of the composer himself. All forms of artistic creation are a portrayal of some level of the inner self of the creator. And so, if music patterns should indeed be found to affect life patterns, biographical details of those composers whose music is still played today can become extremely important to us. They may well hint to us what the outer effects upon society of that composer's music may be. And the importance of Debussy in determining the nature of twentieth-century music is inestimable: not only is his own music still played, but, even more importantly, his works effectively directed the course of much subsequent music by other composers.

This feline Frenchman was also a poet. His literary works are characterized, as Corinne Heline has described them, as being 'of night and of dawn, of moonlight and of velvet shadows, of mists and of perfumes'.[18] Further, Debussy also took an interest in occultism. And as it so happens, his output of music can only be accurately categorized in occult terms.

Experienced occultists often speak of an 'astral' plane of existence, which corresponds closely to the purgatory of Catholicism. The lower reaches of the astral plane are described as being realms of illusion, of ill-defined shadows, of lost souls and of strange perils. Ultimately, the astral plane results from a corresponding state of consciousness – an 'astral' consciousness, as it were. A typical example of an 'astral' state of mind is that induced by hallucinogenic drugs. And this gives a good idea of the kind of art which can be expected to result from the astral consciousness. Astral art is illusory rather than objective, sensuously seductive rather than genuinely spiritual. And it is in such a way, through the use of the adjective 'astral', that Debussy's art can most accurately be defined.

Generally considered to be Debussy's most accomplished work is the opera *Pelléas and Mélisande,* upon which the composer was engaged from the age of thirty-one until he was forty. To call in and ensure an unbiased viewpoint, let us quote from the brief description of this opera in the *Larousse Encyclopedia of Music*[19], where we find reference to, 'its dream-like quality, its enigmatic characters and settings in a never-never land ... the other-worldliness of the text ... a mysterious orchestral score'. To which is added the comment that, 'it is devoid of any definite action and the characters themselves are unreal'(!).

In his personal life, Debussy also maintained actual occult contacts. It is not so widely known that he was for years the head of the secret society, the Priory of Sion. This bizarre and professedly ancient group (still in existence today) believe themselves to be the geneaological offspring of Jesus Christ, who is supposed to have married. They are dedicated to the overthrow of all European governments, that the lineage of Christ might step into power. Moreover, in his later years Debussy became an intense admirer of the works of Edgar Allen Poe. Poe's art is thrice as astral as anything of Debussy's. His horror-fantasy yarns are still among the most potently effective stories of evil and of diabolical terrors in existence. Such was Debussy's fascination with Poe's tales that he set about composing a series of operas based upon them. What manner of music might be expect from a composer who had allowed his consciousness to become seduced by such writings? As it happens, we shall never know: Debussy was still at work upon the operas when he was finally overtaken by the cancer which had threatened him with death since his thirties. His death was a miserable one, and he greeted it with intense bitterness. The prospect of a chilling wedding between the shadowy literature of Poe and the already powerfully influential music of Debussy seemed to have evoked Fate itself in resistance.

IMPRESSIONISM VS. EXPRESSIONISM

As a quasi-reaction against the *impressionistic* music of Debussy and other composers there arose a music of equally uncertain spiritual value which was by nature *expressionistic*. The impressionists had at least been content to take the music of the eighteenth and nineteenth centuries, with its tonality, as a starting point, even though from there they allowed a good deal of innovation and extrapolation to dictate new musical directions. No matter how radical, impressionistic music was still, at its root, tonal. But the new breed, the expressionists, felt moved to call the entire preceding tradition into question. New systems of tonality and harmony were tried out, while whatever forms and rules music had previously conformed to were irrelevant to the expressionists. Or more – something to be particularly avoided.

In his authoritative book, *Music in Western Civilization*, Paul Henry Láng comments:

> The impressionist abandons himself; the expressionist seeks the utmost concentration ... Against the worldly, hedonistic nature of impressionism, expressionism opposed the unnatural, the clashing, the torturing ... In its most uncompromising utterances expressionism carried the anti-romantic zeal to the point where it refused to recognize sentiments, thus basing its new aesthetic doctrine on the mental stage of emotional suspension ...

– To which Láng perspicaciously adds that this was 'really ... the emotion of avoiding emotions'.[20]

In a century which has so often granted Western nations, at election time, the 'freedom' of choosing between two equally uninspiring and insincere political party-leaders, music lovers found themselves confronted with a choice between two schools of music which were of equal abhorrence to the spiritual idealist. Though some good and spiritual music appeared under the impressionist banner, for the most part the 'choice' between the two schools represented the equivalent in the world of art of an election campaign fought between Marx and Mussolini.

Yet it was still only the beginning. Having been cast adrift from the spiritual elements and upward striving essential for all great music, the new musical culture fell prone to over-technicality and an impatient, vacillating hunger for sensationalism. For a few years such increasingly nervous, decadent and materialistic art ruled the roost of the new output of music, until the outbreak of the First World War put an end to an entire era of human history. And yet, following these earliest stages of the non-idealist music, what was to come next? As Paul Henry Láng puts it:

> New life could be infused into the music of this rapidly disin-tegrating world only by an even more nervous, sophisticated and surcharged emphasis on the already overtaxed elements of effect and technique. Experiment then became the final aim ...[20]

THE SERIALISTS

Had they possessed the seismological equipment to do so, the scien-tists of 1874 would no doubt have registered a seismic disturbance of high degree on the Richter scale emanating from the region of China during that year: the bodies of thousands of ancient Chinese philosophers energetically turning over in their tombs at the birth in Vienna of Arnold Schoenberg. For during the course of his career, Schoenberg was to renounce the entire concept of tonality for the first time in human history.

Tonality, the practice of basing music upon one particular key, the melodies and harmonies all gravitating around that key, had been an inherent aspect of music since the beginning of recorded history. The ancients believed that the key which was used for a piece of music had tremendous cosmological significance. We have seen how the Chinese used whatever key they believed to be the earthly reflection of the particular Cosmic Tone which was sounding upon the earth at the time of the musical performance. In this way, the tonality of all Chinese music became associated with astrological Tonality and the harmonic relationships between the signs of the zodiac. Yet even in modern times most music remains tonal in nature, for there are also very practical artistic reasons for the use of tonality. There are special relationships between the 'tonic' or keynote of a piece of music and the other notes such as those removed from it by an interval of a fifth or of a fourth. The note-relationships which are the basis of tonality are grounded upon fundamental mathematical and aesthetic principles. This results in the fact that tonal music automatically 'sounds right' to the human ear, whereas music which is not tonal, at least upon our first hearing it, sounds incorrect and unmusical.

Children all over the world, when they first begin to speak or sing, do so in melodies based firmly upon tonal intervals. The harmonic and melodic principles of tonality, then, seem to be by no means arbitrary or theoretical, but are naturally meaningful to the human psyche. In fact, scientific research has discovered that the traditional harmonic intervals and chords really are special: the physical study of sound vibrations has confirmed that traditional tonality conforms to certain unique and objective vibrational relationships between sound-pitches. Moreover, these same mathematical relationships have been found to be present throughout many and diverse phenomena of nature, in everything from the laws of physics to the geometry and the ratios present in the forms of living organisms. It is only one small step from all of this to the postulate that the ancients were correct: that there truly is something about tonal music which puts it in tune with the entire universe, thus making it a real source of healing and regeneration. We can see, therefore, what might underlie the age-old concept that some music is objectively 'right' or 'correct' while other forms of music are wrong and even dangerous. If tonal music heals and regenerates the body, the mind, and society as a whole, then atonal music might be expected to do the opposite.

It was due to the fact that tonal music comes so naturally to man that, even when the ancient wisdom itself had faded from the memory of the race, the great classical Western composers continued to create music within the principles of tonality and the diatonic scale. In moving fully outside of this traditional system, Schoenberg had made a momentous move indeed. Many fellow composers of the twentieth century hailed it as a great breakthrough. It is dubious, however, whether Beethoven or Bach would ever have done so. And had they still been present to witness the event, the reaction of the sages of antiquity is certain: their conclusion would have been that, provided that Schoenberg's music caught on and became sufficiently popular, the days of Western civilization were numbered.

Schoenberg's music encompassed several different periods. In the first of them tonality, while present, became increasingly uncertain. Then, from around 1908, he entered a second period in which atonality reigned. This has been called 'the phase of unlimited anarchy and liberty' (the very concept being in direct contradiction to the principles of spiritual idealism). In this phase, the seven major and five minor notes of the scale became simply twelve notes a semitone apart. The twelve notes were all treated equally, no form of logical organization being placed upon them. Thus, the resultant music was in no key, and its melody and harmony paid no allegiance to the traditional emphasis upon the intervals of the fifth, the fourth, and so on.

Next, in the important third period of his career, Schoenberg replaced his previous 'unlimited anarchy' with a new system of note organization of his own invention, which came to be called 'serialism'. Under the serialist system, the twelve notes of the octave were arranged into a certain sequential order, and this order then became the series or 'tone-row' upon which an entire piece of music was based. The series of notes could be played forwards or backwards, in its entirety or only partially, and in inverted form. But since the series contained the entire twelve notes in a pre-determined order, it was therefore not possible to play a note a second time within the sequence before all the other notes had been sounded. Webern, Berg and others also adopted the serialist technique from Schoenberg, and the school of 'twelve-note composers' was born.

Though with the introduction of serialism Schoenberg had reverted from absolute anarchy to some form of logical order, the technique nevertheless poses a number of important philosophical questions. For example, what if there truly are some manner of Cosmic Tones, and that works of music attune themselves to one particular Tone through the use of tonality? What would this mean for atonality, as practised in serialism, which does not make use of keynotes? Could it possibly be that, in abandoning the system of tonal music which comes so naturally to man, Schoenberg had, unwittingly or otherwise, attempted to usurp divine Will with human will? Could systems such as serialism represent the rebellion, at some level of the human psyche, against the Harmony of the Spheres?

In his later years, Schoenberg's third phase of strict serialism gave way in turn to a less rigid style in which, while serialism was maintained, elements of tonality were increasingly introduced. Upon first founding the method, the originator of serialism had at the time been criticized by the traditionalists. But serialism had since then become well established in the musical world. Now, for abandoning it in its pure form, Schoenberg was criticized almost as much again!

ENTER: THE COMMANDOS

Music normally evolves as an almost 'natural' development, one composer after another extrapolating and building upon the ideas of his predecessors. To the esoterically-minded thinker, however, the coming of the 'new music' in the early years of this century is particularly intriguing in that, in many respects, it did not so much evolve as appear as though from nowhere. For centuries at a time during earlier periods of world history the face of music had changed comparatively little. A composer had once felt it his prime responsibility to create new *compositions* of music. But in the case of the 'new music' the emphasis radically shifted: the major purpose became to create new *kinds* of music altogether. Now it was as though a veritable wave of individuals were born in the late nineteenth century who all shared the inherent trait of being seemingly incapable of conforming to the traditional standards — and purposes — of the tonal arts.

Nobody illustrates this factor of the 'wave phenomenon' more than does Charles Ives (1874-1954), America's first composer of real significance. Born and raised in Danbury, Connecticut, Ives was almost totally cut off from the radical musical developments which were taking place in Europe. Ives studied music at Yale University at around the turn of the century, but in later years had little way of knowing what was taking place musically across the Atlantic. During these years of his own creative work he heard none of the music of Schoenberg or Hindemith, and of Stravinsky only *The Firebird* and *The Nightingale.* And yet it was as though the composers of the 'new music' had been some sort of commando squad trained in either heaven or hell (depending upon one's viewpoint) to parachute into Europe and re-channel the entire course of music, and that Ives' parachute had been caught in an almighty gust of wind which had blown him off course to the other side of the Atlantic. For there, alone and in virtual seclusion from any other musician or any outside influence, Ives quite independently developed bi-tonality, polytonality, atonality, multiple rhythms or polyrhythms, the use of chance factors within music, and all the other trappings of the 'new music'. In his output, Ives not only paralleled, but even preceded such developments as they took place upon European soil.

As Ives once wrote to his copyist upon sending him a new work:

'Mr Price. Please don't try to make things nice. All the wrong notes are *right.*'

And again, Ives' jotted comment on the margin of the manuscript of his Second String Quartet:

... as a Cadenza to play or not to play! If played, to be played
as not a nice one – but evenly, precisely unmusical as possible!

Experiment was the name of the game; after Ives tried out any
technical innovation in one composition the innovation was seldom
returned to in his music in anything like the same way again. Yet to
the ears of his contemporaries, Ives' music was not merely dissonant,
but mad. Ives was trying to reflect in music the dissonances and
stark realities of the world around him. Yes – in a way this was
Mussorgsky's 'realism' all over again, and again in contradiction to
the greatest musicians of all earlier epochs of human history who
had sought, through music, to impose order and meaning upon
earthly chaos.

It may tell us something about the psychological effects of Ives'
music that, while decades of life still remained to him, his ability to
creatively compose did not. His wife was later to recall the pain and
tragedy of those months and years during which Ives had tried to
compose, only to discover that the fount had dried up. He lived out
his many remaining years as an invalid in almost complete isolation
from other musicians.

Nevertheless, their parachutes well buried, others among the
commando team were ready to strike elsewhere in the world. . . .

To what extent are we justified in speaking of a 'wave
phenomenon' in the way in which the radical musicians burst upon
the scene? It might be said that it was difficult for a young musician
not to be radical in that period – it was in the nature of the times,
was it not? And yet, let us attempt to adopt an Oriental manner of
viewing events: what, ultimately, was the *cause* behind the
radicalism and cultural revolution of the new century? Were the
'new musicians' a sign of the times . . . *or have the times, or at least
some degree of the nature of life in the twentieth century, been a sign of the
coming of the 'new music'?*

But back to the cultural commandos who fell upon European
lands. During the time of Ives, half a dozen composers in Paris set
out upon their own particular revolutionary mission. Known as the
Six, their aim was deliberately to write music which was devoid of
any stirring or lofty feelings. In order to help accomplish this, jazz
and other popular idioms were borrowed by them, and the resulting
sound was 'successfully' noisy and cheap. Serious composers first
became widely aware of jazz during the 1920s, and few of the
proponents of the 'new music' failed to incorporate it into their
work to some extent. Stravinsky, Ravel, Hindemith, Copland and

many others — composers good and bad — all allowed jazz-like effects into their work. By this time, spiritual standards were either non-existent or had been turned upside down. Regrettably few musicians of the 1920s seemed to realize the difference between mysticism and moodiness; or if they did, they preferred the latter.

And still this was only the beginning. . . .

IGOR STRAVINSKY

In the early stages of the 'new music', one work above all others marked the arrival, not to mention the sheer, irrepressible force, of the revolution. Today, music students listen to this revolutionary work in what is usually passive humility. They are academically trained to analyse the structure, rhythm and harmonies of a piece of music rather than its overall effect and impact. No thought at all is given to such considerations as the work's level of spirituality, of course. Yet there are still many people out in the world who, having found it natural to love eighteenth and nineteenth century music, have scarcely heard the works of the 'new music'. Some have rarely, if ever, heard this particular composition, and on occasion I have played a recording of it for them. Invariably its reaction upon them has been one of powerful disturbance and shock. While admitting its intellectual genius and originality, they nevertheless found it to sharply lower their state of consciousness, and not a single one professed the desire ever to hear the work again.

In the reaction of these divine innocents, who had somehow shielded themselves from the presence of the 'new music' in the world about them, we must be coming very close to the initial impact of the work upon its first audiences. *The Rite of Spring* is without doubt the most famous work of Igor Stravinsky. Stravinsky (1882-1971) based the work upon the concept of a pagan ceremony. Certainly the music of *The Rite of Spring* is nothing if not pagan, being wild, aggressive, and fiercely ungodly. The melodies seem designed to frighten; the harmonies to disrupt the mind. But more than anything it was the complex rhythmic side of the work which was so unique. The rhythms race compellingly, driving relentlessly onward, breathlessly, and with dark undertones of violence and dread.

For the première performance of the ballet in 1913, Nijinsky directed the choreography, and none other than Nicholas Roerich, in a rare misjudgment, agreed to create the décor. The choreography followed the only general pattern possible, given the music upon which it was based: a primitive ritual of pre-Christian peasant

Russia which culminates in the sacrifice of a virgin. Even by itself, the music alone of *The Rite of Spring* reaches such a crescendo of hedonistic abandonment as to suggest the sacrificial virgin, intoxicated by the pagan ritual and violent rhythms, literally dancing herself frenziedly to death.

We are familiar by now in this book with the very real powers which music seems able to wield; also one would have had to have lived as a hermit for many years not to have heard of the acts of violence and riots which sometimes take place at rock concerts. It should little surprise us then that the première of *The Rite of Spring*, over forty years before the coming of rock, and yet strangely akin to this music of later decades in the irrepressible violence of its rhythms, likewise resulted in a riot. Accounts written at the time record that the audience sat and listened in silence ... for two minutes. Then there came catcalls and shouts of outrage. People seated next to each other began to fight with fists and canes. Next, the attention of the audience became directed towards the orchestra, towards which everything conceivable that was loose and remotely aerodynamic was thrown. But resolutely, the musicians played on through a hail of abuse and a torrent of missiles. The conclusion of the ballet was greeted by the arrival of the gendarmes. Meantime, the composer at the cause of it all had escaped through a window backstage. Such scenes had never been heard of at a ballet before, and the incident caused a great scandal.

But Stravinsky, at 30, had only as yet begun to get warmed up, and certainly was in no mood for apologies. 'I heard, and I wrote what I heard,' he said. 'I was the vessel through which *Le Sacre du Printemps* passed.'

Stravinsky had written *The Rite of Spring* while still only 29. It marked only the beginning of his world-renown, and only the end of the beginning of his output. He went on to compose for a total of over six decades, and had become the acknowledged grandmaster of the 'new music' long before his death in 1971. Hardly a single style or movement of the 'new music' went untouched by him. As the general in the field, he bustled through the ranks, showing his face in this division and that, encouraging here, advising there, adding confidence by the fact of his presence. Along the way, Stravinsky became one of the first composers of serious music to include elements of jazz in his work. This tendency he capped with the *Ebony Concerto,* composed especially for the 'big band' jazz orchestra of clarinettist Woody Herman and trumpet player Shorty Rogers.

For decades, even as he developed his art and gained wider

recognition, Stravinsky remained next to penniless. But this did not prevent him from becoming closely acquainted with almost all the major names in the European arts. Picasso, a similarly commanding and avant-garde figure, drew Stravinsky several times. During World War I, while attempting to cross the Italian border, Stravinsky was stopped by the guards who accused him, as he later wrote, 'of trying to smuggle a plan of fortifications – in fact my portrait by Picasso – out of the country'.

Neither did his long-standing poverty deter him from maintaining a whisky intake of the kind that would be expected to kill most men. He once preceded the conducting of a concert in Moscow by downing ten drops of opium and two tumblers of whisky. (Given the youthful age at which he gained notoriety, his degenerative lifestyle, and the radical nature of his music, Stravinsky was not very dissimilar, within the context of his own era, to, say, the Rolling Stones and other rock stars of today.) During this Moscow concert he then suddenly felt sick. Finding his pulse weak, a doctor forbade him to continue conducting. But this outraged the composer, who went on to finish the concert after indulging in his own 'remedy' of brandy and coffee.

One of Stravinsky's most famous works for the stage is the opera-oratorio, *Oedipus Rex* (1927). In this work, however, the institution and established conception of the opera is completely ridiculed. Though based upon the classical work by Sophocles, the libretto is sung in Latin – which no doubt most of the audience cannot follow – while a commentator in evening dress stands to one side of the stage and interprets the action in modern jargon to the audience, which has the effect of utterly alienating the singers from the onlookers.

Was the 'new music' *so* different to that of previous centuries? Stravinsky's treatment of *Oedipus Rex* furnishes us with the answer.

The narrow-minded critic will argue here that the new musicians did not break with the past, but merely followed the course of the natural evolution of the art, following the innovations of Beethoven, Liszt, Wagner and others. To which, in reply, it must be emphasised that the prime distinction between twentieth-century music and that of classicism and romanticism was never the obvious technical one, but the difference between the spiritual level of the two. It is a question of *motive,* of the *goal* of the music; it is a fundamental question of morality. We must ask ourselves of any piece of music: Does this build up or does it tear down? Ultimately, it is a question of *the consciousness of the composer.*

It is necessary to be sufficiently detached as to be impervious to intimidation by the materialist twentieth-century musical intellectuals. These, proud to belong to an artistic movement which 'the average person doesn't understand', would throw scorn upon all who could dare to be so 'old-fashioned' or 'boring' as to question, at this late date, the validity of *The Rite of Spring.* They shall claim to our face: *The Rite of Spring* and Beethoven's Ninth Symphony are each equally valid within the context of their respective ages. To which the discerning shall reply: True it is that each are music, each consisting physically of air vibrations and each being performed by similar musical instruments; but these works are the result of two diametrically opposed philosophies – atheistic humanism and spiritual idealism – which have warred since before the dawn of history for the possession of the minds of men.

If we should doubt whether or not *The Rite of Spring* and the other early works of 'new music' are really so bad as all that, then we have only to glance further on in time to see what they led to. What manner of art did the 'new music' go on to become following these first beginnings? After all, the real nature of the seed becomes inevitably outpictured in the flower! The seed itself may give little or no indication as to that which lies within it, and the non-botanist might easily put the name 'rose tree' to the seed of a Venus fly-trap. But in the process of its growth all becomes revealed.

Is there a difficulty in discerning the subtle nature of a music, whether it is beneficial or destructive in effect? Then the answer to the dilemma was put into our hands two millennia ago:

— *Ye shall know them by their fruits* . . .

BALLET MÉCHANIQUE, AND AFTER

The date: 10 April, 1927. The place: Carnegie Hall, New York. A quarter of the way into the century now. And an American audience prepared themselves for a concert of the wonderful new music. The composer, George Antheil, had produced a work befitting the new century of progress. Building steadily upon each other's work, composer after composer had pushed the grandeur and sublimity of Western music ever higher. J. S. Bach, Handel, Haydn, Mozart, Beethoven, Wager – and now George Antheil, with the first performance of *Ballet Méchanique,* his newly wrought creation. And 'wrought' it had indeed been: 'musical engineering', Antheil called it. The instrumentation for the work included various odds and ends and items of hardware – anvils, bells, horns, buzzsaws and an airplane propeller. Oh, and also some pianos. (Ten, to be precise.)

One can imagine that for such a grand occasion as the première at the Carnegie Hall only the world's leading virtuoso buzzsawists will have been employed, and perhaps one of the Wright brothers on propeller for the uplifting finale. (For a much later 1954 performance, the composer feared that *Ballet Méchanique* might by then sound — well, old fashioned — and replaced the airplane propeller with a recording of a jet engine. After all, the 'new music' must move on!)

Edgar Varèse (1885-1965), another American, dedicated his life to seeing that the 'new music' did indeed 'move on', and became one of the leaders in the field. Born a French-Italian in Paris, Varèse emigrated to America in 1915. He saw around himself a concentrated life of hustle and bustle, and a world which, some said, had entered into a machine age. Both the speed and the machinery of twentieth-century city life were to be an important influence upon his music. Said Varèse:

> Speed and synthesis are characteristic of our epoch. We need twentieth-century instruments to help us realize those in music. [21]

And had the people of the day taken him to mean buzzsaws etc., they would not have been far wrong. His work echoed the sounds of city life. Motors, pistons, car horns and other such sounds are distinctly evoked in the music. Melody and harmony were at a minimum; all the emphasis Varèse placed upon rhythm. His insistent rhythms reflected the throbbing, whirring industrial life and the hectic bedlam of rush-hour.

Yes — again we find ourselves meeting our old friend, 'realism'. Of course, the 'new music' is something which the likes of you and I 'just do not understand'. But nevertheless, perhaps we can summon sufficient courage to tentatively enquire: *Why* such music? Why *reflect* city life? (And how objective was Varèse's vision of city life in any case?) Observe the difference here again between twentieth-century 'serious music' and that of earlier times. Formerly music raised and sublimated; now it 'reflects'. What good does such music do for anyone? (But here our questions are drowned out by orchestrated peals of sarcastic laughter. '*Good?* Why should music have to *do good?*')

After the early 1930s Varèse virtually ceased composing, and took up research into electronic instruments. Meanwhile, the tape recorder had been invented in 1935, though it only became widely available after about 1950. Varèse received one as a gift in 1953, and immediately began using it to enter an entirely new field of tone production for 'artistic purposes', which was just opening up. Now it was possible to pre-record exactly the sounds one required, to produce tones artifically, to mix them, slow them down, speed them up, or play them backwards.

Needless to say, the 'new musicians' were going to have a field day.

And so, following a gap of two decades, Varèse began composing once more. His tape-recorded work, *Déserts,* was completed in 1954 and premièred on 2 December in Paris. *Déserts* consisted of sections of recorded industrial noises (more hissing, grinding and puffing – Varèse had apparently not advanced *so* far during those twenty years!) alternated with instrumental percussion passages. The effect was to suggest both a musicality present in industry, and also a mechanization of human musicians. Broadcast in stereo radio, the piece gained instant fame. Like *The Rite of Spring* four decades earlier, *Déserts* had broken new and starkly revolutionary ground, and resulted in a wave of music which followed in its wake. Within but a year or two, the production line for electronic music was in top gear.

Déserts had originally been intended to be accompanied by a film 'purely of light phenomena'. As we might by now expect, however, Varèse stipulated that 'the film must be absolutely in opposition with the score'. (Opposite visual and auditory perceptions, it seems reasonable to assume, could exert a disastrously mind-splitting effect, resulting in possible psychosis. Could it have been that at some level of his being, Varèse *desired* such results?)

Of *Déserts* and the later work, *Poème Electronique,* Francis Routh has pointed out that Varèse 'does not seek to assert the human will so much as to submit it to the timeless void that is nature. We move through a wasteland of sound ...'[22] Routh further indicates the similarity between such music and the literature of existentialism, as championed by Jean-Paul Sartre. (Existentialism was particularly prominent in Varèse's land of birth, France, and especially from the late 1940s onwards.) Perhaps here we find as clear a pointer as any to the philosophy underlying the 'new music': existentialism, of course, is the general doctrine which denies objective universal values or morals. A man, so it is claimed, must create values for himself through his own actions. He has absolute liberty to do as he chooses; thus allowing for anarchy. In fact, *Poème Electronique* (1957-8) was described by Varèse as 'a protest against inquisition [i.e. the maintenance of standards – D.T.] in every form' – a strikingly anarchistic statement.

Poème Electronique, though only eight minutes long, came to be recognized as 'a masterpiece of tape music'. Amid a strange, fearsome background of harsh, artificial sounds, a solo soprano voice enters towards the end, sounding as though invoking some unimaginable form of evil. The composition of the work was suggested in the first place by Le Corbusier, so that it could be played in the Phillips Radio Corporation pavilion which he had designed for the Brussels Exhibition. The tones were projected by four hundred loudspeakers placed at every position conceivable within the building, which itself resembled 'a circus tent with three poles somewhat inaccurately pitched'.[23]

Déserts and *Poème Electronique* were the only major works to be composed by Varèse after the 1930s, and yet, judging by the aftermath, they could not have been better calculated to stir up a new movement of the revolution. Within months of the première of *Déserts,* there followed the first live concert in the world at which every sound was electronically synthesized. Four years later, in 1958, there appeared Berio's *Thema − ommagio a Joyce,* which seemed to be an attempt to portray, in electronic tone and electronically-manipulated speech, a progressive mental disintegration.

Another 'first' came for the electronic musicians in 1967 − the first commission of a piece of electronic music by a record company where the music was not initially intended for broadcast performance.[24] Morton Subotnik was the lucky man, the creator of such previous artistic masterpieces as *The Wild Bull* and *Sidewinder.* Utilizing a Buchla synthesizer, he now unveiled for the world − *Silver Apples of the Moon.*

How to describe this 'music' of Subotnik? At first it sounds merely monotonous. Yet somehow the title is eerily apt: it is as though silver balls are raining from space and exploding on the ground and in the air all around one, doing so with 'bleeping' noises. And so it goes on. Then, for a moment one comes to feel that there might after all be genuine aesthetic interest in these bleeps ... if only one listens, that is; listening more closely ... more attentively ... to the sounds, the silver sounds ... the bursting apples ...

Would the reader allow me here to offer one opinion? No proof, no scientific discussion about the pros and cons of the conviction I find myself with − just a simple gut reaction: that there is something distinctly dangerous to the consciousness in such music as this. Dangerous in a perhaps surprisingly tangible and immediate way. It is as though there exists a chasm within each of these electronic compositions: a dark, yawning crevasse which, if we allow it to, will gladly swallow up whatever portion of our mind we offer it by the directing of our attention towards it.

While Subotnik's work was emerging, another new development was also under way, coming to fruition in 1968. One Walter Carlos, taking up the music of J. S. Bach, produced what could be called a style of 'neo-classicism'. Afraid that there might yet be life in the old boy and his work, Carlos took Bach by the neck and attempted (if he could) to utterly throttle and destroy him. Bach *performed by synthesizer* was the appalling outcome. (More seismic shocks from China.) Needless to say, the synthesizer proved utterly incapable of capturing the most meagre essence of the many shades of warmth, power, awe and reverence, serenity and delicate beauty which Bach's works demand of their usual instruments. This was of little, if any, concern to Carlos or the record company producing the atrocity, however. Their thoughts were no doubt elsewhere: the LP recording swiftly became by far the most popular (and lucrative) electronic recording of all time. Sporting the title *Switched on Bach* on the cover, along with a number of repetitions of Bach's face illustrated in psychedelic style, it became the kind of record which is up for sale by the dozen on Woolworth's swing-racks, and which is piped through as 'easy listening' into dentists' waiting rooms.

What is more, it must be remembered that this was 1968: the 'new music', jazz, and rock music had by now, between them, reigned supreme for decades. Tragic to relate it may be, but nonetheless absolutely true, that for thousands of households into which this atrocity gained admittance, for untold adults and for their children, *Switched on Bach* represented *their very first, if not their only encounter* with this giant of the history of great music.

But it was not to be their last. Not sluggish to cash in on a good thing, Carlos followed up within a year with *The Well-Tempered Synthesizer*.

By this time a certain cross-fertilization was becoming apparent between the 'new music' and the general jazz and rock style. It came to be seen that the technical differences between 'serious' music, jazz, rock, or any other form of modern music were less important than the unifying factor that their philosophical basis was more or less one and the same: hedonism and anarchy. In an era during which the musician was constantly searching for 'new sounds' with which to distinguish himself from the pack, the breakdown of the divisions separating the different musical forms offered tempting possibilities. Jazz took on rock elements, and rock took to itself many of the techniques of jazz. Rock, which had arisen from the most primitive of beginnings, spawned groups such as Soft Machine and Velvet Underground, which were sufficiently avant-garde that no book about the 'new music' was complete without mentioning them. Meanwhile, one noticed with amusement that a certain atmosphere of 'the rock star' had attached itself to a number of the 'new musicians' in the magic of adulation which became associated with their names.

From the loftiest viewpoint, the different forms of modern music began to look like the various branches of what was, at its root, one revolution. The sleeve notes of Terry Riley's *A Rainbow in Curved Air,* for instance, could have been taken directly from a sixties' rock album sleeve, in their naive, anti-patriotic, left-wing vision of an LSD-tinted future:

> And then all wars ended ... The Pentagon was turned on its side and painted purple, yellow and green ... People swam in the sparkling rivers under blue skies streaked only with incense pouring from the new factories ... National flags were sewn together into brightly coloured circus tents under which politicians were allowed to perform harmless theatrical games ... The concept of work was forgotten [despite the 'new factories', where *some* people worked – while *others* outside swam! – D.T.] ... The energy from dismantled nuclear weapons provided free heat and light.[25]

MUSIC BECOMES CAGED

One of the most influential contemporary figures in terms of his effect upon the course of the 'new music' is John Cage (b. 1912). It will be worth while to describe a number of Cage's most important works, since he is at the very cutting edge of where the 'new music' is attempting to take us today. By virtue of the sounds which he produces, by virtue of the length of his career and his prominence within the field, by virtue of the number of new sub-movements within the tonal arts which he has initiated or helped to initiate, and by virtue of the fact that he has gone to the lengths of specifically stating the philosophical foundations underlying his own work, it is perhaps John Cage above all others who, among the 'new musicians', deserves to be regarded as the arch-enemy of spiritual idealism.

Cage's initial claim to fame was the to-some-dubious honour of completing the first known electronic composition. In *Imaginary*

Landscape No. 1 (1939), Cage played two gramophone records of the sine continuum which is used by telephone engineers to test telephone lines, at the same time including the sound of a tam-tam, the result of it all being recorded onto another record. Cage also deigned to include a more conservative instrument, the piano – played by one hand while the other hand was used to damp the strings ...

Again Cage bowed to such 'classical influences' for the 1942 composition, *Credo In Us*. But this time not merely a piano, but classical music itself was inserted directly into the work: *Credo In Us* made use of a record player which Cage, as 'composer', suggested should be playing a classical work such as that of Beethoven, Sibelius, Dvorák or Shostakovich. But unfortunately the classical recording had to share the sound-vibrations of *Credo In Us* with the playing of a radio and recordings of *gamelan* music and jazz, according to the laid-down instructions of the 'composer'. Furthermore, the 'performer', sitting at the classic-playing gramophone, was obliged to regularly raise and lower the needle. Thus, the classic became subjected, in the words of Paul Griffiths, 'to piecemeal presentation in a quite alien context'.[24] We must decide for ourselves to what extent the elements of *Credo In Us* were all chosen for purely 'artistic' purposes, and to what extent the ridiculing of the classical composers, some of whom were still alive and composing, might have been a form of dictatorial attack. (Peter Yates, who knew Cage during these early years, describes him as having been stubborn and argumentative.[23])

It was also in the 1940s that Cage brought out his 'prepared piano' pieces. To understand the concept behind these works, it is necessary to realize that though pianos had previously been considered adequate enough as they were, the 'new music', based as it is of course upon the ideal of continual progress, needed to furnish the instrument with certain improvements. Therefore Cage took it upon himself to do so, 'preparing' the piano by placing various objects within it, resting loosely upon the strings – scraps and bits of wood, odd nuts and bolts, weather stripping, etc. – thus introducing what *Larousse* politely calls 'unusual timbres',[19] and Virgil Thomson 'a ping qualified by a thud'.

Another Cage masterpiece, which no doubt took considerable pains to compose, was rather less discordant. *4 minutes and 33 seconds* consists of performers who arrive on stage, lift up their instruments, poise themselves to play ... and remain that way for – yes, 4 minutes and 33 seconds.

Are we being unkind in ridiculing *4 minutes and 33 seconds?* I believe not. It is true that all sorts of lofty mystical concepts can be associated with silence; this work, it could be argued, brings *silence* to our attention. Yet one feels that this is grossly to underestimate the majority of the audience. Those who cannot normally sit still and appreciate silence will not genuinely do so during this 'composition' either, whereas those who are meditatively inclined do not need John Cage to make them so – they enjoy meditation and the stillness of silence frequently. *4 minutes and 33 seconds* might therefore be viewed as nothing but a joke; cheap, unnecessary and, perhaps also, egocentric.

Imaginary Landscape No. 4 appeared in 1951. This piece, in one respect, was in the best tradition of the ancient wisdom, involving as it did the mystical numbers of 12 and 24. The work required 12 radios as the instruments and 24 performers (one performer for each volume dial and one for each frequency dial). The première performance was delayed for quite a while, until late evening in fact, with the result that when it finally did take place, many radio programmes had changed and some stations had gone off the air entirely. Some critics scoffed that the performance had therefore flopped, but Cage himself, turning defeat into victory as it were, brought forth his new doctrine of music. The whole point, it seemed, was that Cage's work had involved chance factors, factors out of the composer's control, and so the late performance had, in fact, succeeded in demonstrating these all the more successfully! Again the critics attacked: they pointed out that the performance had not involved pure, random chance, but only relative chance, since the composer had still laid down a number of stipulations. Cage therefore renamed the new doctrine 'Indeterminacy'.[23]

Indeterminacy was a radical concept for music. The composer, according to the work he envisaged and the constraints he either did or did not impose, could allow for anything from a slight degree of indeterminacy to a very large, almost total, degree of indeterminacy. (Such music is also sometimes called aleatory music, from the Latin term for dice, *alea*. And yes – Cage *did* use dice to decide the sounds for some compositions.)

A good example of indeterminate music in action was the work, *Concert,* of 1957-8. In this piece, each player was simply instructed to play any, all or none of his notes. The result could have been anywhere between total noise to total silence, with a more likely area of partial noise in-between. Whether the result could ever have been *music,* however, is another matter entirely. (But then, of course, those who question the validity of such sounds 'do not understand'; their 'conception of music is too narrow'.) It might be felt that such antics could have little or no bearing on the stream of serious music as a whole. Yet nothing could be further from the truth: Cage has exerted a great influence, over the years, upon other musicians. Indeterminacy in music, for example, has actually become quite widely practised since Cage first began twiddling his radio dials and throwing his dice.

In time, Cage's own use of indeterminacy also grew more sophisticated. He left off his dice-throwing as a determinator of the tones, and took up *I Ching*. Then later, as the computer field developed, Cage made use of computers also, thus having progressed from gambling with dice, through psychism with *I Ching,* and arriving at the mechanization concept of life. One might imagine that the idea of music as being sounds produced without the intrusion of human will is as near as the art can be taken to the edge of the crevasse of cynical nihilism. However, Cage's *Concert for Piano and Orchestra* and *Atlas Eclipticalis* may be said to succeed, through another method, in pushing music completely over the edge. To borrow Peter Yates' description of the works, these 'may be called an antimusic, as a scientist speaks of antimatter. The many motifs do not harmonically draw together but are mutually rejecting . . .'[23]

Personally, I am attempting to explain to myself here what manner of mind it can be that feels moved to actively pursue the creation of a literal antimusic. Once more, we must not avoid the necessary enquiries: What is the inner motive? *What is the consciousness* which has brought forth these works? *In what direction is such a music likely to take civilization, should it be true that life patterns are influenced by music patterns?*

Cage himself has offered a number of insights into his mental processes and his personal attitude to music. In 1952, in a lecture at the Juilliard School of Music, he explained to the breathless, open-mouthed students (the blanks indicating his musical interludes):

I have nothing to say   and I am saying it   and that is
poetry as I need it   contemporary music is changing.
But since everything's changing   we could simply decide
      to drink a glass of water   To have something to be a
masterpiece you   have to have enough time to talk when
you have nothing to say.[26]

So then they knew.

Also, one other statement by Cage deserves mention. While nevertheless composing more and more works, he has simultaneously insisted that he is 'less and less interested in music'. Not exactly encouraging to the audience!

Cage's style of poetry, it will be observed from the above, is very reminiscent of Kerouac, Ginsberg and the '50s' beat generation. And the parallels also go further: Cage lived in the same state, California, at the same time, the 1950s, as did the early movement of pot-smoking, 'spontaneous prose'-writing drop-outs. Cage likewise professed an interest in Zen Buddhism, and Cage's concept of Zen was likewide a perversion of the genuine article.

In fact, Zen actually became the mainstay of Cage's defence of his doctrines. Genuine Zen may be defined as a mystical path to self-realization based upon methods designed to stretch the limits and break the over-automated habitual patterns of the mind. Certainly its goal and its effect are positive and constructive; with insight, Zen can be seen to be entirely in conformity with the great world religions and mystical paths. The 'Zen' of Cage and of the self-professed 'monks' of beat California, however, is altogether less well-defined, and takes the form of an excuse for artistic and behavioural anarchy. Cage uses Zen as a philosophical basis for his techniques of indeterminacy; and yet, as Christopher Small has pointed out, true Zen does not teach a doctrine of luck or chance, but one of a different kind of *order*: a spontaneous *order*, but *not* randomness.[27]

Francis Routh, who is actually considerably involved himself in the 'new music', nevertheless dismisses Cage's philosophy as being seriously in error. States Routh:

> John Cage represents the point of no return; nothingness, zero. We are bidden to leave the world of reality as if in a trance. The sound has no beginning, middle or end; disembodiment is the ideal; the music is not to be 'listened to' so much as 'experienced', which is not easy for a Westerner ... But, Cage says, forget all you have ever heard, all traditions, musical associations, everything; forget life.
>
> The flaw in this is unmistakable; if the listener is to enter such a state of nihilism, he will also forget John Cage. Moreover, has not King Lear already told us what can 'come of nothing'? And in denying its past, the Cage aesthetic inevitably denies any possible future.[22]

Alas, not all modern musicians can boast such penetrating sanity. Following Cage's lead, a number of others have also worked mainly or entirely within the 'Zen'/indeterminacy framework; the majority of them living in America, and most of these in California. Terry Riley, the sleeve notes to whose record we quoted earlier, is among them. Among his creations we find the composition, *In C.* For this work any number of performers may be used. Each plays as many times as he desires a short melodic fragment, before moving on to the next. Fifty short melodic fragments are included in all, each being diatonic on the scale of C. Through all the noise in which this set-up results, some semblance of cohesion is provided by a piano; upon this the note C is repeated rapidly and continuously.

LaMonte Young's *Composition 1960 No. 7* consists of nothing more than the instruction: 'B and F sharp. To be held for a long time.' As in Cage's *4'33"*, any pretensions at mysticism are here overshadowed by the overwhelming and gigantically egocentric attitude of cynicism. And any suspicions that such cynicism stems from some form of actual, suppressed malevolence may not be ill-founded. For to Young also goes the dubious distinction of having pushed concert programmes inside a violin and then having burned the instrument on stage.

Another 'new musician', David Tudor, has on more than one occasion attacked a piano with various weapons — a chisel, a rubber hammer, a bicycle chain and a saw — while in live performance. Sounds familiar? During those same years sundry rock musicians were doing the same: smashing guitars, burning drum kits and amplifiers, biting the heads off live chickens and bats, and so on. Clearly there is no real difference between these patterns of activity within the two musical movements. True it is that 'serious' music and popular music stem from different origins and have tended to be widely divergent in style, form and purpose. But there is today a common element moving within them: something motivated by hatred rather than by love or any other higher emotion; a force unmistakably destructive and malignant.

Some compositions seem almost to have been envisaged specifically as a means of channelling this malevolence into the direction of the audience. LaMonte Young's *The Tortoise, His Dreams and Journeys* expects the audience, no doubt composed of innocently wide-eyed, admiring college students, to sit through several hours of aural and psychological onslaught. Young and three associates chant an open chord through vastly powerful, ear-splitting amplifiers, and maintain this solitary chord non-stop for almost two hours — all this within a darkened room in which the only light comes from projections of astral, psychedelic-patterned art. Then there is a break; following which comes another like session of similar duration – another two hours. It is possible in one hundred per cent seriousness to equate such practices with the modern brainwashing techniques of Communist and other dictatorial regimes. (Yet who is the more imprisoned and brainwashed – he who is kept under lock and key due to his activities on behalf of freedom, or he who, from the free world, goes willingly into the prepared and darkened chamber of psychological onslaught?)

A friend and fellow composer of Young, Steve Reich, has seen fit to study – not at any established school of music, nor even in the Orient – but under a voodoo drummer in Ghana. Now, voodoo is one of the few musics which, rather than cloaking its innate hedonism and malevolence behind a mask of intellectualism, openly admits to being intended as a means of inducing orgies and of inflicting harm and even death upon other individuals. This is the intent of the voodoo ritual, whatever we may think of its objective ability. And, in view of our data thus far on music's power, the idea that voodoo does possess some actual destructive power should not, perhaps, be lightly dismissed.

A sign for the future, then? Are the avant-garde going to be returning from Africa by the dozen as trained voodoo priests? How long before the first voodoo rite at London's Royal Festival Hall? (A ridiculous concept? Think how inconceivable it would have been to, say, Haydn, that concert audiences would ever sit through violin-burning, dice-throwing, and the biting off of the heads of chickens.) The glorious dream of the experimentalists fulfilled: Western music improved and evolved in our time from Bach, Beethoven and Wagner – to the jungle beat!

Meanwhile, the subtleties of Cage's own artistic style have continued to evolve. But, to ensure an unbiased report, let us hear from Peter Yates, who himself has much sympathy with most of the 'new music':

Some of these compositions are a type of glorified play, for example *Cartridge Music.* Phonograph-needle cartridges are attached to an overhead boom and the edge and centre of a table, chosen for the resonance of its vibration when shoved back and forth across the floor. Cage and a companion, each following a different graphic pattern of events by chance, insert slinkies, pipe cleaners, miniature flags, even a tiny birthday candle which is then lighted, into the needle slots of the cartridges and agitate them, producing noises in the loudspeakers, which accompany the performance with low-frequency vibration sounds culled from records of his music. One watches the actions of the two performers as in other days one watched the actions of the clowns circulating around the three rings of the circus, and the more one relaxes into uninhibited attention the funnier it gets. The action, like great farce, treads with dangerous steps, as if unaware how narrowly it avoids the precipitous inane.[23]

And of Cage's *Variations IV,* as performed by the ONCE group of Ann Arbor, Michigan:

On a small platform an interview was being mimed (an American composer interviewing another American composer), while a tape of the actual interview, taken from a broadcast, played through an inconspicuous loudspeaker. The interviewee blasted several of his more popular contemporaries, saying many things about musical conditions and personalities as true as embarrassing, while the mimed 'feedback' turned it all into parodic comedy, the audience laughing at truth and parody together. Meanwhile a girl was being tied to a table and elevated by two men to the top of a metal pole. Firecrackers were exploding, an automobile running outside an open door. A man appeared, bemused and carrying a baton, as if expecting an orchestra. A girl approached him with a scarf, wound it around his neck, returned with an overcoat to put it on him, returned to exchange his glasses for dark glasses, to outfit him with a piano accordion, finally to replace his baton with a blind man's white, red-tipped cane. The image of the reduced conductor was led up the aisle, bleating his accordion. An allegory of 'the end of music as we have known it'![23]

Thus music becomes theatre; not as a synthesis of the two, but as a disintegration of each.

Neither has dance been allowed to escape the treatment. In witnessing the activities of Merce Cunningham's dance troupe, one recalls the original psyche-splitting plan of Edgar Varèse, that his *Déserts* should be played in conjunction with a film of light-phenomena, 'absolutely in opposition with the score'. In Merce Cunningham's dances – yes; the reader's anticipation leaps ahead of us – the dance movements bear no relation whatever to the accompanying sound.

Cage himself has in the past worked with the Merce Cunningham group. But the relationship, if 'relationship' it can be said to have been, was of the following kind: each composer or dancer would go off quite separately to plan and practise his or her own individual stage performance; then they would come together to perform on stage.

— All of them, performing simultaneously.

When one thinks about it, such a situation — with everybody playing or dancing his 'own thing' — must be the way music and dance actually began, one day back in the steaming primeval forests. But then, at some point, there arose co-operation and organization — which, in retrospect, is after all considered to have been a point of evolution.

A VISITOR FROM SIRIUS

Not for no reason did the face of Karlheinz Stockhausen (b. 1928) peer out at us from the front cover of the Beatles' *Sgt Pepper* album of 1967. The numerous faces and objects on the cover represented a synthesis of the Beatles' pet loves and hates; and Stockhausen was included by those four leading figures of one revolutionary field of music in recognition of this leading personage in another branch of what was, in some ways, the same basic musical revolution.

Though Stockhausen has never been quite as radical as Cage, the difference between the two is in fact one of degree, and not of type. Stockhausen's music is still of the style which the majority of people would not consider to be music at all. Nevertheless, Stockhausen is acknowledged within the realm of modern 'serious' music to be the most important composer since the Second World War. His work has influenced very many young musicians. Given this notability and influence, into which direction then has he directed the tonal arts, this 'most important composer since the Second World War'?

At first composing within the bounds of total serialism, Stockhausen then went on to introduce electronics into his music. And next there came indeterminate music, still largely working with electronic materials. Stockhausen has therefore become the virtual embodiment of the major trends of music within the last thirty years. Not as a follower, however, but very much as the leader. Among his flashes of genius is the use of electronic modulators into which are fed the live sounds of the performers, these sounds then being subject to electronic potentiometers, filters, generators and the like.

If all this sounds worryingly inaccessible to the layman, there may yet be cause to take heart. For as everybody knows, music with words is always easier for the man in the street to understand; and a number of Stockhausen's influential works do contain text. For example, the 75-minute work *Moments* (1964) includes the listed names of Stockhausen's wife, children and friends, small portions from letters he received while creating the work, odd lines from William Blake, clapping and shouts of 'encore'. (With these last items, however, the composer may have been slightly jumping the gun.)

Soon after *Moments*, Stockhausen unveiled *Mikrophonie 1* (1964), a work requiring four players, two of whom, with the ultra-serious and self-important concentration normal to performers of the 'new music', excite a large tam-tam from opposite sides with a multitude of different objects made of everything from wood and paper to plastic and glass. The resultant sounds are picked up by microphones. Ah, the usual raucous 'new music' sound once again? Not a bit of it! For, not to be outdone, Stockhausen has seen to it that this − well, 'acoustic material' − is then fed into the gadgetry worked, or 'performed', by the other two participants, who process and alter the volume and timbre of the material. Four speakers emit both the original and the electronically treated sounds simultaneously for the ears of the audience. (John Cage has not reacted favourably to the idea of the raw 'new music' sound being thus tampered with by the will of human beings. It is said that Cage was present for one of Stockhausen's concerts, but that when Stockhausen began using potentiometers etc. to alter the acoustic produce of the other performers, Cage stood up haughtily and walked out.)

Upon composing a lengthy piece which he chose to call *Sirius*, Stockhausen went on to explain a number of things about the work. The jumble of sounds comprising the piece he claimed to reflect the cosmic music which inundates the earth from the heavenly body of the title, and from the cosmic beings dwelling thereupon. (*Sirius* was released in a format most akin to the presentation of rock recordings: the psychedelic cover depicted an unclothed Stockhausen, as though in the role of rock 'star', lying on the sea-shore and photographed stylistically while gazing up at a cosmic sky.) Following the release of the work, Stockhausen claimed with intense seriousness to have actually descended from a civilization of the 'Dog Star'. For their part, esotericists found much of significance in this statement ... Certain critics, however, contented themselves with the observation that it was probably time for the *enfant terrible* of contemporary music to be returned home.

THE B.F. SKINNER SHOW, OR MUSIC TO GET UNDER YOUR SKIN

Now, as we approach the close of the twentieth century, the dream of those 'new music' composers who began it — that the works of Haydn, Mozart and Beethoven would be left far behind by the wonderful new advances which the 'new musicians' heralded — seems without doubt to be close to full realization. The orchestra has been successfully replaced by electronic filters and potentiometers. With typical twentieth-century ingenuity, it has been perceived that when music is indeterminate in any case, and relies fully upon a network of electronic connections to determine the resultant sound, then the old-fashioned score-sheets are therefore not only unnecessary, but even unemployable. Thus, the instructions for music today often consist only of circuit diagrams and notes on how the various items of electronic equipment should be connected up.

Lest conditions become ripe for B. F. Skinner himself to go on the road, perhaps it is time to get back to simplicity. And what could be more simple than the solo performer?

In Alvin Lucier's (b.1931) 1965 'composition', *Music For Solo Performer,* the 'performer' has three Glass Instrument silver electrodes placed upon his head. These pick up his alpha-waves and amplify them through speakers; the resultant sound is then used to activate a variety of percussion instruments placed in front of the speakers.[19] Very well, let us put it down to typical 1960s' exuberance; but striking a more sinister note by far are the statements of a growing number of individuals who — all humour apart — *actually are* musical Skinnerians. Their ideas have already assumed sufficient importance to gain an honorary mention in the *Larousse Encyclopedia of Music:*

> The new music made possible by the [new] instruments and procedures ... *will not be less, or more valid* — it will be different [my italics]. It has been said that in a few years' time, our understanding of the reactions of the central nervous system will have advanced so far that it will be possible to produce 'functional' music predetermined according to parameters defined by the laws of sociology and human behaviour. Knowledge of sensory systems will permit the diffusion of this music by direct application of electrical stimuli. The musical element will be established by an electronic synthesizer fed with a score in the form of a computer programme. The 'instruments of music' will have become a clinical electrode applied to the forearm.[19]

If the commercial proliferation of such 'music to get under the skin' has not arrived yet, the same cannot be said of the commercial proliferation of musical vibrations applied directly onto the surface of the skin. The inventor, David Lloyd, received the idea one day when another of his inventions, a musically-vibrating flying saucer which hung from the ceiling, fell down and onto his lap. The sensation 'felt good' to him: 'It made my whole body tingle.' (And hence, the dividing line between the musical arts and the 'feelgood' drug-like experience becomes less distinct.) Lloyd began marketing the idea in the form of a two-inch disc which can be attached to the waistband of shorts or panties. While listening or dancing to music, the vibrations can also be transferred directly to the body. Lloyd first put out the discs 'as a joke', but found that the 'rock 'n' roll hot pants' idea caught on fast. However, certain implications associated with these musical vibro-discs are somewhat less of a joke. Researchers have discovered that when vibrations are applied to one part of the anatomy, as for instance during a workman's use of a pneumatic drill, the vibrations travel throughout the body and to every organ. As we shall see in the next chapter, the acoustic effects of the rhythms of much modern music have already been found to be harmful to the human organism. One wonders, therefore, what effects might be expected when those same rhythms are transferred directly to the body by means of raw vibration. The spiritual/philosophical implications of using music in this way are also sobering. To the idealist point of view, music should be used in order to influence man's spiritual nature, inspiring his soul with feelings of love, beauty, resolution, altruism and all good emotions. With this commercial invention of David Lloyd's, however, we have the application of music, not to the spiritual nature of man, but to the physical body, and in order to cause 'tingles' and other bodily sensations which 'feel good'. A photograph, published to show the musical vibro-disc in action, displays the torso of a near-nude female with the disc's lead disappearing down the front of a pair of very brief panties.

It can be seen, then, that with the coming of new *types* of music come also new *uses* of music, the music and its uses being of a similar orientation. The new breed of musician, being fully Skinnerian in outlook, can be said to constitute the ultimate and inevitable result of the reductionist-materialist approach to the art. If the purpose of music is not to sublimate man's being and spiritualize society – if the aim of all art is not to direct consciousness ↑ , 'because there is no ↑ ' – then it logically follows that music should instead be used to pursue hedonistic goals. Music becomes not so much an art as a method by which the musician can experience sensuous pleasure, amass wealth, boost his ego, and gain power through the ability to control others. All of this we see today in the endless production-line of the rock-muzak 'industry' – which *is* an industry, and not an art, since the prime moving motive of the musicians, managers and technicians is those wads of greenbacks. In the rock *industry,* money is basically what it is all about; and thus music is directed, not upward (thus stretching the minds of the people and expanding their consciousness), but to the lowest common denominator. The question of questions is: *Will it sell?* The standard of artistry could not be less relevant.

Yet certain Skinnerians, who have emerged from the serious, rather than from the popular, musical culture, are not satisfied with the bodily 'feelgood' effect of rock, or with the industry's lucrative potentials. More than this, these individuals are seeking, in true behaviourist fashion, to discover the ultimate secrets of how to control living beings by acoustic means. Their questions are: Is there a chord that can make a man go mad? A melody that, accompanying a TV ad, would absolutely *compel* the viewer to buy? Are there rhythms that can disintegrate matter?

The electronic composer, Vorhans, is attempting to produce music that goes straight to the nerves, bypassing the conscious mind. His aim is to compose electronic music capable of manipulating the brain, inducing orgasms and bringing about LSD-like experiences.[28] Elsewhere, at the time of writing, certain scientists and researchers are attempting to discover a sound or tonal phrase that can kill a man.

It would be most unwise to dismiss such developments as impossible; history tends to demonstrate all too convincingly that men have been able to develop, eventually, almost anything their imaginations seized upon. The acoustically-induced human orgasm or anything approaching it would certainly bring the behaviourist brave new world a giant leap nearer to completion. It could be expected to be only a matter of time before industrial interests found some means of overtly or subtly introducing the 'acoustic kick' onto the factory floor in one form or another. Like rats in a Skinner box, which are wired up to receive electrical stimulation of their brain's pleasure centre each time they press a lever, and which press repeatedly and frantically until their bodies no longer possess the strength, so the specially formulated 'music' fed to industrial workers could be controlled to give less or more of a 'kick' according to the level of output. It is difficult to see how the acoustic kick for factory workers could be detected, or at least proved, by investigative bodies. And in any case, from the first discovery of such a technique, if it proved to work very well, we can be sure that the attention of the industrialists and of the nations' ministers of the economy would be very much alerted; and the behind-the-scenes pressure would then be on for the technique not to be outlawed in the first place.

Even more difficult to legislate would be the individual, free-will choice to experience behaviourist music. Modern Western nations have rarely, if ever, legislated against any form of music, and it would be a dilemma to know where to draw the line between legal and illegal tonal art. Yet Skinnerian music could be as addictive and dangerous as any chemical drugs such as heroin. (The reader will not have missed that ominous line from *Larousse*, that 'The, "instruments of music" will have become a clinical electrode applied to the forearm.'[19]) If unchecked, the scope for the cold-blooded exploitation of Skinnerian music would be varied and vast.

By the twenty-first century, it is altogether conceivable for Skinnerian principles to have been successfully implanted into music to the extent of there being music junkies, music pushers, and a multi-billion dollar industry sprung up to exploit the practice to the hilt. Music could be not an art for the uplifting and spiritual emancipation of humanity, but a ruthless, mechanized industry designed to milk the last penny from the pockets of the enslaved, and to utterly control human behaviour for political purposes.

SOME FURTHER ADVANCES IN THE ART
Meanwhile, the evolution of the 'new music' progresses from glory to glory. May we present some further advances in the art:

Terretektorh (1965-6) by the Greek composer, Yannis Xenakis, requires 88 musicians. One could even call them an orchestra. With the slight difference that, in addition to their usual instruments, each player also performs upon maraca, woodblock, siren-whistle and whip; all of which can hardly be likely to relax or reassure an innocent and unsuspecting member of the audience — since the players are all seated among the ranks of the listeners.

One aspect of the total anarchy of contemporary music is the growing body of musicians keen to demonstrate that there is and should be no limit to the variety of means of sound production. In other words, why *should* a musician have to stick to the old violin, trumpet, and so forth to produce tones? Or even the guitar and drum set for that matter? A foremost exponent of this theory is Max Neuhaus, a percussionist who has worked with Pierre Boulez. Among the wondrous inventions of Neuhaus are instruments such as the Water Whistle, for example. The Water Whistle consists of a series of rubber pressure hoses whipping around underwater in a pool. The hoses have whistles attached. Music (or at any rate, *sounds*) are produced beneath the surface, and can only be heard by submerging the ears.[29] Inventions of such genius should of themselves serve to demonstrate why the more traditional instruments, which possess such a huge range of possible tones and subtle touches of beauty, yet reign supreme. The Water Whistle and its brethren may provide remarkable fun for the children on a Sunday afternoon, but each is surely doomed to join the ranks of all other nine-day wonders.

And yet, as though programmed to the one inflexible goal, the 'new musicians' persist. Increasingly, he who would perform contemporary music is, like a 1960s astronaut, apparently expected to be an accomplished scuba-diver, an athlete, and an electronics expert, not to mention a dab hand with a whip. The modern performer is expected to succumb to all and every crazy whim of the composer; to embody the composer's own schizophrenic humour and pretentious concentration upon the frankly inane. When an orchestra is not prepared to do so (and there have been instances of renowned orchestras rebelling at the demands of the radical avant-garde), then they are chided as being backward, and dismissed as unprofessional.

Relentlessly, increasingly, live performances of contemporary music continue, for all appearances, to combine an episode of *Dr Who* with a heat of *It's a Knockout* and an operation of the SAS. Christopher Janney, a 'sound artist' (yes, the quaint old term, 'composer', could never last) from Boston, has engineered a musical instrument from a stairwell. Photoelectric cells are attached to the steps, and each individual photoelectric beam, if broken, releases a series of notes stored in a computer. The 'instrument' is played by one or more people running up and down the stairs.[29]

COMPUTER MUSIC

Christopher Janney's use of a computer conforms to the rule rather than being an exception among contemporary 'sound artists'. The computer, like many other technological devices, is of course neither good nor bad in itself; the extent of its usefulness, and whether it works for good or evil, depends entirely upon the human being who operates it and feeds it information. (As every programmer knows, GIGO – Garbage In, Garbage Out – is an irrepressibly inflexible rule.) In music, as in many other areas of life, the computer admittedly offers much as a labour-saving device. The computer, as a morally neutral implement, may even be capable of aiding in the process of composing music of real worth. Some young composers already find that computers are useful to them since it is possible to compose in computer memory, the machine then being able to play or print out the completed work. However, some would debate the aesthetic purity of even this practice. After all, how well can a computer play back one's latest symphony? Certainly one can hardly imagine that Beethoven was at all the worse for not possessing a computer, or even that he would have had the slightest use for one in the forging of his masterpieces.

But (inevitably, one must by now suppose) the use of computers has been at the forefront of the works of the modern materialist composers; works which seem to be almost consciously designed for the specific purpose of turning the age-old human values of aesthetics and the principles of beauty upside down and inside out. As was reported in a recent article by Doug Garr, computers 'have successfully broken music and vocalization into their component parts and reassembled them as new, hybrid sounds. Voices have been transformed into emotionless tonal instruments.'[29]

Something of the kind was tried in the early '70s by the rock group Curved Air, human speech being vocoded and played back through an electronic keyboard instrument. The 'ghost in the machine' said a little poem with the acoustic arena all to itself, all other sounds having halted, as though the listener were expected to applaud this ultimate flash of genius as it appeared in spotlight. As it happened, however, the end result of the experiment was emotionally cold as ice, and more than a little dull even to Curved Air's mainly undemanding audience: the artistic low-point of the entire piece; a mechanized sound for mechanized minds.

But progress marches on: at the present time we have the research being undertaken by Charles Dodge and the computer music department which he runs at Brooklyn College, New York. Dodge 'grafts' different variables and factors of the sound of different singers together. Voices are first digitized at 15,000 samples per second, and this analysis is then reduced to 120 samples per second, which is easier to work with. A number of factors and 'filter coefficients' vary within each time frame – factors such as pitch, amplitude, and the sounds generated by windpipe, tongue, jaw,

mouth, glottis and vocal-cords. By combining the 'filter coefficients'
of different individuals, then, it is possible to produce a speech graft.
For example, the pitch and amplitude of one voice can be 'played
through' the tongue, jaw and glottis of another voice.[29]

Doug Garr reports on the development that, 'From simple
melody to complex, eerie harmonies, the musical breadth is as if the
Andrews Sisters had suddenly become baritones.' Comments music
professor Tom Jerse, laughing, 'It's like taking one person's vocal
cords and putting them in someone else's mouth. It means you can
mix Mick Jagger and, say, Luciano Pavarotti in one voice
track . . .'[29]

Marvellous! (... Yes?) No doubt the Ph.Ds are being handed
out thick and fast these days down at the Brooklyn College
computer music department.

If we hold, even just to some degree, to the axiom *As in music, so
in life,* then where a runaway, popularized art of voice-grafting
would lead us is both difficult to predict and sobering to contemplate. At best it would seem to point towards a further
dehumanization of the tonal arts, and to yet another force present
within society to increase the incidence of alienation and mental
illness. Actually, in such descriptions as that above of voice-grafting,
it is possible to note a certain parallel with the grafting of genes in
genetic engineering: a parallel in the seeming lack of respect towards
Nature as given to us; in something of a desire to play God; a
certain hint of arrogance.

We can at least be thankful that the 'engineers' of genes are con-
strained, at least for the present, to the combining of *biological* traits
with other *biological* traits. The sound grafters, to their glee, are
subject to no such constriction. Computer experts at Stanford
University, California, for example, can mix the sound of one
inanimate musical instrument with another, or of an instrument with
the voice of a singer. The results can sound like a piano-guitar, a
talking flute or a trumpeting soprano. Stanford researcher John
Serawn, who calls the process 'cross-synthesis', says that the resulting harmonies are 'quite spooky'.[29]

Incidentally, I have yet to come across a written account of
computer vocoding or other such practices which does not, in
describing the resultant sounds, use adjectives such as 'spooky',
'weird' and 'eerie'. If life patterns do tend to follow music patterns,
do we really want the eeriness and spookiness of voice grafting or
cross-synthesis to be the sound of music to come?

COURAGEOUSLY EXPLORING BACKWARDS

We should probably be grateful that cross-synthesis is not as easy to get into as playing the guitar: the high cost of computers prohibits voice-grafting and the like by all but the more wealthy musicians and music departments. IBMs are still not something you can sling over your shoulder and take with you along the overland route to India. But all praise then for Skip LaPlante, who has placed the ability to make music right back among the more usual social stratas of society.

A graduate of Princeton University, New Jersey, USA (where he studied Mozart and Schoenberg), LaPlante performs on sound generators which usually cost less than $US25 to build. He has about 60 of them, all different; wind and percussion instruments.[29] And the secret?

The secret of this latest advance in the art is to raid scrap-heaps, kitchens and old farmhouses. LaPlante has discovered pace-setting new timbres from 'huge cardboard rug tubes, broiler pans, catfood cans, even shards of glass'.[29] Enthuses LaPlante: 'You can get really clean pitches from cinder blocks broken into L-shapes. And cut-down wine jugs make excellent cloud-chamber bowls.' According to Doug Garr, our erstwhile, new-arrival sound artist 'hunts for battered and discarded wine jugs on the Bowery in New York City'. And: 'He has even created music by bouncing a Superball on a piece of glass.'[29]

Yet the fact is that Skip LaPlante has heard nothing! Many times I have encountered such music, and always performed by experts in the field; even once while passing through a district of his own New York City – here too I witnessed the neighbourhood toddlers gathering together. In this particular instance they had two toy tin banjos, a kazoo and a couple of wooden spoons with which to beat an assortment of pots and pans (for as long as their parents would stand it). No doubt toddlers in every city of the world do much the same. All of them quite unsuspecting that they are 'new musicians'!

However, can LaPlante's music really be called 'new' when its sounds are such a close kin to those produced by the first cave man to think of banging a bone on a hollow log? We have already posed this same moot point in reference to the work of John Cage and the Merce Cunningham group. Question of questions: Could it then *possibly, conceivably be* that the self-professed musical 'avant-garde', way out in front, ahead of all the others and pointing the direction, are leading us all ... *backwards?!*

If so, it may be pointless to struggle against the inevitable. Or at

least, so the 'avant-garde' and their supporters would have us
believe, for it is startling with what confidence they are able to map
out our musical future for us in advance. Doug Carr, for instance,
whose illuminating article, 'The Endless Scale',[29] has been quoted
from several times above, assuredly informs us that, 'The music of
tomorrow will not limit expression: it will· free it of virtually all
restraints', and confidently concludes: 'Our aural experience will be
eclectic and electronic.'

ASSESSING THE AVANT-GARDE
Not all who work within the field of music have followed the
views in their entirety of the new 'sound artists'. A number of sane
and timely comments have been forthcoming even from musicians
who themselves profess some interest in the new theories and styles.
In particular, attention has been focused upon the peculiar and
questionable consciousness of the radical avant-garde themselves as
individuals. This is to get right to the core of the matter. Stephen
Walsh writes candidly of the 'pretentious solemnity with which
many of [modern music's] lesser exponents continue to regard themselves'.[19] Yehudi Menuhin, the humble and perspicacious 'patron
saint' of good Western music, refers to the avant-garde as 'mechano'
composers, since they display mind without heart.

Even by the early 1930s the direction taken by some composers
had become sufficiently bizarre for Thomas Fielden, in a chapter
entitled 'What is Good Music?' to warn us that:

> ... we have to remember that while we may discard the vulgar,
> we go to the other extreme if we spend our time posing and
> adopting eccentric outpourings as great, just because they happen
> to be unusual. The one is just as inartistic and non-contributory to
> culture and character as the other.[30]

In his excellent book, *Music in the Life of Man,* Julius Portnoy
clearly defines the problem:

> A composer must be imbued with a deep sense of spirituality, but
> many of our contemporary ones confuse it with sentimentality
> and associate it with an age of romantic chivalry which no longer
> has a place in a world explained purely in mechanistic ter-
> minology. Many contemporary composers will not toil and
> become proficient in their craft. They would rather be vague and
> subjective, and cloak themselves in aesthetic purism so there is no

way to communicate with them musically. They simply follow their impulses, which is very good as therapy for them personally; but unfortunately, they do not go beyond that point and the end result is often chaos, not a well-ordered musical work. Many of our younger composers have lost the quality of humility, a most important element for serving the Muse. Without humility there is no love or charity, and dogmatism usually follows.[4]

WHAT IS THE *PURPOSE* OF MUSIC?

Should we desire to help reveal the actual inner nature of the 'new music', and its possible effects upon the listener, then there exists a very effective method of doing so. Let us recall our previous analogy of the seed and its end result: that the real nature of the seed is only fully discovered when it has sprouted and flowered. What then, we should ask, is the ultimate goal of today's radical composers? What manner of flower do they envision for their seed? What is the purpose behind their endeavours? To what do they aspire? Do they believe, as did J. S. Bach, that music is for the glory of God and the betterment of man? Do they believe, as did all the major classical composers, that their art should be consecrated to the spiritual uplifting of society?

No, for such concepts cannot in fact be contained within the mind which precludes the possibility of the vertical ↑ dimension of reality, with its mystical implications.

It is true that many, and even most, twentieth-century composers have claimed to hold to some form of spiritual belief, and have sometimes included supposedly mystical elements within their music; but these 'beliefs', like Cage's 'Zen', have usually tended to be vague, watered-down and mixed-up; they have been, for the most part, a severe compromise of genuine religious and moral principles, and even, at times, a sham. We would usually be correct in ignoring the token words of such composers, and realizing that they remain, for all their intellectual posturing, atheists and reductionists.

Towards what goal, then, do they envision their art as being directed? Suggestions as to the purpose of music from even the most well-intentioned and humanitarian of materialists are inevitably found to be substantially wanting. Theorists with a biological background, for instance, have frequently stated with remarkably unruffled confidence that all music is an imitation of animal cries. Charles Darwin himself, while proceeding rather more tentatively, suggested that musical tones and rhythm first originated when the half-human progenitors of man evolved the sounds in order to attract a mate, and to ritualize the process of courtship. If this was so, Darwin believed, then it also provided the reason for man's still enjoying music and finding it beautiful today: ' ... from the deeply laid principles of inherited associations, musical tones would be likely to excite in us, in an ... indefinite manner, the strong emotions of a long-past age.'[31] Darwin was saying, then, that Beethoven's Ninth Symphony is enjoyed and acclaimed by us because it reminds us of sex and courtship with hairy beauties of aeons ago.

A more recent theme is stated by Marvin Minsky, who is the head of a project at the Massachusetts Institute of Technology to investigate computer music, and a pioneer in researching the field of artificial intelligence. The purpose of music, believes Minsky, might be 'to relax the brain'.[32] This, we might allow, is probably an improvement over the Darwinian hypothesis. At first sight the idea can even seem quite acceptable: haven't we all used music 'to relax the brain' now and again? Yet the hypothesis – which is shared by many besides Minsky – is glaringly materialist on two points. First, note the use of the word 'brain'. The implication is obviously contrary to the spiritual viewpoint, which views man's being as being something which includes but also by far transcends the physical brain. But no, to the materialist, you and I are merely biological robots; Minsky and his friends are all getting ready to relax our brains with those electrodes implanted into our forearms.

And second, is the purpose of music *only to relax* us? That idea is surely full of holes. Are we *relaxed* – by the incidental music to an action-packed suspense movie? Do football crowds chant – to *relax*? For that matter, does *The Rite of Spring* or the Sex Pistols' 'Anarchy In The UK' – *relax* us? And, still more to the point, are works such as Beethoven's *Missa Solemnis* or Vaughan Williams' *Lark Ascending* designed to *relax* us – and not to move us, melt our hearts, and awaken thoughts of piety in our minds? Rather, good music is designed to expand our consciousness, and such an activity demands of us not so much a state of relaxation as a definite attitude of creative tension.

It seems that the idea of the purpose of music being to 'relax' us occurs to the mind which is locked into the → philosophy simply because this supposed purpose of music is the most constructive of which such a mind can conceive.

The theoretical reduction of music to being an agent of 'relaxation for the brain' is symptomatic of the times. We live in an age when even the deepest of spiritual practices, such as meditation, are frequently regarded in such materialist terms. Meditation, described millennia ago by the authors of the Upanishads as 'knowledge of the Self as pure and immortal ... pure unitary consciousness, ineffable peace, supreme good ... unity with the light that is in the sun, freedom from evil, ascension to God's dwelling place ... the transcendence of physical consciousness' is assessed by modern scientists according to the meditator's brain's ability to move a needle on an EEG display. Self-acclaimed twentieth-century 'gurus', such as the Maharishi Mahesh Yogi of TM (Transcendental Meditation) fame, advertise techniques of 'meditation' guaranteed to fulfil the needs of man in the modern world by helping him to be 'unburdened of tension' and, of course, 'relaxed'.

In addition to what we can call the 'relaxation theory' of music are those other → ideas that the entire purpose of all music is to 'entertain', or that the function of music is to provide 'an emotional catharsis'.

Another such deficient concept provides the foundation stone for the music of Stephen Halpern. Halpern has become connected in many people's minds with the New Age movement – the general belief that as we pass deeper into the age of Aquarius, a new era of brotherhood, peace and spirituality will progressively manifest. Yet it can be of no little importance that the New Age movement, for all its high mystical hopes and commendable moral values, has thus far adhered almost exclusively to the music of the → and even ↓ directions.

And what, to Stephen Halpern, is the purpose of his music? In all of his talks and writings the same criterion keeps appearing by which all music, it seems, should be judged: that music should be 'healing'. Again, hardly a despicable idea at first sight. However, the term 'healing', as used and understood by many, is frequently as far from the genuine meaning of the word as is the 'peace' of the Kremlin or the 'love' of the sexually permissive. For Halpern, 'healing' means soothing and pacifying; music to calm – and yes, to 'relax' us – after a busy day at the office. All much along the lines of a musical TM.

A wider and more acceptable definition of 'healing music' would include tonal art which helps to perfect and align the totality of man's being. In this sense, classical and all genuinely good music is certainly healing: healing in the word's truest and fullest sense, as a harmonizer and improver of each aspect of man's being – physical, emotional, mental and spiritual. In his talks, however, Halpern has never seemed particularly enthusiastic about classical music. After all, works such as Elgar's tremendous *Pomp and Circumstance* marches or Verdi's *Aida* are hardly 'healing' in the sense of being soporific, marijuana-music (as is the output of the supposedly New Age musicians). Besides being both inspirational and spiritual, classical music is also usually very demanding intellectually, if it is to be fully absorbed. The listener is active, not passive.

If a new and better era awaits humanity, its successful manifestation will certainly require men and women of *true spirituality* – which is to say, men and women of both mystical heart *and practical mind.* Active and capable intellects will be an essential. It demands little foresight to realize that planet earth will never be improved by sitting back in a cloud of incense or by falling asleep to an electronic sound-massage. Is, then, the music of Stephen Halpern, Steve Hillage and others truly New Age music? Does it raise our hearts with inspiration to be self-sacrificing? Does it divinely organize our minds? Does it impel us to awaken to the challenges of the hour in the world at large, as, directly or indirectly, any genuine New Age music must? Not when it is an impulsive chaos of jazz. Not when it is over-electronic and divorced from human feelings. Not when, as it so often is, it is a synthetic mist of psychedelic miasma.

Such music could never have been possible under the system of beliefs held by the composers of former times. Musicians of the past humbly placed themselves in subservience to the eternal principles which have governed, and always shall govern, the laws of aesthetics of all art.

What happened at the beginning of our century is that these principles came to be considered as not being eternal and immutable at all. When one thinks about it, the doctrine of flexible and transient artistic standards was the only basis upon which the revolution could ever have taken place. Francis Routh, the composer and writer on contemporary music, spells the new course of things out for us in his chapter on Schoenberg and the Viennese school:

Once Schoenberg had accepted the break-up of the traditional syntax as a *fait accompli,* it is no longer reasonable to consider his music by the traditional standards. Fresh ones are needed.[22]

To this one might wonder: but are not the principles and standards by which we judge music and the other arts basically the same as those by which we govern *our lives,* and by which we structure *our view of the world?*

No problem – Routh takes the fact completely in his stride. If the choice is between not altering our artistic standards because it means altering the standards by which we also live, or else changing both our standards of art and of life, then we must apparently choose the latter. Routh continues: 'If the musical ideas appear arbitrarily linked, unconnected sections juxtaposed, the harmony illogical, then Schoenberg invites us to reconsider and revise our view of the musical art – *and with it, our view of reality* [my italics].'[22] (Invoking the *As in music, so in life* maxim, the kind of music described by Routh above would therefore lead to life-phenomena paralleling the above-described musical phenomena. That is, *mental* ideas would become arbitrarily linked and unconnected, *actions* would become strangely juxtaposed, and the *emotions* illogical.)

Upon what, then, should we base our value judgments regarding a work of art? Plato and the other sages of old believed that, to be of value, art should contain and display the three sisters of Beauty, Truth and Goodness. These three qualities were conceived as being intimately interrelated: like the Trinity of the world's religions, the three qualities were, in fact, different aspects of the Supreme. Moreover, they were *inseparable:* a work of art which was beautiful was so since it contained elements of Truth and Goodness. Art which did not contain such elements was automatically ugly, and to be shunned. It might be said that the definition of Beauty was that it contained Truth, in that it was aligned to the eternal principles of the Above, and that it contained Goodness, since its effect upon the perceiver was always a beneficial one.

Enter now the 'new music', to the proponents of which the objective view of art – that art affects people and society – is anathema, since it demands of the artist a sense of moral responsibility. Hence, in order to clear the way for anarchy in music, the objective view of the art *must* be refuted; the inseparableness of Beauty, Truth and Goodness *must* be denied, so that we can claim that Beauty, or artistic value, does not depend upon the Goodness, or objective effect, of a work. Over again, then, to Francis Routh:

The three goddesses of Beauty, Truth and Goodness are independent and jealous ladies, each with her own particular sphere of activity ... we must clearly differentiate their distinct roles if we are to lay the basis of a valid aesthetic judgement; and it would be perverse to allocate music to any except the first.[22]

These are outstandingly twisted sentiments as they stand. But Routh
has not yet finished:

> Let us be quite clear about this from the outset. The sense or
> faculty with which we judge music is on a different intellectual
> level from that with which we decide whether an action or
> institution is good or bad, or whether a scientific theory, or
> religion, or philosophical system, is true or false.[22]

If we reduce that philosophical concept of music to its naked
essentials we are left with: 'The sense or faculty with which we
judge music is on a different intellectual level from that with which
we decide ... good or bad ... true or false.'

Thus, we are invited to embrace a doctrine of aesthetics in which
not only have morality and spirituality been discarded as unnecessary, but no firm standards of any form whatsoever remain.
The wavering, subjective mortal will has ousted, or attempted to
oust, the universal laws of immutable beauty. Yet more radical still
than the make-it-up-as-we-go-along moralists is the philosophy
implicit in indeterminate music, in which not even mortal will, but
mere chance, rules unrivalled. Thus, there remains no scope for the
making of value judgments at all, since we are called to accept and
applaud whatever sounds turn up. John Cage, indeterminacy's
godfather-supremo, informs us that:

> Value judgments are destructive to our proper business, which is
> curiosity and awareness. How are you going to use this situation
> if you are there? That is the question.[33]

And again, Cage snaps at us:

> Why do you waste your time and mine by trying to make value
> judgments? Don't you know that when you get a value judg-
> ment that's all you have?[33]

In conclusion, let us stress once more that the flower reveals that
which always was contained in the seed. In order to get to grips
with the real nature of the 'new music' it is necessary to discern
where the composers are trying to lead us. And when Cage speaks
of discarding value judgments in relation to music, we can be sure
that he envisions an exactly similar fate for the value judgments by
which we live and relate to our fellow man. The contemporary

musician, Christopher Small, is certain that in twentieth-century music, we see 'the shape of a society to which it aspires'.[27] It's a society we may be familiar with in advance from the works of George Orwell and Aldous Huxley.

ROLL OVER BEETHOVEN; ROLL OVER MAN

To the spiritual idealist, man is essential to the process of creating music on two counts: as a composer and as a performer. In composing, only man, and no machine, can discern those elements of spiritual value and beauty which are essential to good music; and in performing, it is only the heart, head and hand of man which are capable of infusing into the tones those subtle nuances and touches of deep sublimity which makes each performance unique and worth while. The contemporary 'sound artists' left, early on, much of the performing to their computers and synthesizers. But beyond this, they have not been slow in realizing the further possibility, which is a reductionist-materialist's dream: why not let the machines get on with all the composing as well?

As early as 1956, Lejaren Hiller and Leonard Isaacson of the University of Illinois programmed their computer to compose by selecting notes from a chromatic scale with a range of two and a half octaves. The program had the machine select notes at random, but rejecting those notes which did not combine well melodically according to the traditional rules of key, and so forth.[34]

The following year, Max Mathews and John Pierce, upon attending a concert, decided that a computer could do better. The two were colleagues at Bell Laboratories, New Jersey and had soon invented a computer which, they believed, could reproduce any sound able to come out of a loudspeaker. Within a year, their computer had become the first in the world actually to generate the sound of, er ... 'music'.[34]

Despite the 1956 composing computer of Hiller and Isaacson, the title of 'the world's first composing machine' is also claimed for the electrical engineering creation of Salvatore Martirano, who is also at the University of Illinois, deep in Ray Bradbury country. The 'Sal-Mar Construction' is certainly more complex than the Hiller-Isaacson programme, however: by activating various combinations of 291 switches the computer is directed to create variations on basic melodic themes. It can also emit its own artistic creations through 24 independently controlled speakers.[34]

Meanwhile, Max Mathews, the same electrical engineer from Bell Laboratories, is continuing his efforts to do better than those human beings at that concert in 1957. Now also Bell's director of acoustic and *behavioural* research, he works with machines such as the Crumar synthesizer to program and create new sounds. Mathews admits that computers may never write the equivalent of a Bach cantata. Rather, ' ... they will write something very different, but something present and future generations find just as satisfying'.[34] (No doubt another case for the old electrode on the forearm ...)

And if computers are to compose and perform our music for us from now on, then it would, of course, be unthinkable to deny them the right to run the music classroom. Should it for some reason be considered necessary to continue to teach music to human beings, then it would obviously be ridiculous to leave the task to a mere mortal. Hence, the Systems Development Corporation of Santa Monica has come to the rescue in conjunction with the Wurlitzer Corporation. In an article entitled 'Teaching Music by Computer', we read:

> The new computerized music experiment will have a class of youngsters simultaneously playing electric pianos connected to a computer. The classroom is silent. Through headphones each child hears only his own playing and the instructions or musical notes generated by the computer. Different combinations of musical notes are generated in response to each student's activities ... Each child can control his own program to a degree ...[35]

As we might expect, the music-teaching computer described above is but a variant on the standard designs for computer-assisted instruction which resulted from the mechanical 'teaching machines' developed by B. F. Skinner at Harvard in the 1950s. Skinner's 1984-like dream was to see all teachers, with their ability to be genuinely compassionate and to care individually for each child in their care, replaced by consoles and flashing lights. Absolute values have never meant any more to Skinner than they do to the 'new musicians', we should also note, as was reflected in the very title of his book in which he set forth his ideas on how to reform 'human organisms' and civilization by way of mechanical teaching machines and other conditioning methods. The title of this famous behaviourist book might also be taken as a most accurate description of the music of behaviourist 'sound artists': *Beyond Freedom and Dignity*.[36] Both Skinner and the 'sound artists' have hurled the challenge to us, proclaiming such notions as freedom and dignity to be antiquated and defunct. If the world does not take up such challenges, and give answer, then the B. F. Skinner Autonomic Orchestra may as well be correct in their proclamation.

EMPTY SEATS

We have, then, briefly surveyed the cold, barren landscape of the 'new music'. The question we must now seek to answer is: What has the effect of this music been upon twentieth-century man? How have the music's characteristics, such as everything from atonality and serialism to indeterminacy and Skip LaPlante's cardboard rug tubes, influenced life patterns?

Later in this book we shall note that whenever, during the course of history, a traditional, classical style of music has been supplanted by a revolution of musical materialism, such revolutions have tended to succeed by means of the same general tactic. By introducing a cheaper and more boisterous form of art, the revolutions have won popularity with the masses. Almost overnight it seems, virtually the entire populace begins listening to and craving for the new, cheaper sounds. And the traditional, more demanding music becomes all but forgotten.

The revolution of the 'new music', however, has taken on a different shape. In this instance, the stream of classical music has been led astray down a wayward path into realms of cold-hearted abstraction and mentalism. Serious Western music has been led to its death, and the fount of genuine creativity and beauty has all but dried up.

The result of this particular revolution, therefore, is that there is scarcely any serious contemporary music which the music-lover who possesses the slightest iota of spiritual attunement can enjoy. A century ago, concert halls were filled with audiences who had come to listen to the latest work of the composers of the romantic era; today we have few, if any, composers of serious music who are worth mentioning. If we would listen at all to a contemporary work, then we are bidden to subject ourselves to the latest crazed creation of a Stockhausen or a Cage.

Faced with such a prospect, the public have 'voted with their feet'. During the writing of this very chapter, in 1982, John Cage, then aged 70, arrived in London to perform his latest work, the title of which one does not even care to remember. And neither, apparently, did many others, for midst the political and artistic capital of Great Britain, this leading figure among all 'sound artists' was forced to accept as a venue the Almeida, a backstreet café/bar which sports its narrow entrance between a derelict house and a flypostered shop-corner off Upper Street, Islington.

Of the effect of the 'new music' upon civilization we can therefore say that, actually, its *direct* effect is not so very great. Few non-musicians listen to or even know of the work of today's 'sound artists'. True, electronic and anarchistic music crops up with disconcerting frequency on cinematic sound-tracks which are heard by millions; and the philosophy behind the 'new music' has no doubt filtered, unnoticed, into many areas of life. But for the most part, in the attempt to shift music into their own peculiar chosen direction, the 'new musicians' have lost virtually all popular support. The most unfortunate result of their 'revolution' is that, since it has supposedly 'advanced beyond' the more traditional styles, little music of true beauty and inspiration is currently on offer.

Yet there still remains to us the towering and vastly varied array of works produced by the composers of the eighteenth and nineteenth centuries. And it is these works to which music-lovers continue to flock; it is these sublime creations of art which continue to fill the great music halls of the world. Indeed, the music of Handel, Bach, Beethoven, Chopin and others has actually never been more widely listened to than today, with the modern availability of radios and hi-fi sets. We therefore certainly must not suppose that music such as Beethoven's influenced only the mentalities of the people of his own day. Indeed, many of his masterpieces were scarcely known in Europe during his own lifetime. To take Beethoven's magnificent late string quartets as examples, not all of these were performed even once while he lived, and they were played only infrequently for nearly a hundred years after his death. Therefore people have only really had the opportunity to familiarize themselves with these stupendous creations during our own century – a fact of perhaps deep significance.

TWENTIETH-CENTURY TRADITIONALISTS

The music of the classical and romantic eras contains a beauty which is eternal and immutable, and therefore, in the spiritual sense, is entirely contemporary. Aesthetically, Bach is as meaningful and important to us today as ever, and to the works of such a genius the adjective, 'dated', can never apply.

Yet, ultimately, we must also begin to look ahead once more; to reawaken within ourselves the confident hope that a genuine New Age music is about to dawn; a music of equal or even greater sublimity as the great works of the past, and yet possessing a character and effect which is entirely new. And as a laying of the foundations for such a music, a minority of twentieth-century composers have clung tenaciously to the more traditional approach to music. Refusing to succumb to the whirlpools of anarchy around them, they have produced, even in this century, music of unique and lasting greatness. I refer, of course, to composers such as Sibelius, Rachmaninoff, Shostakovich and Khatchaturian, and to the major twentieth-century English composers.

These modern traditionalists have retained a more conservative and basically tonal position whilst nevertheless experimenting and evolving their art along many lines. Almost to a man, the modern traditionalists have maintained the viewpoint which is anathema to the 'sound artist' — that music *does* exert an influence over the character of man, and that the artist therefore has the solemn responsibility of composing only that which purifies and spiritualizes man and society. When they have not explicitly expressed such sentiments, the altruistic orientation of their music has nevertheless spoken for itself. And nowhere is this more so than in the works of the modern English composers.

England had, in the nineteenth century, been devoid of good composers to the extent that the Germans sarcastically referred to the nation as 'the land without music'. Yet England in particular was, in the twentieth-century, to be blessed with a flourishing of native musical beauty, and even, at times, sheer genius. One thinks not only of Elgar, Delius, Holst and Vaughan Williams, but of others such as Cyril Scott, Arnold Bax, John Ireland and Michael Tippett.

The works of Ralph Vaughan Williams (1872-1958) combine past tradition with new musical forms, an unmistakable 'Englishness' and a wonderfully poetic lyricism, a deep love of nature and what is at times a soaring mysticism. Among his greatest works are *In The Fen Country, Norfolk Rhapsodies, Towards The Unknown Region,* the unforgettable fantasias, the song cycle *On Wenlock Edge,* the symphonies, and the superb piece *The Lark Ascending.* It is interesting to note that throughout Vaughan Williams' work, and especially in *Job,* the forces of good are represented by diatonic and modal music, while unstable chromatic music demonstrates evil.[19]

The career of Gustav Holst (1874-1934) began under the early influences of the music of Wagner and the spiritual texts of ancient India. (In order better to understand and translate the original language of these texts, Sanskrit, Holst studied it in depth.) These twin influences led to Holst's composing of a number of choral hymns from the *Rig Veda,* as well as the operas *Sita* and *Savitri.* Much later, towards the end of his life, he composed that which he believed to be his greatest work, the orchestral piece, *Egdon Heath.* But between these two phases his mystical leanings had deepened and widened, and there had appeared from his pen the two works for which he is now chiefly known. *The Hymn of Jesus,* a highly original and exalted choral work, is based upon an apocryphal Gnostic text which Holst translated, while the popular suite *The Planets* resulted from an interest in astrology. The seven parts of *The Planets* demonstrate all of Holst's mastery of rhythm, harmony, melody, meaning and mysticism, along with a dazzling choice of orchestration.

Vaughan Williams, Holst, Elgar and others have demonstrated clearly that a refusal to renounce the foundation stones of past tradition and the immutable principles of true aesthetics nevertheless leaves open a vast scope for artistic exploration. For the purification and redirection of the tonal arts, the young composers of today would do well to begin with the signposts left to us by the twentieth-century English composers. It is perhaps in their work, more than in anything else created in this century, that is to be found that art which is fully deserving of the title, New Age music.

And the key to their artistic success? A comment by Vaughan Williams, spoken in reference to Sibelius, provides the archetypal pattern of all the significant English music of this period: ' ... *great music is written, I believe, not by breaking the tradition, but by adding to it'.*

Notes

* It is for this reason that we cannot bring ourselves to write the phrase 'new music' without recourse to quotation marks: not only do many people query whether the humanistic tones of modern composers are music at all, but it is also open to question just how 'new' the 'new music's' basic essence of musical anarchy and materialism can be said to be. Whether one thinks of the 'serious' stream of contemporary music known as the 'new music', or of the more popular rock music, the fact is that nothing of their basic elements are really all that new at all. Back in ancient Greece, the revolutionary 'music of the future' was publicly attacked and ridiculed by the writer of comedies, Pherecrates, who presented the Muse as a violated virgin. In the Middle Ages, the traditional music of the troubadours – an esoteric group of artists – was overwhelmed by the coming of the revolutionary minstrels. The troubadours' songs, outwardly about deeds of courage and of a high form of romance, had deliberately been implanted with deep spiritual allegory which only the initiated understood. But the minstrels were the Middle Ages' equivalent of the rock or folk-rock musician: they dressed and lived as hippies, their music was pessimistic and cynical, their numbers grew constantly and they met together in gigantic gatherings or 'fests' (as they would be called today). The minstrels very powerfully affected the social climate of their day. In China, Lü Bu Ve, the author of *Spring and Fall*, struck out at the vulgar music of the tyrants Hia and Yin in words which could equally apply to the musical 'revolutions' of any age, including our own. They are words well worth keeping in mind during the course of this chapter:

> They deemed the loud sounds of big drums, bells, stones, pipes and flutes beautiful and thought that mass effects were worth while. They aimed at new and strange timbres, at never heard of tones, at plays never seen before. They tried to outdo one another and overstepped the limits.

None of this, then, is at all new. It has all been seen before. The outbreak of musical revolution in the seeking of ever-greater excesses of anarchy and novel 'effects' is actually no more of a 'new' phenomenon than the very struggle between good and evil itself.

3.

Assessment:
Music, Man and Society

In the one corner: the ancients and traditionalists; the conviction that music affects character and society, and that therefore the artist has a duty to be responsibly moral and constructive, not immoral and destructive. In the other corner: the materialists, disclaiming responsibility and the need for value judgments, paying no heed to the outcome of their sounds. This second camp contains not only the radical avant-garde, but also the entire mass of the much more popular and culturally significant jazz and rock musicians.

Who, then, is correct? Upon the answer could depend the entire future of music and civilization. It is time for a detailed appraisal of this crucial issue. *Do life patterns follow music patterns or do they not?* This chapter must be an arena from which only one of the two opposing philosophies can emerge intact.

How valid were the beliefs of the ancients? What modern, scientific evidence is there in support of their concept of music's objective power? Let us examine in turn, in this chapter, the questions of music's possible influence upon the physical body, upon the emotions, upon the mind, and upon society at large.

MUSIC AND THE PHYSICAL BODY

To the question, 'Does music affect man's physical body?' modern research replies in the clear affirmative. *There is scarcely a single function of the body which cannot be affected by musical tones.* The roots of the auditory nerves are more widely distributed and possess more extensive connections than those of any other nerves in the body (a fact which may be of deep inner significance).[37] Investigation has shown that music affects digestion, internal secretions, circulation, nutrition and respiration. Even the neural networks of the brain have been found to be sensitive to harmonic principles.

According to the nature of the music which plays its vibrations upon the body of man, so is the body affected — a very real and physical verification of the aphorism, *as in music, so in life!* Researchers have discovered that consonant and dissonant chords, different intervals, and other features of music all exert a profound effect upon man's pulse and respiration — upon their rate and upon whether their rhythm is constant, or interrupted and jumpy. Blood pressure is lowered by sustained chords and raised by crisp, repeated ones.

It has been found that the tension of the larynx is affected by melodies, becoming, for instance, tightened during a descending series of chords. Since the larynx is very sensitively influenced by the ongoing stream of man's emotions and thought processes, its reactions to music are probably indicative of what is basically an effect of music upon the psyche. We can see, then, that music affects the body in two distinct ways: directly, as the effect of sound upon the cells and organs, and indirectly, by affecting the emotions, which then in turn influence numerous bodily processes. As the indirect effect of tones upon the larynx indicates, melodies cause a constant saga of tensions and relaxations to occur within many parts of the body. If the musician is playing his instrument, then he and his instrument can also be said to be 'playing' the bodies and minds of the audience.

In his studies on the effects of sound stimuli upon the skeletal muscles, Dr Tartchanoff discovered that:

1) Music exercises a powerful influence on muscular activity, which increases or diminishes according to the character of the melodies employed.
2) When music is sad or of a slow rhythm, and in the minor key, the capacity of muscular work decreases to the point of ceasing entirely, if the muscle has been fatigued from previous work.

The general conclusion is that sounds are dynamogenic or that muscular energy increases with the intensity and pitch of the sound stimuli. Isolated tones, scales, motifs and simple tonal sequences have all been found to have an energizing effect upon the muscles. [38]

A further possible effect of music upon the body is described by Bob Larson, the one-time rock guitarist who gave up his playing upon becoming a Christian. Larson writes:

Drs Earl W. Flosdorf and Leslie A. Chambers found in a series of experiments that shrill sounds projected into a liquid media coagulated proteins. A recent teenage fad was that of taking soft eggs to rock concerts and placing them at the foot of the stage. Midway through the concert the eggs could be eaten hard-boiled as a result of the music. Amazingly few rock fans wondered what that same music might do to their bodies.[39]

Not the most appetizing of thoughts. Anyone for hard-boiled punk rocker?

And on the subject of modern popular music, with its great emphasis on fast, loud and syncopated rhythm, it is worth remembering that rhythm in music exerts a very strong influence over the heartbeat, tending to bring it somewhat into conformity with the rhythm of the music itself. Since many young people listen to hours of rock music per week, one shudders to imagine what effect this must have upon their health and lifespan; there is no doubt that while the music is being listened to, the heart also beats unnaturally fast and strongly. Musical syncopations are also reflected in syncopations, or unnatural emphasis, of the heartbeats. Jagged jazz and rock rhythms have been experimentally demonstrated to cause the beating of the heart to lose its perfect rhythm. Research has discovered rock music to be bad for digestion; it is also dangerous while driving. Further, since rock raises the blood pressure, it is bad for cases of pre-existing hypertension. And since the heartbeat in turn affects one's mood and emotions, these too become subject to the influence of rock rhythms when they are heard, tension and inharmony of the mind being increased. Indeed, rhythm affects not only our bodies, minds and emotions, but even our subconscious. Who has not suddenly realized that his leg was moving to the beat of some background music while the conscious mind was entirely directed elsewhere?

Those rhythms which are more harmonious and healthy have been found, depending on their tempos, to be very effective stimulants or sedatives, and they are of course much more beneficial in the long run than toxic, addictive chemicals such as Valium. Julius Portnoy tells us:

> music can definitely change metabolism, affect muscular energy, raise or lower blood pressure, and influence digestion. It may be able to do all these things more successfully and pleasantly than any other stimulants that produce those changes in our bodies.[4]

Whether rhythm stirs us up or soothes us down seems to depend primarily upon how its frequency of beats relates to the normal heartbeat of 65-80 beats per minute. A tempo at about the same pace as the normal heartbeat soothes us, as if our body thinks to itself: 'Ah, that's right, we're both together in unison.' In fact, if you put your hand over your heart while listening to such music, you will find that the heart tends quickly to correct any discrepancy in its tempo, and comes into perfect rhythm with the music. Rhythm which is slower than the heartbeat, however, builds suspense, as though the body is getting ready for the music's sudden speed-up in rate to the normal rate of the heart. ('Any moment now . . . any moment now . . .'). At the other end of the scale, fast rhythms raise the heartbeat rate, and therefore emotional excitement, right up. Anyone can test this for himself, as there's certainly nothing subtle about it. Count your number of heartbeats over a minute of silent sitting in a chair, or if listening to averagely paced music. Then switch on some fast music and, after a minute or two, count your heartbeats per minute again.

Since fast rhythm releases into the bloodstream chemicals which excite the organism, such music can literally be said to give a 'kick'. When a young person is used to listening to fast rock music for a number of hours per day, such kicks literally become a form of addiction, and a sense of emptiness is experienced if for some reason the music cannot be listened to for a prolonged period of time. Although no research has yet been conducted on the subject to the author's knowledge, it also seems likely that the heart-rate of such people is faster than that of other people *even throughout the day, while they are not listening to the music itself.* If so, this would have sobering implications for the physical and emotional health.

In part, the powerful effect which different rhythms have upon us may be determined by the first rhythm which we ever hear. This is our mother's heartbeat, heard by us continuously over the months which we spend in the womb. In an experiment conducted by Dr Lee Salk, a recording was played of a normal heartbeat for newborns in a hospital nursery. Most of the newborns were soothed to sleep. Then Dr Salk put on the accelerated heartbeat of an excited person. The two recordings were both at the same volume, but when the second was played every single one of the infants awoke, most of them tense and some crying.[40]

A rather off-beat and less common effect of music is the mysterious melody malady known as musicogenic epilepsy. Some of its victims have been tormented to the point of committing suicide or of muder. Seventy-six cases of this malady have been documented, but there are no doubt many other sufferers who simply do not realize the source of their problem and have received no specific treatment. In each documented case the sufferer experienced seizures which were brought on by certain kinds of music, though the causative music was different in different cases.

One instance involved a 39-year-old British woman who always felt anxious and sweaty when certain tunes were played in places such as the supermarket or at the local pub. At first she did not connect the music to the symptoms. She knew only that at these places her thinking would often grow cloudy, and her lips, eyelids and fingers would twitch convulsively. Then she would lose consciousness. Only at length did she connect the seizures with the background music. The woman was examined by neurologists Peter Newman and Michael Saunders who attempted to induce a seizure under controlled conditions. Various kinds of music were tried, such as music from Gilbert and Sullivan, Handel's *Messiah* and Beethoven's Ninth Symphony, but with no result. Only when a single by the Dooleys was played, 'I Think I'm Gonna Fall in Love With You', did an attack occur.[41] (By the sound of the singularly original title it would probably have had the same effect on quite a few of us!)

But if only 76 people have been found to suffer from musicogenic epilepsy, the same cannot be said of other unfortunate aspects of some types of music. Take one of the most basic elements of modern music — its sheer volume. Sound is measured in decibels, and experts believe that human health is endangered by any sound at 90 decibels or above. It has been found that at dance halls the average decibel rate in the middle of the dance hall is a little under 110 decibels. In front of the band the sound often reaches 120 decibels. Remember that coagulating protein? Should the reader, upon speaking to a regular disco-goer, find that the reply comes somewhat inarticulately, it may be because the disco-goer's brains are still calcified from the night before.

Or perhaps the person just can't hear you. The Environmental Protection Agency in America has discovered that current generations of youth suffer from hearing problems normally associated with fifty- to sixty-year olds.[42] *Time* magazine has further reported that permanent loss of hearing among rock fans is a much more common complaint than is generally realized.[43] (So now it becomes clear. That's why disco music has to be played so loud: the higher the volume, the more the hearing degenerates, and the higher the volume ...)

If the ears of a rock fan happen to have so far stood up to the battering, it is nonetheless certain that his body has been internally affected. To quote from Bob Larson once more, who, having once been a rock musician, is now a campaigner against the music:

> The hormone epinephrine is shot into the blood during stress or anxiety or the simulated experience of submitting oneself to an abnormal volume of music. When this happens, the heart beats rapidly, the blood vessels constrict, the pupils dilate, the skin pales, and often the stomach, intestines and oesophagus are seized by spasms. When the volume is prolonged there are heart flutters.
>
> A three-year study of university students by investigators at Germany's Max Plank Institute showed that 70 decibels of noise consistently caused vascular constriction – particularly dangerous if the coronary arteries already are narrowed by arteriosclerosis.[39,44]

And that's 'only' 70 decibels; we must remember that the volume at the average dance hall reaches much higher.

In conclusion, we can say that insofar as the physical body is concerned, the notion that music has no effect upon man, or that all music is harmless, is absolutely in error.

MUSIC AND PLANTS: SOME PRELIMINARY FINDINGS

What of the effects of music upon non-human life? Certainly the denizens of the animal kingdom do not seem impervious to the influence of either harmonious or discordant tones. In one experiment conducted by psychologists, rats were given the free run of two separate but connected boxes. Music was being 'piped through' into each of them – Bach into one, rock into the other. Though the two boxes were identical and all other conditions except the music were equal, the rats all spent their time in the Bach box. To test further the purity of the experimental conditions, the music broadcast into the two boxes was changed around; and gradually the rats all moved into the other box. Such an experiment does not, of course, mean that the creatures preferred or 'comprehended' Bach on the same level that a human being can, but the result does indicate that at some level, the degree of pleasure or pain which the rats experienced in the two boxes was tipped in favour of the master of Baroque.

Other experiments have found that certain types of music cause hens to lay more eggs and cows to give more milk. (Stockhausen once visited a site at which battery hens were laying more eggs to the strains of *The Blue Danube*. Recalling the incident later, he commented that his own music would have given the hens diarrhoea!) There are also long-standing traditions from various parts of the world that singing and instrumental music causes farm animals to thrive.

In order to produce the most precise and unambiguous results from experiments, however, scientists often revert to the study of the more primitive forms of life. In the investigation of the effects of music upon life, a number of preliminary experiments have been conducted with plants. Paradoxical as it may seem, music's effect upon the more primitive vegetable kingdom is one of the most convincing methods of all for proving that music does affect life, including human life. For experiments conducted with humans, and even, to some extent, with animals, have the extra factor of the mind to contend with. This means that while men or animals may be demonstrated to have been affected by tones, the effect may not have been a direct or objective one. Rather, the effect upon the body may have been caused by the mind's subjective reaction to the music heard. In the case of plant-music research, however, psychological factors cannot really be said to be present. If music can be shown to affect plants, then such effects have to be due to the objective influence of the tones directly upon the cells and processes of the life-form.

And such results have been forthcoming. While plant-music research is still to a large degree an unexplored and beckoning field for researchers, some preliminary investigations have turned up some pretty unambiguous findings.

Two quite independent series of experiments, one conducted in the Soviet Union and the other in Canada, have each discovered that seeds of wheat can be made to grow faster when treated with tones. The Canadian sound-treated wheat seedlings, in a carefully controlled laboratory environment, grew no less than three times as large as untreated ones.[45] The Soviet seedlings were dosed with ultrasonic tones, with the result that they germinated faster, were more frost-resistant, and yielded more grain.[32] These are obviously findings of great potential for practical application in the world.

Another series of experiments treated plants with (to?) Bach's brilliant Brandenburg Concertos, with which, at an early stage in this book, I mentioned my own experience. The Brandenburgs made geraniums grow faster. As an interesting side-experiment, other geraniums had not the concertos themselves, but only their dominant frequencies broadcast to them. This group grew faster than a group which had no sounds broadcast at all, but not as much as the Brandenburg group proper. This suggests that while the individual tones of Bach's music exert a certain regenerative influence upon plant life, the effect is greater if the frequencies are played in the precise and beautiful rhythmic, melodic and harmonic orders in which Bach actually placed them. Investigations of a similar fashion have also been conducted upon bacteria. These have been found to die when certain frequencies are played to them, while they multiply in response to others.

An intensive series of studies carried out by Dorothy Retallack of Denver, Colorado, demonstrated the effects of different kinds of music on a variety of household plants. The experiments were controlled under strict scientific conditions, and the plants were kept within large closed cabinets on wheels in which light, temperature and air were automatically regulated. Three hours a day of acid rock, played through a loudspeaker at the side of the cabinet, was found to stunt and damage squash plants, philodendrons and corn in under four weeks.

Mrs Retallack played the music of the two different Denver radio stations to two groups of petunias. The radio stations were KIMN (a rock station) and KLIR (a semi-classical station). The *Denver Post* reported:

> The petunias listening to KIMN refused to bloom. Those on KLIR developed six beautiful blooms. By the end of the second week, the KIMN petunias were leaning away from the radio and showing very erratic growth. The petunia blooms hearing KLIR were all leaning toward the sound. Within a month all plants exposed to rock music died.

In another experiment, conducted over three weeks, Dorothy Retallack played the music of Led Zeppelin and Vanilla Fudge to one group of beans, squash (marrow), corn, morning glory and coleus; she also played contemporary avant-garde atonal music to a second group; and, as a control, played nothing to a third group. Within ten days, the plants exposed to Led Zeppelin and Vanilla Fudge were all leaning away from the speaker. After three weeks they were stunted and dying. The beans exposed to the 'new music' leaned 15 degrees from the speaker and were found to have middle-sized roots. The plants left in silence had the longest roots and grew the highest. Further, it was discovered that plants to which placid, devotional music was played not only grew two inches taller than plants left in silence, but also leaned towards the speaker.

Such plant-music studies are crucial for the reason we have already stated: assuming that they are well-controlled and the results accurate, they are able to prove something which experiments with humans or animals are unlikely to: that the effects of music are *objective,* and not dependent upon the subjective preconditioning of the psyche. Let us recall that besides the ancients' belief that music affects the body, emotions and mind of man, they also claimed that music's power was *objective,* not subjective. That is, they claimed that different types of music are *inherently good or inherently bad;* that certain combinations of tones are objectively life-enhancing and evolutionary in nature, while others are unhealthy and dangerous. Should the ancients' belief be true (and Mrs Retallack's work suggests this to be the case), then it would be a fact of vital significance. No longer could modern musicians possibly claim that music is a matter of 'taste', or that the musician should be allowed to perform anything he chooses. Moreover, those types of music which are objectively good or objectively bad might not always be found to conform to people's own subjective likes and dislikes. Since all types of music are liked by some individuals and disliked by others, it stands to reason that there must be instances where objectively bad music is nevertheless 'liked' by a certain misguided segment of society. Plant-music research, then, in supporting the ancient wisdom teaching on the objective power of music, apparently disproves in one sweep the entire contemporary hedonistic, anarchic viewpoint on the art. In short, it seems to offer to us a scientific basis from which a permanent and inflexible aesthetics of music can be constructed. Permanent and inflexible because true aesthetic principles are not subjective, but, as we noted in the previous chapter, are universal. Good music is still good music even if there is no human listener. There is still a life-giving force within it.

The question of what constitutes good or bad music can be answered in just eight words: good music gives life; bad music gives death. There is more to life and death than the two sides of the grave: *every moment of music to which we subject ourselves may be enhancing or taking away our life-energies and clarity of consciousness, increment by increment.* From the point of view of the ancient Chinese sage, the phenomenon of individuals today 'liking' or 'enjoying' bad and destructive music, while not being able to enjoy or understand genuinely good music, would be explained by the fact that such individuals have become 'tuned into' the wrong tonal patterns, simultaneously losing their attunement with Reality and universal principles.

In Dorothy Retallack's own words: 'If rock music has an adverse effect on plants, is the rock music listened to so long and so often by the younger generation partly responsible for their erratic, chaotic behaviour?' And: 'Could the discordant sounds we hear these days be the reason humanity is growing neurotic?'[46]

Dr T. C. Singh, head of the Botany Department at Annamalia University, India, has also conducted research into the effects of music on plants. He discovered not only that constant exposure to classical music caused plants to grow at twice their normal speed, but also went on to find what seemed to be one of the main causes of this accelerated growth. The sound waves of a musical instrument, Dr Singh found, cause increased motion in cellular protoplasm. As a further test, a tuning fork was sounded six feet away from a plant, and this also caused streaming movements in its protoplasm. (Protoplasm is the basic material of which all plant — and animal and human — life is made up.) All sorts of intriguing options for further study occur to one here. Would the protoplasm be found to stream at a different rate when tuning forks of different tones are sounded? Would there be a distinction between major and minor notes? Do certain instruments *inhibit* growth, irrespective of what they play? In Dr Singh's experiments, the violin was found to be one of the most life-enhancing instruments of all. Altogether, life-enhancing characteristics as a result of music were shown in balsam, sugar cane, onions, garlic, sweet potatoes and other plants besides.[38,47]

Yet perhaps the most interesting and significant of all of Dr Singh's findings was that *later generations* of the seeds of musically stimulated plants carried on the improved traits of greater size, more leaves, and other characteristics. Music had changed the plants' chromosomes! Presumably the same effect can result in the negative sense, from bad music. The possible significance of this finding to the human kingdom is evident, and not a little concerning.

MUSIC, MIND AND EMOTION

So real and open to practical usage are music's psychological influences that the art has been applied throughout the ages in order to bring about emotional and mental effects. From the earliest times, fishermen, harvesters and other workers have sung in unison in order to inspire themselves to work at an optimum capacity. With the coming of the radio, we might note, this basic practice did not cease, but was simply adjusted: scientific researchers have discovered that melodious, cheery music on the factory floor boosts productivity considerably.

Paradoxically, one form of music which has long been used to practical effect has the dual result of inspiring one group of people whilst striking fear into another. This is martial music, used since the dawn of history with often devastating results on the battlefield. So efficacious have bands of drummers, trumpeters, and such like proved to be in warfare that the defeated opponents, recognizing that the victors' martial music played a large role in defeating them, have often adopted an identical or similar music for themselves — even though the particular form and style of music has often been quite alien to their own cultural background! To refer to one such instance, the early Crusaders, having been defeated by the Saracens, adopted the arabic martial tones for themselves, with the result that victories once more came their way. In our own day, since warfare itself has altered in form, there no longer exists a role for battlefield musicians; but the expanded usage of patriotic and inspiring songs of freedom and honour could still prove to be of great benefit to the sometimes demoralized or apathetic forces of the Western Alliance, billeted on the European Front or in America.

The psychological influences of music are almost infinitely varied. In particular, man has always turned to the beauty of good music as a source of balm and joyous uplift. Shakespeare knew that good music:

> ... can minister to minds diseased,
> Pluck from the memory a rooted sorrow,
> Raze out the written troubles of the brain,
> And with its sweet, oblivious antidote,
> Cleanse the full bosom of all perilous stuff
> Which weighs upon the heart.

Who can doubt that music influences our emotions? It is surely true that music is only listened to in the first place because it makes us *feel* something. But now this is very interesting, for if music gives us feelings, then these feelings — of uplift, joy, energy, melancholy, violence, sensuality, calm, devotion, and so forth — can certainly be said to be *experiences*. And the experiences which we have in life are a vitally important factor in the moulding of our character.

Psychologists have devoted a great deal of study into discovering just what it is that determines our character — how intelligent we are, what our particular skills are, whether we are civilized in our behaviour or rebellious and destructive, and so on. Not a single serious psychological project or experiment on this topic has failed to conclude that the experiences of life play an extremely important role in the shaping of character.

Two factors are concerned with the formation of one's character. The first is experience, which can also be called learning in the widest sense of the word; the second factor consists of the innate traits with which we are born, and which psychologists believe to be genetically inherited. It is agreed that each of these two factors is extremely important. All that psychologists do not agree upon are the exact percentages to which each factor plays its part in the formation of the total character. In the case of one important character trait, that of one's IQ, psychological studies have indicated that experience accounts for a good proportion of our intelligence. Exactly what proportion the studies have arrived at has depended upon factors such as the type of data analysed. However, estimates for the extent to which environment determines IQ range from 13 to 55 per cent.[48] It would be reasonable enough to assume from this that the actual proportion involved is roughly one third. The other two thirds is the result of heredity and other innate factors.

The logical sequence of connections which we have developed is thus: music is an experience; experience moulds about a third of our total character, judging from psychological studies; therefore some portion of this proportion of our character traits is the result of the music we hear. We find ourselves spanning several thousands of years, and standing hand-in-hand with Confucius! *Music moulds character.*

Basically, it still all boils down to *As in music, so in life.* Widening this aphorism, we find that all psychologists do indeed agree that *As in EXPERIENCE, so in life.* Are the parents interested in art? Then the child too might be expected to become interested in art. Are the friends rowdy? Then the child too might tend to become more rowdy. Does the child watch proudly strutting rock musicians on the screen? Then he too may proudly strut. In study after study, children have been found to copy adult behaviour which they have seen either live or on television. For example, Bandura and Huston conducted an experiment in which children were divided into two groups. Each group was able to see an adult going through a variety of unusual and striking actions while the children themselves were busy with a discrimination problem. Each group of children was able to see a different set of actions by the different adults; the adult might talk to himself or knock a small rubber doll off a box. Later, the children of each group were seen to imitate the particular actions they had been able to observe.[49]

These were children of the same age as those who, in millions of homes in Britain, each week watch *Top of the Pops* on television. Not having seen this programme for many years, I happened to switch on a television set recently – and witnessed what this programme and its music have become. Near-naked men and women danced sensuously in the midst of an occult pentacle which had been drawn on the floor. The men wore animal masks with antlers and horns. The music and its lyrics (as far as these could be discerned) were complementary in their lustfulness and violence. One almost wishes that one did not know of studies such as those of Bandura and Huston ...

In denying the fact that music and the behaviour of musicians tend to shape people's character and behaviour, the materialist musicians are by implication attempting to refute the entire body of carefully documented psychological research conducted and established over the last several decades by hundreds of responsible researchers. Not only music, but all forms of experience mould the way in which we think and behave. To take the example of television, which in modern times has also come to hold a powerful sway over society: according to the National Viewers' and Listeners' Association of Great Britain, there now exist no less than *six hundred* pieces of scientific study which have demonstrated that there is a link between televised and social violence.[50]

Experiences affect our character throughout our lives, but their influence is particularly strong during childhood and adolescence, when the personality is still taking shape and is more malleable. Not for nothing is schooling conducted during these years. Music too, then, can be expected to be particularly powerful in the moulding of character during childhood and the teenage years.

MUSIC AS AN ENCODER

The strength of music's effect upon man can be inferred from detailed studies conducted by psychologists into the effects of other environmental factors which influence man. Language is one such environmental factor, and one particularly similar to music in that it also involves sound, pitch and rhythm. There are unmistakable indications that one's native language does mould character and the way in which we perceive the world around us. Researchers have discovered that when a society does not possess a word for something, that something frequently becomes incapable of being conceived of or identified by them. Some African tribes do not contain within their language the words for certain colours; hence they cannot distinguish those colours even though their eyes are perfectly normal. On the other hand, some societies, possessing terms not present in our own language, are thereby enabled to distinguish that which we could not hope to. Since their snowy world is almost entirely made up visually of white and light-grey, Eskimos possess dozens of names for dozens of minutely different shades of grey to white. These shades all look about the same to us, even though our eyes are as good as the Eskimos'. In having a word for each shade, the Eskimos are able to specifically conceptualize, refer to, remember, and hence perceive and recognize them. Elsewhere, the Hanuóo peoples have no problem whatsoever in distinguishing between *ninety-two* varieties of rice, since they have names for each of the ninety-two varieties.[51]

Psychologists call the ability of a referential word to enhance man's perceptual and conceptual abilities *codability*. The words of a language clarify and *encode* concepts and phenomena for our minds and memories. The process is very marked during childhood, the child's intellectual abilities increasing in close accordance with his or her mastery of language. It is as though words provide the specifically-shaped chalices into which our otherwise vague and fluid thoughts can be poured.

It seems highly likely that different types of music, in giving to us various kinds of emotional experiences − romantic love, lust, religious feelings, patriotic fervour, rebellion, etc. − also encode such feelings and their various hues. A style of music which we have never before heard, and now hear for the first time, may open our minds to an entirely novel feeling or way of looking at the world. A stirring, patriotic song during wartime can encode, unify and intensify the thoughts of an entire nation. And in combining words with music, many concepts can be encoded as never before. The word 'Lord' may not move or mean anything to the non-religious person, but in hearing it sung in paeons of rising, fugal praise he can realize and feel its power and glory for the first time.

Music has often encoded entire movements of human life which were virtually non-existent until the musical referent made its appearance. The Beatles' early singles began the creation of an entire sub-culture by encoding it in music. A few years later, the album *Sgt Pepper* did the same again.

Is it not possible that music, like language, gives us a framework of emotional experiences and mental concepts which tend to shape how we view the world? It is not only possible, but it has to be the case! And it may well be that music, like other perceptual experiences, can affect us in exceedingly specific ways, moulding our way of thought in direct relation to the specific elements of the music.

In his book, *Music, Its Secret Influence Throughout the Ages,* Cyril Scott stated his belief that the music of each great composer of the past played a vital role in very specifically altering the minds and hearts of the people of the day, and thus paving the way for civilization as we know it today.[5] For example, Handel was born into a period during which morality and piety in England were at a low ebb. Yet the effects of Handel's music, and especially his devotional works, according to Scott inspired a reawakening of true religious feeling, while Handel's very formal style brought about the formalism, and even over-formalism, of the Victorian era.

Scott cites two typical tributes to the awe and reverence which Handel's *Messiah* invokes. The first is from the *Quarterly Review,* which runs:

> We feel, on returning from hearing the *Messiah,* as if we had shaken off some of our dirt and dross, as if the world were not so much with us; our hearts are elevated, and yet subdued, as if the glow of some action, or the grace of some noble principle, had passed over us. We are conscious of having indulged in an enthusiasm which cannot lead us astray, of tasting a pleasure which is not of the forbidden tree, for it is the only one which is distinctly promised to be translated with us from earth to heaven.

The second quotation is from Dr Gregory's biography of the Rev Robert Hall, and reads:

> Mr Hall was present in Westminster Abbey at Handel's commemoration. The King, George III, and his family were there in attendance. At one part of the performance of the *Messiah* (the Hallelujah chorus) the King stood up, a signal for the whole audience to rise; he was shedding tears. Nothing, said Robert Hall, had ever affected him more strongly; it seemed like a great act of national assent to the fundamental truths of religion.

Concerning Handel's style, Scott himself writes regarding what he sees as having been its subsequent effect upon English society with the coming of the Victorian era:

> Those who have closely examined Handel's technique will

observe that he had a strong predilection for the repetition of single chords, for two or more bar phrases, and for *sequences*, – viz.: the reiteration of a phrase in a different position or on a different degree of the scale. Thus, apart from its emotional content, Handel's music was pre-eminently formal in character, consequently it was formal in effect. If, however, we combine its emotional qualities with its formalism, and to repetition and musical imitativeness – for sequence is but imitativeness – add grandeur, the net result is the glorification of repetition and imitativeness; and if we translate all this from the plane of music to that of human conduct, we get love of outward ceremony and adherence to convention.

MUSIC AS A COMMUNICATOR AND MULTIPLIER OF STATES OF CONSCIOUSNESS

Some philosophers – and even the occasional musician – have categorically denied that music contains any meaning whatsoever, declaring its sounds to be purely abstract. Yet the emotional content of music seems so obvious to most of us that we simply accept its existence *a priori*. There is surely no doubt that music actually conveys very real and sometimes very specific emotional states from the musician or composer to the listener. For this reason, thinkers have from time to time postulated that music is a form of language. Yet in fact music is both less, and more, than any language of words. Words are highly specific: it would be difficult to communicate in pure tone form that, 'Jack called: he will meet you at 3.45pm by the bridge on the A45. Bring your report.' But on the other hand, while words may be specific on the mental level, they tend to be little more than conveyors of information. Though some emotion is contained in all spoken words, words nevertheless tend to be mere *symbols* of reality; only symbols, what is more, of real inner feelings. Music, however, conveys the very emotional essence or reality behind the information. To listen to Handel's *Messiah* is not to debate intellectually about religion; it is to feel and become one with that surging inner flame of devotion. In this sense, music is more than a language. It is the language of languages. It can be said that of all the arts, there is none other that more faithfully conveys the inner state of the artist; none other that more powerfully moves and changes the consciousness.

Yet if music can so move and transform the inner feelings and the outer behaviour of man, what exactly is it that determines what effect any given piece of music has upon people? What, in the final analysis, is the origin of the emotional effects of music?

Is it not the state of consciousness of the musician? Surely the lowest common denominator which determines the precise nature of any musical work is the mental and emotional state of the composer and/or performer. *It is the essence of this state which enters into us, tending to mould and shape our own consciousness into conformity with itself.* Through music, portions of the consciousness of the musician become assimilated by the audience. To spell it out so bluntly is almost too shocking. Yet if we accept that music does fulfil such a function, transferring elements of the consciousness of the musician into the listener, then the moral implications for the use and misuse of the tonal arts can no longer be denied.

We have seen that thinkers down through the ages have warned of the social dangers attached to the misuse of tonal art. But there is also the positive side. When used correctly, music is perhaps unequalled in its power to instil in man the beauty of true morality and those higher, inspired purposes for which our lives are intended. Thomas Fielden, the musician and writer, felt this most strongly. He asked:

> Which is to be preferred? The jingo and the shouting, easily excited Philistine, satisfied to be told that all he says and thinks is the criterion for the minds of men: or is it the serious, humble student, sitting at the feet of masters, striving to achieve skill, perhaps himself to become a master, and in any case to have a dwelling on Parnassus, whose lowest slopes cannot be reached without effort? Who shall deny that character is engendered, that exaltation and triumph, as well as the tender things of the spirit, can reach greater heights, through this art of music which has always inspired men to achievement, and strengthened their minds to fine and noble thinking?[30]

MOTIVES FOR MUSIC

For argument's sake we have tended to assume thus far in this book that hedonistic artists perform their anarchistic music because they do not believe that music influences people. And yet the more one looks into the subject, the more it is discovered that even the performers of violent contemporary music *do* believe that their music has an effect on their listeners. That is, they do not perform such music out of the belief that it is harmless, but out of a deliberate desire which in former days would only have been called evil.

The fact is that *all* types of musicians, good and bad, tend to be quite aware of the communicative power of tonal art. Through this communicative power, the emotional state of one artist can be transferred to a hundred, or even to ten million, listeners. Musicians of all genres have thereby seldom been ignorant of their vastly enhanced ability to direct the minds and affairs of men. Often this has been the prime motive behind their art. The subject of the *motives* of musicians is one which should not be ignored.

A most revealing statement is attributed to Mick Jagger, spoken during the 1960s. At that time, millions of concerned parents were certain that this lead singer of the Rolling Stones was nothing but 'a long-haired, thick-lipped, thick-headed layabout' (to quote one I remember from the time). As I write, it is now twenty years on, and the dust has settled, so to speak. The hair is still there, and the thick lips. But it is doubtful that Mick Jagger ever was all that thick-headed, or quite such a layabout. A former student of the London School of Economics, Jagger, along with his group and all the other rock bands, has in his way worked extremely hard at the proliferating of his music, message and lifestyle. In the '60s, while all the dust was still up in the air, an awful lot was spoken and written about the music of rock artists, but almost nothing about their motives. Obviously money was and still is one prime motive. (The Rolling Stones' 1981 tour, carefully planned by Jagger to be a money-spinner, gathered in forty million US dollars, breaking all previous records for such a tour.) But there was, and is, another motive. Jagger was the one who, on that occasion during the '60s, spelled it out absolutely clearly. Said he: 'We are moving after the minds, and so are most of the new groups.'

Many would argue that, in retrospect, the Stones had succeeded to a remarkable degree even before that decade was out.

The rock star, David Crosby, has also confided in an interview:

> I figured the only thing to do was to swipe their kids. I still think it's the only thing to do. By saying that, I'm not talking about kidnapping, I'm just talking about changing their value systems, which removes them from their parents' world very effectively.[52]

Sometimes the effects of rock upon the audience have been immediate. Violence and rioting have hardly been unknown at rock concerts, but according to John Phillips of the group, the Mamas and the Papas, 'by carefully controlling the sequence of rhythms' any rock group can create audience hysteria consciously and deliberately. 'We know how to do it,' he said. 'Anybody knows how to do it.' And according to the *Saturday Evening Post* of 25 March, 1967, Mr Phillips and his colleagues were not at all satisfied to allow his words to rest unproven. Prior to a concert they were to perform in Phoenix, Arizona, they decided to put their theory to the test. And during the concert, by making use of a certain combination of rhythms, they actually did create a riot among the audience.

The Rolling Stones were the protagonists in a similar story. When, during the 1969 Altamont rock festival, they performed the song, *Sympathy for the Devil,* the Hell's Angels 'bodyguards' went on a rampage, attacking the audience with such violence that people were severely injured and even killed. Afterwards, Mick Jagger did not seem too concerned about the incident. He and the other group members even refused to attend court in order to identify the murderer or murderers who — perhaps because of this — went free. However, one thing Mick Jagger did have to say: 'Something like that happens every time I play that song.'

Music for 'moving after the minds'; music for the instigation of mass violence ...

The motives for music were not always so. Hence: Beethoven, submerged in the bliss of reverence of God, sacrificing his entire life to the mission of transferring such states of being abroad throughout the world. In the margin of the manuscript of his *Missa Solemnis* he penned: 'From the heart, may it reach other hearts.'

Thus: the towering figure of Wagner, of whom Paul Henry Láng has written:

> Never since Orpheus has there been a musician whose music affected so vitally the life and art of generations ... Wagner himself wanted to be more than a great musician; the new music he created was for him merely the path to the complete reorganization of life in his own spirit.[20]

Therefore: Sibelius, whose innate national pride remained undaunted by the occupation of his native Finland by the Russians, and who therefore sought to capture and fan the flames of national freedom through his magnificent work, *Finlandia.* The piece succeeded so instantly and unmistakably in its task that the occupying forces were compelled immediately to ban it.

J. S. Bach wrote that he composed for the spiritual uplifting of man, and to the glory of God. Franz Lehar during his final days, stated: 'I wanted to conquer people's hearts, and if I have succeeded, I know I have not lived in vain.' And in Monteverdi's words, 'The end of all good music is to affect the soul.'

Do musicians affect those who listen to their music? *Is* music a medium for the communication and multiplication of states of consciousness? If our answer be yes, then we must therefore also affirm that morality in music matters. The morality *of the musician* matters. Even quite apart from such blatant examples as those of rock music quoted above, music must *always* have a moral effect. Either overtly, or in subtle ways which are communicated from subconscious to subconscious, musicians always express through their performances whatever level of psychological harmony or inharmony they have within themselves. This is inevitable. Even the slightest inner hang-up manifesting through the slightest shake of the performing hand or through the minutest weakness in composition becomes registered upon our own subconscious as we listen. No matter how one might try, it is impossible not to express in one's music the reality of one's own inner state of being, even if only in subtle ways. This affects others, the attainment or weaknesses of the performer or composer tending to become the attainment or weakness of the hearers. Music therefore has influences as varied and diverse as the minds of the musicians themselves. As Dr Howard Hanson, Director of the Eastman School of Music at the University of Rochester, has stated:

> Music can be soothing or invigorating, ennobling or vulgarizing, philosophical or orgiastic. It has powers of evil as well as for good.[53]

MUSIC THERAPY: THE UNIVERSAL CURE?

Remove the magnet from beneath a sheet of paper, and iron filings, if they had been placed on top of the paper, become scattered and chaotic, losing the pattern imposed upon them by magnetism. Return the magnet beneath them, and the former pattern is renewed. Likewise was music in ancient times believed to be able to renew the divine harmony and rhythm of man's body, emotions and mind. All forms of sickness and disease, mental or physical, were regarded as being ultimately musical problems. The sick man had lost his inner harmony; he had allowed dissonance to enter the symphony of his being. He was no longer in tune with the universe and its laws. Therefore outward, audible music was used in order to realign man with Universal Sound.

Primitive societies often placed a greater emphasis on magical chants and ritual dances than on medicinal herbs in order to cure their sick.[4] Then, from the earliest appearance of civilization we find that music therapy, far from falling into disuse by being regarded as impractical and primitive, remained in high regard, even becoming formally institutionalized. From their surviving writings we know that music was used as a therapeutic tool by the ancient Chinese, Hindus, Persians, Egyptians and Greeks. In the first book of Samuel it is related how David freed Saul of an obsessive depression by music.[54]

Homer, in the *Iliad*, relates how a rampaging plague was halted by the God Apollo because he was so delighted 'with sacred hymns and songs that sweetly please', sung by Greek youths. In the *Odyssey* Homer tells how, after Ulysses' knee had been wounded while boar hunting, the pain was eased and the wound itself healed by the 'chanting of lays'. These two Homeric accounts give an interesting insight into the early Greek period, revealing that music was found efficacious in countering injury, illness and plague. Music was also used extensively to heal emotional disorders.

The Greeks' use of music as a healer was originally passed down to them from earlier civilizations, but after the life and work of Pythagoras the practice of music therapy also lent itself as a natural extension of the beliefs of the Pythagoreans. Bringing the ancient wisdom teachings to bear within the civilization of Greece, the Pythagoreans conceived music to be the stepping-down in frequency of the Music of the Spheres (Cosmic Sound). Therefore good music was in tune with the rhythm of Life. It was in harmony with the macrocosm; and it was also in harmony with the physiological activities of the healthy man as microcosm. Good music could reinfuse a man whose body had lost its health, re-establishing him in conformity with the divine harmony. Hippocrates, the 'father of medicine', is said to have taken his cases of mental illness to the Temple of Aesculapius to listen to the stirring music there.

The temple priests and physicians of Rome used music therapy up until the point when the Empire was completely Christianized.[4] The Arabs of the thirteenth century had music rooms in their hospitals. Paracelsus practised what he called a 'musical medicine'. He used specific compositions for specific maladies; mental, moral and physical.[55] Medieval physicians often used minstrels to play for convalescing patients, thus speeding their recovery. Even from the latter years of the nineteenth century we have reports of an orchestra being used to treat nervous cases, and of a mental institution near Naples where musicians were used in a curative capacity.[56]

Apart from a few mediocre exceptions (such as the piping through of muzak into dentists' waiting rooms in order to calm the patients' nerves), music therapy is not in wide or institutionalized use today. Due to its seeming intangibility, music is not considered by a materialistic age to be capable of producing significant healing effects. But it seems likely that we are missing out here on a potential boon of great proportions. A small number of private therapists do specialize in the use of music, and find it to be capable of affecting a wide variety of healings.

At present it is up to the therapist as an individual to assess the patient's needs, to decide which music can help to fulfil these needs, and to determine how it should be presented. Modern music therapy is still a pioneer art/science. Intuiton, wisdom and knowledge is required of the therapist.

One music therapist, Julienne Brown, writes:

> The objective of a music therapist is to make contact with the patient through music and personality, so that a deep musical and personal relationship can be built up. After this happens, or more exactly, as this is happening, the therapist can guide the patient through musically and emotionally dependent phases towards a freeing of the emotions. If the therapy is achieving its objectives, the patient will begin to function better as a whole person. This includes helping him to achieve his full musical potential and strengthen his personal identity. With a new patient, I almost immediately attempt to discover the extent of his musical responses, and to help him to answer more meaningfully the question about himself: 'Who am I?'[57]

Said William Congreve, 'Music hath charms to soothe the savage breast.' Certainly a powerful and soothing piece of music, an adagio or barcarolle, would usually be at least as effective on the tense patient as an unnatural chemical tranquillizer, and far more wholesome. But perhaps here we have hit the nail on the head ...

For music therapy and other alternative forms of medicine to partially or wholly replace the entire, highly questionable pill-popping style of medicinal industry, business interests which deal in the bracket of hundreds of millions of dollars per year would need to be overcome. Money is power, and it is the economic power, not the objective effectiveness, of the prescribe-a-pill industry which has maintained the industry's predominant influence over the healing profession.

Hopefully, however, music therapy will grow in grass-roots popularity by reason of its sheer efficacy, which needs to be demonstrated by greater numbers of experienced modern-day practitioners. As music therapist Jean Maas has said:

Music is the greatest power I have ever experienced. I doubt if anything else equals its power to act upon the human organism.

Long ago, Novalis stated that *every* illness is a musical problem. Thus far, modern experience has not proved him wrong. In the literature of music therapy, reports can be found of success to a lesser or greater degree in the treatment of hysteria, depression, anxiety, nervousness, worry and fears, tension, insomnia, high blood pressure, headaches, asthma, brain damage, cancer tendency, heart weakness, Parkinson's disease, tuberculosis, and a wide-ranging host of other mental and physical ailments. Even the most unlikely problems have been helped or solved by music's curative effects. The behavioural scientist Johannes Kneutgen reported that debilitated youngsters and the mentally retarded pass quiet nights when tape-recorded cradle songs are played, bed-wetting decreasing in incidence by no less than two-thirds and sleeping pills not being found necessary any more.[58]

Recently there have been major advances in the use of musical instruments to help the handicapped. On the face of it, most instruments would seem to be beyond the ability of the severely handicapped to play, but with imagination this has not proved too vast a problem. Instruments can be adapted to the individual needs of the handicapped performer; or else, special gloves or retention straps can be used to help the person hold or perform the instrument. A guitarist with no right arm with which to pluck the strings might learn, for instance, to play the guitar with an attachment connected to his right foot. With such individual adaptations, many handicapped people have taken to music with profound concentration. The result has been that not only have they found themselves with a genuine interest and well developed ability, but that the mental and physical effort necessary in order to learn to play, happily engaged in for long hours, has proved exceptionally effective in the development of sensory-motor co-ordination, helping the disabled to move.[59,60,61]

Is music a universal curative agent? On the one hand, the practical mind must concede that in cases of the worst kinds of physical ailment, when these are already fully manifested, more immediate and physical forms of treatment are necessary. But it may well be that a more generalized use of the curative powers of sound would prevent such illnesses from appearing in the first place. Indeed, what makes music therapy particularly attractive is the fact that it heals the *cause* behind disease, rather than merely suppressing the symptoms as do most forms of modern medicinal treatment. According to all the evidence presented by contemporary music therapy, good music does indeed appear to harmonize man's being, bringing him back into more healthy patterns of thought, feeling and action, even as was claimed by the wise of antiquity. We have said that the worst kinds of physical ailment, when these are already fully manifested, require physical treatment; yet who in fact can say, ultimately, what the power of acoustics might not accomplish? It may well be that the power of sound, once a major science of the past, is yet to be a major science of the future.

MUSIC AND THE STRUCTURE OF SOCIETY

Having established that music exerts a definite influence upon man as an individual, the question of whether or not music affects society as a whole is merely one of extrapolation. The individual is the basic component of society. All civilizations are houses constructed out of the bricks that are people. If the characters of a sizeable proportion of the individuals within a society become changed, then that society will definitely undergo a degree of similar changes.

The evidence strongly suggests that music's effect upon the individual is similar to that of other perceptual/learning experiences such as the acquisition of language. As we have already noted, there exist definite similarities between the influences of language and music upon society. For example, both act as encoders of intellectual concepts or emotional feelings, and without the key word or piece of music, it is possible for concepts and feelings to be unknown and alien to entire societies. One human faculty which seems to be affected by both language and music is that of, intriguingly enough, the awarness and perception of time. Regarding language, social psychologists and anthropologists have noted a number of instances of primitive peoples in various parts of the world who have few or no terms by which to refer to the passage of time – no words such as 'hours', 'months', 'yesterday' or 'soon'. One result of this is that they are unable to handle the concepts of past and future. Unable to clearly conceptualize or discuss the passing of time, they live in a vague kind of eternal now, and the structure of their society and its activities reflects little or no sense of progress, or even of cyclic events.

This close relationship between language and the conceptualization of time is closely paralleled in the relationship between people's music and their conceptualization of time. In the modern Western world the movement and rhythm of most music is very clearly thought out, written down and adhered to. Musical works may be consciously divided into definite movements and sections. There is a sense of progress from beginning to end. Likewise we grapple with time in very precise, intellectual terms. Days are divided into hours and minutes. The time of day, date, month and year of many historical events are exactly recorded. The future days and weeks of our lives are often well planned out in advance. We are strongly aware of each day's progression from morning to night. Moreover, we tend to live with the feeling that our lives are taking us somewhere; with the sense of progress over time towards a goal.

All this is not necessarily the case in the music and the intellectual framework of other cultures. Balinese musicians do not write their music down, and therefore do not rigidly adhere to a repertoire of inviolable classics. Rather, their love is to improvise (though within certain definite rules).

Building upon this, Christopher Small has recently made a very interesting observation about the music and the people of Bali: that the musicians are not concerned, as we are overwhelmingly in the West, with the ideal of progress, since their very concept of time itself is not linear but circular. Moreover, and most important:

> This circularity of time is revealed not only in the music but also in many of the rituals and social customs of Bali ...
>
> The calendar similarly reflects the circularity of the Balinese sense of time. It measures, not the elapsing of time, but the characteristics of the various parts of time cycles.[27]

Such similarities between music patterns and life patterns are unlikely to be wholly due to the nature of the culture in general dictating the patterns of its music. Each must influence the other to some degree. On the one hand, it would be unrealistic to suppose that civilization, as an environmental factor (and including that civilization's already-existing music), does not have an influence upon the course of the music of the present moment, as this music comes forth. Yet civilization, in influencing music, *is itself* affected *by* music. What we have here is a classic chicken-or-egg situation (which came first?). In encoding this or that world-view, music must to some extent be merely reacting to the culture it already finds itself within. But having conceded this point, it must also be affirmed that, as Cyril Scott indicated, a study of history clearly reveals that changes in music have tended to precede outer, 'historical' events. In other words, music does also symbolically encode lifestyles and ideologies which do not yet exist in the outer life, but which come to exist due precisely to this creative quality of the art.

One of the few modern writers who does not deny that music is as important for the shaping of society as society is for the shaping of music is John Shepherd, one of the four authors of a recent book entitled *Whose Music? A Sociology of Musical Languages.*[62] Shepherd writes:

> Music is ... an open mode that, through its essentially structural nature is singularly suited to reveal the dynamic structuring of social life, a structuring of which the 'material' forms only one aspect. Music is consummatory ... because social meaning can arise and only continue to exist through symbolic communication originating in consciousness – communication of which music forms a part.[63]

In the same way that the time-sense of the Balinese seems to have been patterned after the time-structure of their music, John Shepherd points to the spatial, temporal and structural similarities between the Western music of different historical periods and the societies of those same periods. Certainly it is true that in medieval plainchant the individual was submerged in the overall structure of the music, even as medieval man tended to lack individuality within the structure of society. Today, individual expression in music is paralleled by individual expression in life.

Are notational and tonal systems also associated with the structure of society? Shepherd suggests that this is the case, and that tonality encodes the industrial world-view. He writes that:

> the architectonicism of the tonal structure articulates the world sense of industrial man, for it is a structure having one central viewpoint (that of the key-note) that is the focus of a single, unified sound-sense involving a high degree of distancing. It is, in other words, a centre-oriented structure with margins ...
>
> It is, moreover, a dialectic correlate of the spatialised time articulated by tonality that industrial man, in becoming increasingly objective and self-conscious, is able to stand back

and objectify the passage of time ... By bringing the corporeal pulse of music into such *continual* high relief – and thereby altering and negating its original 'timeless' and hypnotic characteristics – the rhythmic structure of tonality helps to maintain industrial man's intense and constant awareness both of the passage of time, and of his own consciousness.[64]

Shepherd therefore emerges as one of the few modern thinkers to suggest in print an at least partially creative role for music. Elsewhere in even the same book, however, this possibility, with its vast implications, is generally avoided. Virden and Wishart, for example, interpret Shepherd's line of reasoning as being merely that (and I have placed their key choice of words in italics), 'medieval music *articulated* an idealisation of its society'; that, 'tonality *expressed* musically the nationalised and centralised hierarchy that was actually emerging throughout economic, political and cultural life'; and that, 'the transformational generative rules for tonality were thus established as a musical *accompaniment* to the emergence of a new general sense and organisation of the human world.'[62] What can be seen here is the opposition in people's own minds to the realization of just how powerful and important music is. The association between structures in music and structures in society would seem to be undeniable, but when it comes to the personal *interpretation* of this fact, the tendency is to become at least rather vague, if not completely reductionistic.

Yet while it may not be difficult for the armchair philosopher to discount the independent, creative role of music in affecting society, it can prove impossible for the practical philosopher 'in the field' to do so. And, even more amusingly, when an armchair philosopher becomes suddenly confronted with the real world, he is often compelled to alter his outlook. A good example of what happens when the materialist philosophy of music comes up against reality is afforded by the story of music under the regime of the Soviet dictatorship. According to strict dialectical materialism, man does not shape civilization, but civilization shapes man. In the words of Marx, 'it is not the consciousness of men that determines their existence but, on the contrary, their social existence determines their consciousness'. Words which B. F. Skinner would have been proud of. As such a materialist viewpoint has it, then, men are merely biological machines which are programmed by their environment. Music, as a creation of the consciousness of individuals, should therefore exactly reflect the structure of society, except in symbolized form. This was an important notion to the Communist dictators who emerged as victors of the October Revolution. Their concern was to keep the masses in order, and to prevent any form of counter-uprising. Thus, as one aspect of this concern it was necessary for them to formulate a definite policy towards the arts, in order to ensure that the arts did not become a threat to their rulership. According to dialectical materialism, however, art should follow political-economic events, and therefore could be left free of political interference. No influence in the other direction was conceived to be possible, since art (from consciousness) could not affect political-economic events (society). In order to direct the nature of music and the other arts, the Soviet dictators believed that no direct intervention was necessary; that their political and economic moves would be sufficient. Initially, therefore, a liberal view towards the arts was adopted.[63]

As seems to be the case in so many activities of Soviet society, however, this 'liberal' outlook was admittedly subject to a certain degree of double-talk from the beginning. For example, Lenin acknowledged that 'every artist takes it as his right to create freely, according to his ideal, whether it is good or not' yet then continued:

> But of course we are Communists. We must not drop our hands into our laps and allow the chaos to ferment as it chooses. We must try consciously to guide this development and mould and determine the results.

Trotsky too felt the need 'to destroy any tendency in art ... which threatens the revolution'.[63]

To the Soviet authorities classical music was perfectly acceptable since, as John Shepherd has pointed out:

> traditionally tonal classical music both encodes and articulates the structure of a centralised political-economic system, and so was entirely appropriate to the 'new' order of things in Russia. Given this affinity, it was hardly likely that music articulating other competing structures would be tolerated. This goes a large part of the way to explaining why the morbid frustration of Tchaikovsky and the neurotic eroticism of Scriabin were tolerated, while the clearer, more vigorous language of Prokofiev has often been castigated.[63]

The problem posed to the Soviet dictatorship was that while

classical music was no threat to their retention of power at the centre of the Communist hierarchy, the century in which they actually lived saw the birth of all kinds of music which were indeed a threat. Not only the 'new music' proper, but also devotional music and some forms of popular music were utterly incompatible with the structure of Soviet society and the Communist ideology. Modern music stressed a different form of hierarchy. It also stressed individual expression, sometimes to the point of anarchy. In coming to power, Stalin saw immediately that music posed a real threat to the stability of his regime. Irrespective of the dictates of dialectical materialism and its theorizations, the practical needs of the real world forced Stalin into a complete about-face of the attitude of the Soviet leadership towards the tonal arts. In 1927 the more avant-garde Association of Contemporary Musicians was absorbed into the conservative, ideological Russian Association of Proletarian Musicians. In the following years, Soviet composers were kept fairly much in place by virtue of the withering criticism of anything remotely progressive. As early as 1936, the Russian Association of Proletarian Composers was itself replaced by the Union of Soviet Composers, an official organ of the government.[63]

In its basic essentials, the story of the Soviet encounter with the power of music is simply that of the Communists' discovery that, despite all of their reductionist theorization, music does possess the power to introduce novel modes of consciousness into society, thus changing the society. The only way of preventing this was to suppress the novel music itself.

It is also important to note that some forms of music, such as classical, are efficient in the preservation of *all* forms of modern society, whether Capitalist or Communist, and probably even whether good or evil. Conversely, anarchistic and disruptive musical forms, like plagues or famines, are destructive to *any* kind of modern society. This means that certain types of music, while being the last thing a politician would want to see let loose within his own nation, are exactly what he would want to see at large within the camp of the 'enemy'. But in order to use music as a weapon in this way, it is obviously essential for the politician to realize and believe in the power of music in the first place. This, Western leaders have rarely done. However, their hard lesson regarding the political and social power of the art was never forgotten by the Soviet Communists. In more recent times the Soviet and other Communist regimes of the world have kept, or attempted to keep, a tight rein upon the importation of rock music into their own countries. Yet there exists evidence that the political (left-wing) nature of the Western rock industry has been significantly influenced by radical subversives from the 1950s onwards.[65] Even more startling is the evidence that, since the 1940s, the Soviets have actually turned to music as a means of upsetting the mental stability of Western infants. David A. Noebel has documented in detail the attempts of Soviet-related radicals to set up record companies in the West for the promulgation of hypnotic and harmful musical recordings for children, as well as for the releasing of left-wing and anarchistic rock and folk-rock discs.[65]

Besides those types of music which have a disruptive effect upon society, music can also be a potent rallying, unifying force, as has frequently been displayed. Music has acted as the central focus for the unification of individuals, movements, classes and cliques. In unity of purpose lies immense strength, so as the agent for the bringing about of such unity, music has often changed the course of history. Songs or musical movements have at times united entire nations. They have even *created* nations: it is seldom realized today to how great an extent the American Revolution was a musical revolution. Eloquent and rousing songs of protest, freedom and brotherhood first unified and awoke a people to their destiny, the revolutionary music eventually being precipitated into a physical revolution, and the United States of America being born.

THE TONAL SIDE OF THE AMERICAN REVOLUTION

Several years before the American War of Independence, resistance songs began to appear in print. These swept the colonies, becoming extremely popular, and being actively sung by many.

Though the effect of the songs was to quickly forge a broad feeling of unity and purpose among the colonists, the works actually originated with small, organized minorities who deliberately used the medium of song as a means of furthering their vision for the future of their land. For the most part, these groups consisted of Freemasons and the Sons of Liberty.

The vital role of the Freemasons in the entire story of the Revolution cannot be overestimated. George Washington, his Chiefs of Staff, the great majority of the signatories of the Declaration of Independence, and almost all the early prominent figures among the colonies were Freemasons. So too, amusingly enough, were the 'Indians' responsible for the Boston Tea Party. The Masons, in fact, lay at the entire cause and core of the Revolution.

The publication of patriotic freedom songs was one of the major methods by which the Masons rallied and awoke a people to their destiny. Many of the political leaders of the emerging nation, such as Francis Hopkinson, Thomas Paine and Benjamin Franklin, were also among the New World's most popular songwriters, in addition to being Freemasons. Francis Hopkinson, as well as being acknowledged as America's first native composer, was also a Freemason and a signatory of the Declaration of Independence. He is also widely believed to have been the designer of the American flag.

The first patriotic music to be published in the New World appeared in 1768. John Dickinson's *Liberty Song* set the pattern for all those which followed in the years before the manifestation of the physical revolution itself:

Come join hand in hand brave Americans all,
And rouse your bold hearts at fair Liberty's call;
No tyrannous acts shall suppress your just claim,
Or stain with dishonour America's name.

In Freedom we're born and in Freedom we'll live,
Our purses are ready,
Steady, Friends, Steady,
Not as slaves, but as Freemen our money we'll give ...

All ages shall speak with amaze and applause,
Of the courage we'll shew in support of our laws;
To die we can bear — but to serve we disdain,
For shame is to Freedom more dreadful than pain.

In Freedom we're born ...

History records that the *Liberty Song* 'became an obsession, being sung everywhere: at political demonstrations, protest meetings, patriotic celebrations, dedication ceremonies for liberty trees, for pure enjoyment, and also for nuisance value to enrage the British ...'[66]

Such songs played a major role in the early formation of the Americans' sense of nationhood. Esotericists may also read significance into the fact that the songs were sung regularly and widely by large gatherings of people: thus, the tones of freedom and resistance were continually and powerfully going forth from 1768 onward. Even discounting the esoteric angle, the connection of such music to the events which followed is unmistakable.

From the beginning, the vision for the future which the songs pronounced was a supremely ambitious one. Given the relatively tiny importance and minor status of the American colonies during the 1700s, the vision was also uncannily prophetic. The songs called for mankind to 'awake to the call of liberty', and predicted that 'freedom's flame' would roar 'with a loud note' even 'to distant shores'. As early as 1774, while British troops were exacting revenge for the Boston Tea Party, the *Newport Mercury* published a song which included the following startling stanza:

> A ray of bright Glory now Beams from afar,
>> Blest dawn of an Empire to rise;
> The American Ensign now sparkles a Star,
>> Which shall shortly flame wide thru' the Skies.

Some years before the onset of the actual War of Independence, the patriotic songsters had already made it plain that they were aware of the martial power of tone. One verse, appearing in the *Boston Chronicle* of 23-26 October, 1769, sombrely warned:

> But when our country's cause the Sword demands,
> And sets in fierce array, the warrior bands;
> Strong martial music, glorious rage inspires,
> Wakes the bold wish and fans the rising fires.

During the war itself, there was no mistaking the Americans' favourite victory music. Thomas Anburey, a member of the surrendered British army, wrote from internment on 27 November, 1777:

> *Yankee Doodle* is now their paean, a favourite of favourites, played in their army, esteemed as warlike as the Grenadier's March – it is the lover's spell, the nurse's lullaby. After our rapid successes, we held the Yankees in great contempt, but it was not a little mortifying to hear them play this tune, when their army marched down to our surrender.

It should be mentioned that the American patriots were convinced that their struggle was divinely supported. In this they were spearheaded by the Freemasons, who had known all along the destiny to which the New World was directed, and who felt that the very angels of God were behind their endeavours, guiding and guarding the sons of liberty, and helping to bring forth a nation which would one day illumine the world. Indeed, at times it was as though the very heralds of heaven were whispering their own lyrics into the receptive ears of the Mason-musicians. Dr Joseph Warren's *New Massachusetts Liberty Song* sounds as much the utterance of a God of Freedom as that of a Boston patriot:

> We led fair FREEDOM hither, when lo the *Desart* smil'd,
> Paradise of Pleasure, was open'd in the Wild;
> Your Harvest bold AMERICANS! no Power shall snatch away,
> Assert yourselves, yourselves, yourselves, my brave AMERICA
>
> Lift up your Heads my Heroes! and swear with proud Disdain,
> The Wretch who would enslave you, shall spread his Snares in
> vain;
> Should EUROPE empty all her FORCE, you'd meet them in
> Array,
> And shout, and shout, and shout, and shout, for brave
> AMERICA.

Thomas Paine's *Liberty Tree* gave praise to the tree of liberty which would take root, flourish and draw 'the nations around to seek its peaceable shore'. The song also acknowledged the existence of supporting celestials – an acknowledgement intended to be taken no more symbolically or poetically than literally:

> In a chariot of light from the regions of day,
> The Goddess of Liberty came;
> Ten thousand celestials directed the way,
> And thither conducted the dame,
> This fair budding branch, from the garden above,
> Where millions with millions agree,
> She bro't in her hand, as a pledge of her love,
> The plant she call'd Liberty Tree.

The song was first published in July, 1775, under the pseudonym, 'Atlanticus'.

Ultimately, such songs were voiced by the early patriots in the genuine spirit of prayer and invocation. Their Freemason leaders believed the nation's destiny to have been mapped out in advance by divine agents, requiring only courage, faith, song and application to bring it forth into manifestation. Considering the subsequent miraculous birth, victory and unparalleled growth of the new nation, there is enough to give one pause before declaring the Americans' earnest beliefs to have been incorrect.

4.
The Ancient Wisdom:
Music in India

The syllable OM, which is the imperishable Brahman, is the universe. Whatsoever has existed, whatsoever exists, whatsoever shall exist hereafter, is OM. And whatsoever transcends past, present and future, that also is OM.

Thus begins the *Mandukya* Upanishad, one of India's oldest writings. Though the terminology may differ, we find ourselves confronted here with the very same concept of the Primal Vibration that we encountered in the philosophy of ancient China. In Hinduism, the syllable OM not only represents the concept of Cosmic Sound but, when uttered, is believed to actually attune the individual to the celestial Tone itself.

The Hindu has always tended to be more inwardly mystical than outwardly industrious. Thus, in India there has been less of a tendency to physically harmonize their civilization with universal principles, as the Chinese did by means of the *huang chung*. Rather, the Hindus have placed an even greater emphasis than did the ancient Chinese upon the sacred alignment of *consciousness*. In this spiritual endeavour the concept of OM, as the earthly sound which mirrors the Sound of the One Tone, is paramount. Intoning the OM, in combination with certain mental and spiritual disciplines, is of prime importance in raja yoga. In some meditation techniques the OM is not actually uttered at all, but simply imagined with the inner ear, consequently attuning the soul directly with the Soundless Sound.

OM

We have used various terms so far in the course of this book in reference to the Soundless Sound, applying first one and then another in order not to limit, but to expand one's conceptualization of that to which the terms refer. Cosmic Sound, Primal Vibration, the *Logos,* the Music of the Spheres, the Word, celestial harmonics, the One Tone – all such concepts are inclusive within the Hindu term, OM.

In the Vedas, India's oldest scriptures, which are far more ancient than the Old Testament, the OM is described as being the basic natural force inherent throughout all of the phenomena of Nature, and from which all other forces are derived. Through the vibratory power of the OM, God created and sustains the entire universe. Descending in frequency from the realms of pure Spirit into the arena of time and space, the OM shapes and organizes primordial matter-energy in such a way as to cause atoms to coalesce, thus manifesting physical matter. All that exists is therefore conceived as being fundamentally vibrational in nature. This applies not only to tangible substance, but to all forms of energy. Light, heat, audible sound – all are stated by the Vedas to be the vibrational force of the OM manifesting at different frequencies and combinations of frequencies.

In a variety of ways there exist indisputable similarities between Hinduism and Christianity, and one of these similarities lies in the concept of the OM, for one can hardly avoid the conclusion that the OM and the Word of Christianity are one and the same (horror of horrors though this may be to the Christian fundamentalist!). Each are associated with the Creation, and each with the Second Person of the Trinity (Vishnu in Hinduism, and the Son in Christianity). To speak of 'the Word' is to refer indirectly to a phenomenon; whereas the OM *is* that phenomenon. OM *is* the Word.

The Vedas place great emphasis upon audible sound, for sound is said to be a manifestation of the Cosmic Sound itself. The Vedic language of Sanskrit differentiates between audible sound and Cosmic Sound, calling the former *ahata* and the latter *anahata. Ahata,* audible sound, can be heard by everybody by means of the ears, whereas *anahata* cannot. However, *anahata* can be heard – or *experienced* – by the advanced yogi sitting deep in contemplation.*

Rather than merely considering audible sound to be the *effect* of vibration, the ancient writers of the Vedas went one step further, considering Cosmic Sound to be the *cause* of all vibrational activities and forces. Light, which consists of vibrations of a much higher frequency than those of audible sound, was nevertheless seen as being a form of sublimated tone. The Sanskrit words for the two – *svar* for light and *svara* for tone – indicate in root syllables how similar in nature the two phenomena were once known to be. The additional 'a' at the end of *svara*, the word for tone, indicates that tones are stepped-down, particularized light.

Music holds a position of vital importance within the Hindu cosmo-conception. Since it consists of audible sound, or *ahata*, it is viewed as being a manifestation of *anahata*, which is to say, of the OM. Therefore, music, like all audible sound, contains some of the very power, energy and consciousness of the Word of God. To the ancient Hindu, as to the Chinese, audible sound was thought capable not only of influencing the mind and emotions of man, but literally of shaping and changing physical events taking place within the world. Sound accomplished this by gradually altering the non-physical vibratory patterns which lay at the root of all objects.

Of all the forms of audible sound, those created by man were deemed to exert the most powerful effect, for the sounds of man – the use of the voice and the playing of musical instruments – were a very specific and intelligently controlled release of vibration. Hence they were capable of resulting in definite and specific changes in consciousness and in the physical events of the world. Shiva is said to have exclaimed, pointing out how best to serve him: 'I like better the music of instruments and voices than I like a thousand baths and prayers.'

Volume I of the *New Oxford History of Music* informs us that:

> The notion that the power of music, especially the intoned word, can influence the course of human destiny and even the order of the Universe, goes back to the very oldest surviving form of Indian music, namely, the music of the Vedas. The intoned formula is the pivot point of the whole elaborate structure of Vedic offerings and sacrifices. It is the power of the words enunciated with the correct intonation, that determines the efficiency of the rites: a mistake may destroy everything. The priests claim that by their activity they not only uphold the order of human society, but maintain the stability of the universe. By means of well-conducted ceremonies they have compelling power over the Gods themselves. The instrument that conveys that power is the word.[12]

It is said that a singing girl, by singing so perfectly a certain *raga*, averted a famine in Bengal by causing the clouds to shed their moisture upon the crops below.[16] Another tradition refers to the fearsome, magical effects of the *Dīpaka raga*, which was said to destroy by fire all who tried to sing it. According to the story, the

Emperor Akbar ordered a famous musician, Naik Gopaul, to sing the *raga*. Akbar's motive in doing so was to prove beyond doubt that the *raga* really did possess such a power. Gopaul tried to excuse himself, but Akbar insisted that Gopaul obey. The singer therefore begged permission to return home and bid farewell to his family and friends. The request was granted; the trip home and back taking Gopaul six months. When he returned it was winter, yet despite the cold and before singing, Gopaul placed himself in the Jumna river, the waters reaching up as high as his neck. Gopaul's hope was that the coldness of the river would protect him — yet no sooner had he sung a few notes than the river grew hot. Gopaul continued to sing, and the river began to boil. At this point the singer, in agony, begged to be excused, but Akbar would hear none of it. Therefore Naik Gopaul resumed the song, upon which violent flames burst forth from his form, consuming him to ashes![67]

THE MYSTICAL BASIS OF MUSIC AND SPEECH

The idea at work throughout the Vedic mysticism of sound is that music and the human voice provide a vehicle for the manifestation of the energies of Cosmic Sound. According to the sounds produced, so will the effect be. Each instrument, possessing its own unique timbre, therefore releases a different form of sound-force. For example, the three classes of instrument — string, wind and percussion — are associated with the Trinity: Brahma, Vishnu and Shiva. The personages of this Trinity actually represent all manner of triune aspects of Nature which are manifested throughout the universe. At their most fundamental level, the Trinity represent three primary and sacred forms of cosmic energy, and it is these energies which are released into the world by means of music.

According to Occidental esoteric traditions, the Trinity are present in music in the form of harmony, melody and rhythm. Though Indian music has virtually no harmony, there are similar references within ancient Indian lore to the role of melody and rhythm. Western esotericism has it that it is the Father-God aspect of the Trinity which relates to harmony; yet not so much to harmony itself as to intervals of pitch differences between the different notes of the scale. In other words, the Father aspect relates to what might be called the 'vertical' axis of music, since pitch differences do not in themselves take place over time at all, but, by themselves, remain abstract and unmanifested. In this sense, Brahma of the Hindu Trinity can indeed be said to be present in all music. Shiva, or the Holy Spirit, represents the presence of God manifested in the material world. In music, Shiva is that which gives music reality within the known world of time and space, for Shiva relates to rhythm, the movement of music over time. Of these two, Brahma and Shiva, is born Vishnu *the Son,* even as melody is born of *the dimensional Cross* between rhythms, or 'horizontal' movement over time, and harmony, or the 'vertical' difference in pitch.

Indian writers have always stressed that primacy in music belongs to the voice. The voice is thought to be a more potent medium for the expression of cosmic forces than are inanimate instruments. Esoterically, the voice is associated with the Mother-God, thus adding a fourth member to the Trinity of string, wind and percussion instruments. There are two reasons for this more potent power of the voice. Firstly, no other instrument can express so perfectly all the delicate subtleties of spiritual feeling that the musician seeks to give forth to others as sound, because only the voice has a direct bodily connection with the intellect itself. Secondly, the voice of man is particularly intimately associated with the OM, the voice of God. Human speech is a lesser, stepped-down aspect of the OM itself, since man is a Son of, and a part of, God Himself. Therefore, through the use of his vocal cords in speech or in singing, man is thought to be a co-creator with God. According to the symbolic writings of the *Aitareya* Upanishad, the Creation involved the formation of a cosmic 'mouth'. 'From the mouth proceeded speech, from speech Agni, fire.' Within the lesser world of time and space, this same creative Holy Spirit force or fire, Agni, is said to proceed from the throat of mortal man. Groups of sadhus roam the land of India or congregate at religious festivals, chanting *bhajans* and yogic mantras for many hours per day, every day of the year; and this for the dual purpose of elevating themselves in consciousness and maintaining the equilibrium of the society. For thousands of years there has never been an instant of time when many thousands of holy men were not chanting Sanskrit verses within the Indian subcontinent, that evil or disaster might not prevail on earth.

A similar function is attributed to the intoning, over the millennia, of the ancient Vedas. The Vedas, which are the basic scriptures of Hinduism, are also revered by the adherents of other religions such as Buddhism and Jainism, and are among the oldest religious texts in the world. A point often missed by Western readers of the Vedas is that these texts never were primarily intended only to be read and quietly studied, but were sacred hymns which were intoned and sung. The Upanishads, which form a

portion of the Vedas, and which are sold in paperback form in the
modern West, are not poems or written dialogues, but songs.
Therefore their function was not merely to convey abstract,
intellectual wisdom, but literally to *release* that wisdom as a real and
sacred energy. Energy was always considered to be released when
the magical Sanskrit formulas were vocalized. This energy then
helped – not only theoretically, but also practically – to create the
spiritual states of mind and of life which the words described.

MUSIC AND SPIRITUALITY

Due to the danger of music being misused by the evil or ignorant, in
classical Indian music great stress is laid on the morality and
spiritual stature of the musician. In learning to become a classical
Indian musician or dancer, the student becomes attached to an
established artist. Invariably the teacher, after the many years of his
own training and association with the music, has developed a keen
sense of spiritual awareness and responsibility. The teacher therefore
becomes both a music teacher and a guru to the student. It is considered inconceivable for the student to attempt to seriously perform
classical Indian music or dance before a solid grounding in the
ancient religious texts and their teachings upon the mystical aspects
of music have been mastered. From the outset, the training is both
musical and spiritual.

As early as the third or fourth century BC, the author of the
Rāmāyama stated that a singer should eat sweet fruit and roots in
small quantities, that he should accept no money or other remunera-
tion for his art, and that he should always sing exactly as taught
without any attempts to improve or change the master's composition with flourishes and the like. Such standards are not always
followed today, yet still the most accomplished performers are
always extremely religious individuals. In the past, however, Indian
musicians were not only great performers, but also advanced yogis.
What their music must have sounded like, fusing so perfectly the art
of tone with the peak of self-control and the heights of mystical
awareness, we can today only begin to imagine. Writing of these
great figures of the past, Ravi Shankar states that they had complete
control over their bodies:

> They knew all the secrets of *Tantra, hatha yoga,* and different
> forms of occult power, and they were pure, ascetic and saintly
> persons. That has been the wonderful tradition of our music –
> and even today, though such miracles may not be performed, one

can see the immense impact on the listener and, as many put it, the 'spiritual experience' the listener feels.[68]

Music assists the Indian devotee to direct his emotions upward in love for the Supreme, to still the rebellious mind and bring it to a point of concentration. Music even aids, it is believed, in the raising of the 'vibration' or spiritual frequency of the body itself, beginning the process of the transformation of matter into spirit, and consequently returning matter to its original state. Thus, as all is OM, the OM as music calls to the OM as manifested in the soul of man, to draw it back to the Source of the OM itself.

NAME AND FORM

The moulding power of sound is attributed not only to music, but also to the spoken word. According to the Hindu cosmology, the name of a thing is actually a vital key to understanding its inner nature. The name of anything is its key-note sound-pattern, the expression in audible sound of the higher vibratory patterns which have created the form itself. This is completely distinct from the Occidental conception of name, which is thought to act merely as a label, much like a reference number. To the studied Hindu, a name is not an arbitrary reference number, but the actual mathematical formula of ratio and vibration upon which the creation and sustainment of the form or living being is based. There can only be one correct name for any person or object, for any other name would be an incorrect formula. To change one's name is to change one's personality.† This is the understanding upon which the language of Sanskrit is based, in which all phenomena are named according to their root-formulas. The language is derived from a long-forgotten, unknown source of great occult wisdom. Sanskrit has always been considered to be a holy language, because its sounds are such a pure expression of God, the Geometry of Divinity. Each letter and syllable of the language is mathematically and mystically precise. To alter the language is absolutely forbidden.

The seed sound of any object, phenomenon or condition is known as its *bija* mantra. By knowing this seed sound, a yogi believes he can achieve a state of absolute knowledge of the thing itself. Likewise, by a certain use of the mantra, the thing itself can be destroyed or changed – or created if it does not yet exist. On the subject of *bija* mantras, the American religious leader, Elizabeth Clare Prophet, has stated:

Over thousands of years, ancient tradition has brought forth the bija sounds of many of the most exalted beings, as well as the elements of earth, air, water and fire. By performing japa, or repetition, with a bija mantra, we create a harmonic resonance with the being or element whose seminal sound is that bija mantra.

In a linguistic sense, bijas have no meaning in and of themselves. But mantra yogis fully realize that the Sákti, or potent force of the Divine Being, is transmitted to the one who is chanting the mantra.

The bija sound for the earth element is LAM (lãm). The bija sound for water is VAM. The bija sound for air is YAM. Fire is the sound RAM. Ether, or akasa, has the bija sound HAM.

As we give these bija mantras, we can attune to the inner pattern of each plane of God's being.

Each one of these five sounds ends in the letter M which is the sound of Mother or MA. It is the sound of the HUM (hōōm) of the Mother flame, and it is the sound that crystallizes what is coming forth from the causal stress into physical matter. Mother is the author of the *Mater* universe.

The first letter of each bija denotes its frequency. The central vowel of each is A – the action of Alpha, or the Father principle. The Father creates, the Mother seals the creation. The three letters of each bija form the Trinity – the Trinity that is always necessary to have a seed.[69]

INDIAN MUSIC AND ITS APPRECIATION

Traditional Indian music can be divided into three general classes: classical music (i.e. the *raga*), purely sacred music (vocal chants to deities such as in *bhajans*), and folk music. All three are readily available to us today in the form of recordings made by some of India's greatest artists in these genres. Moreover, some of India's great artists regularly tour in the West. This practice was largely initiated by the sitar player, Ravi Shankar, who gained great popularity in Europe and America among some of the younger generation during the late 1960s and early 1970s. The brothers Imrat and Vilayat Khan, and Ali Akbar Khan also tour frequently, these being among the greatest of India's living musicians. However, it could be argued that in order to experience the total, committed atmosphere of Indian music, there exists no replacement for hearing it in its natural environment, as the holy men of the hills chant their morning rituals, or as the musicians of the local village spontaneously gather at sunset for the sounding out of the tones of the hour.

Western and Indian classical music have each taken their art to the highest point of beauty and sophisticated tonal expression, but each has done so in a different way. That the qualities of Western music (such as its use of harmony) are not often found in Indian music, and the qualities of Indian music not frequently to be found in Western music is not a failing of either. Since each are radically distinct evolutions of the tonal art, each must be respected and listened to in its own way, according to its own criteria of what the music is oriented towards achieving. To the unaccustomed ear, Indian music can sound strange and alien, and like any music, before one is really attuned to it, it can even sound monotonous – which is exactly what it is not! However, once one has learned to appreciate the music's many deep and beautiful qualities, it is an attunement which is maintained for life. It even seems at times as though the Westerner who develops a taste for the *raga* does himself begin to think and act a little in the manner of an Oriental devotee, becoming more subtle and meditative of character.

In listening to Indian music, one could do worse than to heed the wise words of advice from Peter Hamel, the German musician and writer, that:

> For Indian music, as for the performer himself, it is much more important that the public *should be able to listen with the heart,* rather than observe the musical development or 'appreciate' the music critically and dispassionately ... Once one has 'got the feel of' Indian music, its monotony suddenly becomes so colourful and full of nuances that its riches start to spill over into deeper dimensions.[70]

Among the programme notes for his 1975 European Tour, Pandit Patekar advised his audience that in listening to Indian music they should:

> Temporarily release yourself in thought from the usual way of thinking and concentrate on the higher, spiritual aspects of life. Music offers the best means for such concentration.
>
> Place the universal in front of your contemplation, and endeavour to lay aside or to forget the habit of looking at partial aspects only ...
>
> Try to think your way inside the artist. In other words, try to feel with him and to become one with both artist and theme.

This reveals clearly why it is so important for the Indian musician to be of pure consciousness. In Western classical music the performer is usually 'lost' midst the body of the entire orchestra; and even solo parts are often clearly laid down by the composer. In Indian music, however, and particularly in the *raga*, the entire 'atmosphere' and quality of the piece depends upon the musician himself, who builds up and invents the exact melodic patterns as he goes along. Literally, the *raga* presents a stream of consciousness, and is thereby a very obvious example of our statement in the previous chapter, that music acts as a communicator and multiplier of inner states.

THE *RAGA*

The *raga* (or *rag*) is the basic form of Indian classical music. Indeed, it may always have been so. There exists evidence that the *raga*, or a *raga*-like form of music, existed as early as 400 BC. Though the instruments of ancient India differed considerably from those in use today, it seems that the musical forms and structures of those times were similar to those of today, possibly differing from today's *ragas* no more than the *ragas* of modern India differ between themselves from the north to the south of the subcontinent.

Over thousands of years of musical evolution, the *raga* has developed into an art form capable of summoning up the most intense spiritual feelings. The listener may experience indescribably deep yearnings for something not quite defined, but which seems to be connected with the very core of the meaning of life. These feelings vary in an infinite variety of subtle ways, according to the type of *raga* performed, to the degree of understanding in the listener, and according, of course, to the spiritual development of the performer.

Of the four main dimensions of music — harmony, melody, rhythm and timbre — harmony is again, as in China, virtually non-existent in Indian music. But, and again as in China, this lack is more than made up for in that melody, rhythm and timbre are developed to an extraordinarily sophisticated degree. Classical Indian melody and rhythm often exceeds anything that is to be found in the mainstream of Western music.

As in the Western diatonic scale with its seven major tones, there are also in Indian music seven basic notes, known as SA, RE, GA, MA, PA, DHA and NI. While the notes of this scale are not brought together harmonically, there is a very refined art — one might even say science — to the melodic use of this tone scale.

Modifications of the seven basic tones or *svars* into 'natural', 'flat', 'sharp', 'extremely flat' and so forth produce a total of 22 basic intervals or *shrutis* to the octave which are applied in Indian music. Using these *shrutis* according to traditional and strictly laid down rules gives the basis of the *raga* system of music. From the established *svar-shrutis* (tone-intervals), hundreds of different tone combinations are organized. Each combination of tones is the basis of one *raga*. That is, each particular *raga* is based upon a particular selection of *svar-shrutis*. The relationship and order in which these tones can be played during the *raga* are governed by strict and complex rules. It is up to the musician to display the full range of note relationships and ornamentations of which he is capable, and to do so movingly and artistically, whilst nevertheless remaining within the particular laws of the *raga*.[19]

The *raga* system grants the musician freedom of expression *within the limitations of a certain inviolable mode.* This is a convincingly successful solution to the problem which the music of ancient civilizations always came up against. The dilemma has already been discussed in relation to China: since music was so important a force in altering phenomena upon earth, it would be unwise, dangerous, and perhaps even suicidal in the long run to allow musicians to perform whatever they wished. Therefore it was imperative for music to be regulated, and definite laws applied regarding what could and what could not be played. But if the laws meant that only certain set pieces of permitted music could be performed, and no new compositions brought forth, then people would become bored with hearing the same music over and over, and the art itself would therefore decline. The immensely successful Indian solution was, then, to apply a system of rules which, while effectively determining what *type* of music was performed, and even its spiritual atmosphere, did not actually dictate the notes themselves. So flexible is the *raga* form that the same *raga* performed by different artists, or even by the same artists upon different occasions, can offer entirely distinct delights and experiences. Artistic expression and invention is allowed for, then, yet the necessary barriers provided against anarchy.

One tradition has it that originally there were only seven *ragas,* but this may be the remnant of an ancient reference to the association of different *ragas* to the seven Cosmic Tones. Today there are ten basic *raga* forms in the north of India and 71 basic *ragas* in the south, each *raga* form possessing its own particular combination of tones. Yet *ragas* can differ from each other in even the minutest of details, and as many as 5831 *ragas* have been identified in the south.

Within each *raga* SA is sounded almost continually as a drone, and all other tones are therefore heard in relation to this. (The prominence of SA is therefore reminiscent of the importance of the *huang chung* in China.) Besides the drone of SA, one note is also selected in each *raga* for special melodic prominence, and a second tone as a secondarily important melodic note. Each *raga* has its own name which states the *raga's* emotional character. This might be anything from longing for a loved one, or a mixture of melancholy and hope before dawn, to a mixture of joy and affection, or meditative thoughts on one's life at the close of day.

In India, as in other ancient cultures, specific aspects of music also hold a variety of cosmological associations. And under the Indian system it is the different *raga* forms which hold many of the extra-musical connotations. As in China there are associations between music and time cycles: each *raga* is linked with a particular time of day, and sometimes with a particular season. Even today, the studied Indian would normally consider the playing of a *raga* at the wrong time to be an act of gross ignorance.

Aspects of music in India still hold connotations with things as various and diverse as the signs of the zodiac, the planets, the days of the week, the seven heavens, the seasons, the elements, colours, voices of birds, human complexions, the sexes, temperaments, and man's age. However, it would be unwise to place a great deal of trust in the objectivity of such connotations as they exist today. Not only do they differ between the north and the south, but in both parts they differ from the connotations indicated in the ancient texts.[16] As Curt Sachs relates:

Tradition is hopelessly lost. Every local school has a terminology of its own, and when a northern musician associates the raga *Srī* with love and evening twilight, a man from the south will rebuke him and relate it to grandeur and the hours between noon and 3pm.[16]

As to the musical natures of the *ragas* of different hours of the day, one distinction is clear, however: 'ragas have most flats in the quietest hours, extending from midnight to the hot time of the day, and reach a major-like character in the cooler time between six and midnight.'[16]

If the most important feature of Indian music is the melodic sequences, then the second is certainly its rhythm, or *tāl*.

The *tāl* is a rhythmic cycle, composed of a certain number of beats, or time units, known as *mātrā*. These different rhythmic cycles have many different numbers of beats, but the most widely used is that comprised of sixteen *mātrā*, and grouped into four bars: 4–4–4–4. Each *tāl* or rhythmic cycle has its own name, 4–4–4–4 being *tintāl*. Similarly, for instance, the rhythm of ten *mātrās* divided into the four bars of 2–3–2–3 is *jhaptāl*. There are also more complex rhythms such as *vishnutāl*, which consists of five bars containing altogether seventeen *mātrās*: 2–3–4–4–4.[19]

The structure of the classical *raga,* or the order of the different sections of its music, is fixed. However, the time spent upon each section is left to the performers. In the first part of the *raga* a great degree of improvisation is possible, though always within the laid-down rules of the particular piece. This is the *ālāpa,* in which the main traits of the *raga* are gone over and stressed, ornamented and improvised with more liberty than is possible in the later movements, which comprise the *raga* proper. In the south of India the *raga* proper forms the major bulk of the entire piece, but in the north, where in some respects there are greater deviations from the music of Indian antiquity, the opportunity for virtuosity has led to the *ālāpa* taking on a more pronounced length. Sometimes it is longer than all that follows. However, such virtuosity is not of the kind that has often perverted the great music of other civilizations, but is still kept in subservience to the rules of the particular piece, and allows no cheapness to enter. During this meditative, introductory section, first one and then another of the basic notes of the *raga* are brought in, the music gradually building itself up. It serves as an excellent introduction for the listener to the notes and flourishes of which the *raga* is composed. The notes are played in all three octaves; and at this stage the rhythm is less pronounced.

Next comes the *jor.* This too is improvised, and usually performed on only one instrument, but it introduces more tangibly the elements of rhythm. Then the percussion instrument joins in and the work 'takes off' in a glittering array of varied expression and subtle interrelationships between the notes of the leading melodic instrument or singer, and the tabla or other percussion instrument(s). Much dynamic importance attaches to each first beat of the rhythmic cycle: whereas the soloist and the percussionist are free to explore independent rhythmic nuances throughout the rest of the cycle, they must be sufficiently skilful and rhythmically aware always to come together once more precisely on each first beat. Finally a climax or *jhālā* arrives. This is invariably so brilliant when performed by experienced musicians as to leave one breathless with excited concentration, yet also refreshingly invigorated with its sheer, exuberant energy.

One of the most distinctive and beautiful features of the music is the infinite subtle differences between its melodic notes. The intervals of Indian music are on a smaller division of the scale than is used for the majority of Western works. This results in a tonal art which is extremely rarefied and contemplative. Indian music also differs considerably from that of China. Whereas Chinese music emphasizes the single note to a marked degree, Indian music stresses the intervals *between* the notes of the scale. The intervallic distance in pitch between two notes is not an avoided area of tone as in most musics of the world, but is actually the region of pitch which is actively used in order to constitute a large proportion of the melody itself. In the performing of instruments, the transition from one note to another is often a sliding transition, producing what is sometimes an indescribable effect of longing or of devotion. Quivers and all manner of ornamentations also take the pitch away from the strict notes of the scale.

A similar element of unique beauty is found in Indian singing techniques. The notes of the song do not have to be sounded in a fixed way but can be approached, according to certain definite rules, by a sliding voice from either above or below. Within the sliding note, or glissando, the singer rests at numerous intervals for a matter of micro-seconds at a time, sliding rapidly up and down the scale. This requires great knowledge and skill, for only those intervals which are among the *shruti* of the particular piece of music may be paused upon. In this way an element of freedom and an opportunity for invention is always present. The mood of the musician leads him continually to create and re-create the *raga* or other work afresh; yet the piece itself, in its theoretical framework, remains unchanged.

It is obvious then that Indian music and the music of the West differ considerably in the kinds of moods and spiritual atmospheres which they invoke. Both can express sublimity, but each a different form of sublimity; and so on through each kind of feeling which music can bestow. The two musical traditions lead the mind to flow along different paths of awareness. And from the point of view of our present study, this is a most significant fact.

MUSIC AND INDIAN CIVILIZATION
The music of India affords us some interesting indications regarding the relationship between music and civilization. The distinctions between Indian and Western music – the meditativeness of the

former and the latter's more solid and formal structures – do seem to be mirrored in the contrasting 'inner' orientation of the Indian mind and the more practical and outwardly successful Western mind. Furthermore, musical differences between the north and the south of India may also be mirrored in divergent lifestyles. Certainly the peoples of the two regions do differ, and so does their music, that of the south being more faithful a continuation of the music of the past, whereas the north, in both its style and its instrumentation, has been considerably influenced by the music of Persia and Afghanistan.

That there are many poverty-stricken areas in India, and particularly in the north, is known to all. And thus it might be argued that the music has failed to render beneficial influences upon the people and the land. This, however, is not necessarily the case. We must remember that to the Hindu, Buddhist and Jainist alike, the sole and only purpose in life is to evolve *in consciousness,* little regard being paid to the outer life. The music too emphasizes this retrospective orientation of the soul. While spiritual evolution does not normally preclude the possession of material wealth, it does not require it either. From the point of view of the Indian devotee, India is, then, one of the greatest repositories of wealth and success in the world. For its wealth is of the heart, and its success is in the spiritual height to which so many of its native souls attain. Weighed on the scales of devotion, India is the First World nation, and our own might be said to be the land that is backward.

There is one other respect in which a connection is apparent between the land of India and its music, and this is the degree of change, or lack of change, between the two over time. The music has altered relatively little in at least two and a half thousand years, and so has the civilization. Even the colonization of India by the British, while bringing about certain changes in the outer life such as improved transport systems, had little influence upon the Indian way of thinking.

Yet what of the more recent past, *and what of the future?* Nowadays one can walk for hours around some of the cities and villages without hearing a note of traditional *ragas, bhajans* or the chanting of the Vedas. There is another kind of music to be heard, however. During the 1960s music from the West at last began to gain a significant foothold. Or to be more precise, a music began to flourish in India during the Sixties which was not Western music proper, but an Indian adaptation of the new Western rock 'n' roll. The general style of British and American 'pop' songs was imitated, a number of Indian crooners making their appearance on the scene.

Sometimes Western pop was copied to the extent of particular Western 'top-ten' songs being literally re-recorded by Indian performers, and then broadcast. In other cases the new sounds which flooded the land were a hybrid of the two cultures – a kind of three-minute pop-*raga* about teenage love – and, like all hybrids, inexpressibly ugly. Simultaneously, an Indian film industry grew up, its output including many of the pop-musical kind of productions which had in the West helped to promote the music of Elvis Presley and the Beatles.

By the opening of the 1970s, Indian pop music had secured a similarly strong grip upon the listening habits of the young city-dwelling Indian as had the pop and rock of the West upon Western youth. And, interestingly enough, it is from this period onwards that the civilization and culture of India, the land which has its origins lost in the mists of time, has at last begun to show signs of disintegration. Particularly among the younger generations there are the beginnings of new hedonistic tendencies, the infiltration of radical politics, and a more materialistic outlook.

Coincidence? Possibly. Yet one imagines the wise-eyed, cross-legged yogi, looking down from the Himalayan mountain slopes, watching the social movements taking place upon the plains below. Impassive of face, he observes the events of the passing years. And what is this which, with a slight sigh, he whispers to himself? Let us strain to hear. Is it not, perhaps, *'As in music, so in life'*?

Notes

*It is interesting that the term *anahata* refers not only to omnipresent Cosmic Sound, but is also the name in Sanskrit for the heart *chakra*. The heart *chakra* is one of seven major *chakras* or spiritual centres which the yogi believes to be located at non-physical levels of his form. Of the seven, the heart is the most important, and possesses the most intimate link with the heavens. This reminds one of the Chinese legend of Wen of Cheng, who could perform his wonderful music only after he had reached that which he sought to express, which was within his heart. The Indian yogi-musician also believes that only by purifying and expanding the heart (or *anahata*) *chakra* can he bring forth the music of divinity. As the name denotes, the *anahata chakra* is considered to be the anchoring point within man of the Word of God.

† For this reason, some Western esotericists claim that nick-names are harmful in their effect. They are said to act as 'hexes', the friends

and family imposing a wrong vibrational matrix over the form and personality of the individual concerned. This applies not only to names such as 'fatty', but even to simple abbreviations such as 'Sam' or 'Mike'.

5.
The Twentieth Century:
Jazz and the Blues – Their Nature and Origin

Like human nature itself, music cannot possibly be neutral in its spiritual direction. At times it may exhibit a mixture of uplifting and degrading elements, but ultimately all uses of tone and all musical lyrics can be classified according to their spiritual direction, upward or downward. It is unusual for movements in music which combine truly exalted elements with those of the downward direction to maintain their stability for long; almost always one or the other force gains the upper hand, as can clearly be seen throughout the history of the art. It is actually a part of the essential nature of the majority of styles and movements of music that they either lift people into an awareness of beauty and sublimity, or that they inculcate, subtly or overtly, feelings of indiscipline and hedonism. To put it plainly, music tends to be of either the darkness or of the light.

TONAL ANARCHISTS THROUGH THE AGES
History records that of the music of light and that of darkness, only one is usually prominent within any given civilization. For as long as sublime and beautiful music prevails, so does the civilization flourish both spiritually and in material prosperity. Almost always, whenever the major music of a civilization has been of a more primitive and abandoned nature, the civilization itself has been barbaric, and has usually gone into decline, eventually ceasing to remain a civilization at all. We have already indicated that the classical civilizations of China and India have declined together with a parallel – or even prior – decline in their music. The same could be demonstrated in respect of many other peoples.

The case of ancient Greece provides a particularly clear example. Greek music began to decline during the era of Pericles, around 444–429 BC, this being at a time when Greek civilization and the rest of its arts were at their highest level. It was music which led the way into degeneration.

As Greek classical music became progressively replete with cheap innovation, excessive modulation and decorative shakes, Aristophanes attempted in his plays to counter the rot with parody and humour directed against the cheap new music. He likened the singers with their quivering voices to zigzagging ants, and called the instrumentalists ecstatic, effeminate creatures who were so easily bent that they had to wear stays. (Their wavering music was produced by bending certain of their instruments, such as the *strophae*.) In one of Aristophanes' musical plays the Muse stages a personal protest against the modern wave of innovators who twist her on the rock with their inharmonic notes as they modulate. The play was a foreboding of musical rebellion, an appeal on behalf of the whole tradition of well-educated Athenian citizenship against uncultured or alien ideas.

The appeal came too late. The new music had already set in, supplanting the more refined and disciplined classical styles. One year later the revolution in music manifested tangibly as a violent, physical revolution, and the downfall of the elite of Athens.

Following the Greek revolution of 404 BC, a deliberate blatancy and toughness distinguished the lyrics of the performing rebels who came to the fore as the musical stars of their time. One famous manifesto by Timotheus of Miletus smacks strongly of the mood of Chuck Berry and of the Beatles when they sang 'Roll Over Beethoven', calling for Beethoven and Tchaikovsky to make way for the coming of rhythm and blues. In similar vein, Timotheus repudiated the entire past (also taking care not to miss the opportunity to court the younger generations):

> I do not sing the old things,
> Because the new are the winners.
> Zeus the young is king today:
> Once it was Cronos ruling.
> Go to Hell, old dame Music.

(One can almost imagine it being shouted to the accompaniment of electric guitar.)

Decades later, in his famous work, *Laws*, Plato lamented the musical revolution and its 'unmusical anarchy'. His words are as relevant today as when first written:

Through foolishness they deceived themselves into thinking that there was no right or wrong in music – that it was to be judged good or bad by the pleasure it gave. By their work and their theories they infected the masses with the presumption to think themselves adequate judges ... As it was, the criterion was not music, but a reputation for promiscuous cleverness and a spirit of law-breaking.

Meanwhile, the music continued to deteriorate. Mere *virtuosi* replaced true musicians. Uplifting melodies and the former, disciplined styles were replaced by the novelty-ridden, insubstantial sounds of exhibitionist 'stars'. Greek music became trite and effeminate, and the people followed suit. Homosexuality was rampant, and the nation waned over the years as a military force and as a bastion of culture. Eventually Greece declined totally into the shade and the Roman Empire came to the fore.

Throughout the ages peoples have faced the choice between music of the ↓ direction and music which encourages the contemplation of eternal verities. The story of their choices is in many respects the story of civilization itself. What is also noticeable is that when destructive music appears within a civilization, it usually does so very suddenly. Its onset comes as a veritable wave or blitzkrieg, almost as though by a deliberate strategy. It attains to a position of power and of widespread popularity with the masses within just a few years or decades; and its influence upon society in general is often similarly sudden, bringing about a swift and negative change in philosophies, politics, morals and lifestyles.

ROOTS

Were we to scour the globe in search of the most aggressively malevolent and unmistakably evil music in existence, it is more than likely that nothing would be found anywhere to surpass voodoo in these attributes. Still practised in Africa and the Caribbean specifically as the rhythmic accompaniment to satanic rituals and orgies, voodoo is the quintessence of tonal evil. Often its very declared purpose is to inflict harm upon other parts of life. Its multiple rhythms, rather than uniting into an integrated whole, are performed in a certain kind of conflict with one another.

It would be quite incorrect to consider voodoo to be 'primitive', however. Studies have shown that the mutliple rhythms, performed on a large number of percussion instruments, are actually extremely complex. It is said by some that certain very subtle nuances which are incorporated into voodoo rhythms, while being too subtle for the ear of even the trained Western musician to notice, are actually the source of much of voodoo's claimed occult power. What is certain is that to hear this music is to become instantly encompassed by the sound of its raw, livid power. As for the evil rites to which the music provides the background, the author is informed by authorities of unquestioned repute that human sacrifices continue to occur from time to time in both North Africa and the Caribbean.

During the slave trade, voodoo crossed the Atlantic in the persons of those among the blacks who practised it, and took root in the Caribbean, as well as in the United States. Though the historical records on the matter are sketchy, the original African-style voodoo seems to have arrived in the West Indies more-or-less intact. Laws were passed against the playing of such music as early as 1619, but with little effect. Nor could the voodoo rite be stamped out on the American mainland. It is on record that by 1835 blacks would gather in New Orleans to sing and perform acts of voodoo, including the blood sacrifice of animals. Musicologists and historians are in no doubt that the drum rhythms of Africa were carried to America and were there transmitted and translated into the style of music which became known as jazz. Since jazz and the blues were the parents of rock and roll, this also means that there exists a direct line of descent from the voodoo ceremonies of Africa, through jazz, to rock and roll and all of the other forms of rock music current today.

The first definite documentation of the existence of the blues comes only from early during this century, but early twentieth-century blues performers mentioned the music as having existed some decades earlier. The blues seem to have been performed at least as early as the latter nineteenth century. Enslaved perhaps even more in consciousness than in body, the Negroes sang, 'Sometimes I feel like a motherless child, a long ways from home' and 'Nobody knows the trouble I seen'. Their songs of sadness and melancholy merely served to reinforce the repressed and depressed condition of their physical lives. Many Negroes, however, adhered to the giving of spirituals, their own particular form of praise to God, which can still be heard today. But the first blues singers took the lamenting qualities of the spiritual and transferred them into songs the subjects of which were human lovers.

From a combination of the blues and ragtime, jazz was born. Buddy Bolden is recognized as having been at least one of the first, and probably *the* first individual to play the music that later came to be termed 'jazz'. Bolden was born in New Orleans in 1868 (New Orleans at that time still maintaining its status of being the ostensible voodoo centre of the United States, incidentally). He began playing while in his twenties, during the 1890s. With other musicians, Bolden would march around the streets of New Orleans, performing as he went. His music was a strange, exciting, new and revolutionary sound; and it was a revolution which he literally carried into the streets. Frequently he and his band would march through and stop over in the red-light district. Bolden was said to be well acquainted with all the district's female inhabitants.

A cornet player, Bolden led a number of successive bands. But as the result of his heavy drinking and of syphilis he became insane around 1906. He last performed in 1907, and was then committed to a state institution in the June of that year. There he died, in 1931.

This 'father' of jazz, hardly heroic or inspiring in his biography, seems in many respects to have set the pattern for all that jazz was to become and result in. The music he had spawned first became grounded, naturally enough, in the whorehouses of New Orleans. From there it spread to the brothels of other cities, and thence, over time, transferred to the bars and dance halls.

The first actual appearances of the printed word 'jazz' were in 1917. The Hearst newspapers of 21 January, 1917, contained this notice in the column of one Damon Runyan:

New York. Jan 20. – A Broadway cafe announces, as something new to the big Bright Aisle, the importation from the West of a syncopated riot known as a Jas Band.

On 5 August of the same year an article appeared by Walter Kingsley of the *New York Sun* which seems to indicate that already the music had spread and stirred up an interest. The article was headlined: 'Whence comes jass? Facts from the great authority on the subject', and continued:

Variously spelled Jas, Jass, Jasz, and Jascz. The word is African in origin. It is common on the Gold Coast of Africa and in the hinterland of the Cape Coast Castle ...

Though these are among the first reports of jazz in print, the music is known to have been established in a number of states prior to 1917. Ragtime and the blues had paved the way for this, developing rapidly on both the East and West coasts in the closing decades of the nineteenth century.

One of the chief idiosyncratic features of jazz and the blues was the incorporation into their lyrics of words and phrases of African origin. Languages such as Wolof and Mandigo had taken several generations to pass out of general use among the black slaves. When these languages had eventually given way to English, a considerable number of African words and phrases had nevertheless been absorbed into everyday usage within the general framework of the white language. In their English forms, a number of phrases of African origin are now widely used by both whites and black, such as 'to do one's thing' or 'to be with it'. The expansion of their use is almost wholly due to the music of jazz, and later of rock, since these musical movements formed the backbone of an entire sub-culture. Along with the music came elements of the language. The Western use of the term 'hot', for example, to describe fast, unchanging, steady beat, is mirrored in West African terminology. Some words now in wide use are pure and untranslated African, including *okay*, *rap*, *dig* and *hippie*.

The word *jazz* itself is also of African origin, and is thought to have originally referred to the sex act. This seems quite likely to be true: it can easily be seen how the word could have become connected to the music, since jazz grew up among the brothels of New Orleans, and since the two practices of the playing of jazz and of sexual gratification went hand in hand during those early days. When, in addition, we learn that the phrase 'rock and roll' was also originally an allusion to the sex act, the link between these forms of music and sexuality becomes striking.

By 1917, Storeyville, the New Orleans red-light district, gave employment to hundreds of young jazz musicians. But in that year the US Secretary of the Navy, 'alarmed by the regularity with which his sailors became involved in incidents of violence and dissipation'[19], ordered the bars and brothels closed down. An ironic act indeed; for it was this very event which led to the accelerated spread of jazz beyond the city, as the young black performers sought employment elsewhere. Ten years later the music could be found in dozens of major cities, but with its central 'base of operation' now switched to Chicago.

History, though not recording jazz to have been the cause, tells the story of the way Chicago went: 'A brash, coarse and excitable city enjoying its dubious distinction as the capital of Al Capone's bootleg empire, Chicago teemed with gin mills and speakeasies where illegal liquor was consumed to an accompaniment of loud, aggressive music.'[19]

RESISTANCE

In contrast to the apathetic attitude usually displayed toward the dissonant music of our own day, the people of the 1920s tended to be very aware of the threat which jazz posed to society. As the music spread among a minority of the lower stratas of society, opposing reactions were strong at first. Middle-class moralizers castigated it as the work of the devil. In his *Jazz, A History*, even pro-jazz writer Frank Tirro admits:

> Jazz became the symbol of crime, feeble-mindedness, insanity and sex, and was under constant attack from the press from the early 1920s on ... it is ironic that we preserve, study and enjoy a music today that was felt to be insidious and lascivious only yesterday.[71]

Ironic indeed.

Opposition came from many directions: from classical musicians, from the writers of music journals and books on music education, from newspaper journalists, priests and sociologists. It might be asked: why were reactions so strong against a music which, at the time, was played only by a small minority, whereas in our own day a greater proliferation of a music in similar vein goes virtually unchallenged? The answer can only be that during the 1920s the new, syncopated music came into a world which had hitherto never heard such sounds, and the music was therefore clearly recognized for what it was. Today, on the other hand, our senses have become dulled and our awareness inoculated against such music through sheer familiarity. We therefore do not naturally react to it as would the pristine consciousness.

But in the 1920s it was different. Newspapers cited jazz not merely as a symptom, but as a specific cause of the moral decay. For example, the *New York American* of 22 June, 1922, contained:

Jazz Ruining Girls, Declares Reformers (sic)
Chicago, 21 June — Moral disaster is coming to hundreds of young American girls through the pathological, nerve-irritating, sex-exciting music of jazz orchestras, according to the Illinois Vigilance Association.

In Chicago alone the association's representatives have traced the fall of 1000 girls in the last two years to jazz music.

Girls in small towns, as well as in the big cities, in poor homes
and rich homes, are victims of the weird, insidious, neurotic music
that accompanies modern dancing ...[71]

Writing a few years later, the composer, poet and esotericist, Cyril
Scott, had this to say:

> After the dissemination of Jazz, which was definitely 'put
> through' by the Dark Forces, a very marked decline in sexual
> morals became noticeable. Whereas at one time women were
> content with decorous flirtations, a vast number of them are now
> constantly preoccupied with the search for erotic adventures, and
> have thus turned sexual passion into a species of hobby. Now, it
> is just this over-emphasis of the sex-nature, this wrong attitude
> towards it, for which Jazz-music has been responsible. The
> orgiastic element of its syncopated rhythm, entirely divorced
> from any more exalted musical content, produced a hyper-
> excitement of the nerves and loosened the powers of self-control.
> It gave rise to a false exhilaration, a fictitious endurance, an
> insatiability resulting in a deleterious *moral* and physical reaction.
> Whereas the old-fashioned melodious dance-music inspired the
> gentler sentiments, Jazz, with its array of harsh, ear-splitting
> percussion-instruments inflamed, intoxicated and brutalized, thus
> causing a set-back in Man's nature towards the instincts of his
> racial childhood. For Jazz-music at its height very closely
> resembled the music of primitive savages. A further result of it
> was to be seen in that love of sensationalism which has so greatly
> increased. As Jazz itself was markedly sensational, the public has
> increasingly come to demand 'thrills' in the form of 'crook
> dramas' and plays, the only dramatic interest of which is con-
> nected with crime, mystery and brutality. This also applies to sen-
> sational fiction: for the sale and output of this type is prodigious.[5]

'MY DADDY ROCKS ME WITH ONE STEADY ROLL'
(– THE LYRICAL CONTENT OF THE BLUES)

The perverse elements of the musical tones of jazz had their parallel
in the lyrics of the majority of blues songs. For one thing, the subject
matter and direction of consciousness contained within the blues
was as a rule of a low and suffocatingly narrow-minded nature. The
theme of human love in its imperfect aspects – betrayal, mistrust,
physical love devoid of the higher feelings, and so on – is still the

central core of the repertoire pumped over the airwaves today. Yet it all began decades ago. As is the case today, *loving,* according to the singers, seemed to be only one half of a naturally oscillating polarity, the other half of which was *leaving:*

> Leave you, ol' maid,
> gonna leave you, ol' maid.
> Look out Ju-li', ol' maid,
> look out Ju-li', ol' maid.

Or, if the protagonist of the song decided to stay, he nevertheless did so under his own conditions:

> I'm gonna buy me a bulldog, watch you while you sleep,
> (I said I'm gonna buy me a bulldog, watch you while you sleep.)
> Just to keep those men from making their early mornin' creep.

More sinister themes were also common. But few specialized in them more than Robert Johnson, the 'King of the Delta Blues'. Born in 1914, Johnson's lyrics dealt with, as Frank Tirro puts it, 'three recurring themes: the impermanence of human relationships, incessant wandering, and irrational terrors. His blues are shot through with dark foreboding . . .'[71] One Johnson song, 'Me and the Devil Blues' has these typical lyrics:

> Early this morning when you knocked upon my door
> Early this morning when you knocked upon my door
> And I said, 'Hello Satan, I believe it's time to go.'

> Me and the devil was walking side by side
> Me and the devil was walking side by side
> And I'm going to beat my woman until I get satisfied.

> ... You may bury my body down by the highwayside,
> So my old evil spirit can get a Greyhound bus and ride.

Johnson died in 1938 or 1939, having been either poisoned by a woman or shot by her jealous husband. (Nobody is quite sure which.)

One of the most common subjects was sexual desire. Due to the singers' idiosyncratic turns of phrase, however, the actual meanings of their songs were frequently not realized by the whites who heard them. The early black slaves had found it most advantageous to be able to converse among themselves in African languages which were not understood by their white masters. Now, with the coming of the blues and jazz, a number of African colloquialisms which had survived, as well as more recently evolved slang terms, were used deliberately to veil the bluntly sexual nature of many of the songs. To veil the meaning was only half the reason for the use of such slang, however: another was that the singers actually knew of no other words, such as are found in a dictionary, by which to refer to human genitalia, etc. Hence, to the blacks themselves their songs were not nearly so subtle and veiled as they were to the average white. For instance, when the blues singer sang about lesbianism: 'BD woman can lay her jive/ Just like a natural man' the meaning was quite straightforward to the black listener, though to the white of the 1920s it was incomprehensible. Frequent names for the male genitals were 'roll' or 'hot dog'. Female genitals became 'jam roll', 'bun', or 'shortening bread'. (The extent to which such terms fooled the whites is evident in the continuing popularity – often as a nursery rhyme (!) – of the song about Mama's little baby loving shortening bread.)

Sometimes the imagery was most contemporary:

My baby got a little engine, call it my Ford machine,
(I say) My baby got a little engine, call it my Ford machine,
If your generator ain't bad, baby, you must be buying bad gasoline.

Not only lesbianism, but group sex, various sexual perversions, and the derision of religion are all there, half-concealed among the blues lyrics which were the precursors to the lyrics of modern rock. Homosexuality, too – as, for example, in the instruction, 'If you can't send me a woman/ Send me a sissy-man'.

The most common blues term of all for sexual activities was 'riding'; many a tune about riding having been quite innocently recorded and released for mass-consumption by the white-run studios. From this expression is derived the term, easy-rider, as utilized for the title of the famous film of the hippie era.

In fact, it was particularly for the sake of being admitted to the recording studios that the artists disguised and partially cleaned-up the meaning of their songs in the first place. In private – at home, or within the walls of the brothels – a far more explicit form of the blues was sung. Here, four-letter words that the whites certainly would recognize (unless they had been living in Greenland since the age of eight), abounded, as did sexual imagery of an almost unheard-of obtuseness. Some of these songs were actually recorded unintentionally as early blues singers relaxed with their guitars between formal recording sessions. There existed no possibility whatever of being able to release such songs during the 1920s. And yet – time passed; and yes – a more 'enlightened' world dawned. A few years ago these shockingly obtuse recordings were unearthed from the vaults of the studios and heard once more. Upon which, in the late seventies, they were released in the form of several long-playing discs. Some harbour no doubt that the release was a perfect and fitting symbol of the enlightenment of the age. Others, meanwhile, reserve for themselves alternative musings.*

JAZZ 'ARRIVES'
Even deep into the thirties, jazz was still to a large extent tied economically and sociologically to illegality. During the prohibition period countless illegal speakeasies and small cabarets sprang up across the United States; and it was within them that jazz discovered its expanding market. Most of them employed at least a pianist, and often a small band.

By now many of the jazz musicians were white. Also, whereas there had previously been little or no role for soloists in the earliest jazz (partly because the players needed to hide their musical limitations behind each other), soloists now came to the fore – both actually and metaphorically. In doing so they were following the example of Louis Daniel Armstrong, the first jazz virtuoso. Armstrong was the protégé of Joe 'King' Oliver, the successor of Buddy Bolden as the leading New Orleans performer. In Chicago Armstrong performed live and also recorded with groups he called the Hot Five and the Hot Seven (as though unconsciously perverting the ancient concept of the divinity of these numbers and of their sum, the Twelve). Also in prominence at this time was the white trumpet player, Bix Beiderbecke. Beiderbecke died at the age of 28, in 1931, the same year as the death of Buddy Bolden. (It is impossible not to note that, like the rock performers of our day, the jazz players were extraordinarily prone to early, violent and unusual death.)

With the repeal of prohibition, jazz followed alcohol in the latter's return to 'respectability'. For jazz, however, this meant the attainment of semi-'respectability' for the first time. Following this, by the mid-1930s the music was more widely played than ever before. It was the age of the so-called Big Band, jazz taking over the ballrooms of the Roosevelt era. This period of jazz is remarkably similar in its mass hysteria to the phenomena associated with the rock of the '60s, '70s and '80s:

> Orchestras became as keenly supported as football teams, and their individual stars as admired as boxing champions. Audiences were numbered in thousands, Hollywood beckoned to the more successful bandleaders, magazines conducted annual popularity polls evoking response from people all over America. Police had sometimes to be called out to control adoring crowds, and the profits soared into five figures, then six, then seven. Jazz now enjoyed the questionable prestige of its first millionaires ... Although Louis Armstrong had by now succumbed to the fleshpots of Hollywood, and his influence as a developing musician was on the wane, his effectiveness as a player remained enormous.[19]

THE EFFECTS OF THE MUSIC

Jazz had now arrived in earnest. Its adherents were sufficiently de-sensitized to be unaware and ignorant of its continuing effect upon them. But to the sensitized mind the harsh rhythms of jazz were brutalizing to the consciousness. On the physical level the rhythms of jazz, like their parent sounds of Africa, literally forced the listeners to do something rhythmic with their limbs. The faster the tempo, the more the emotional tension created. As for meter, Alice Monsarrat has commented that:

> The normal easy meter ... like that of a waltz, is 1–2–3, 1–2–3, or a fox trot 1–2–3–4, 1–2–3–4. But with the advent of the twentieth century, the meters began to gallop brokenly stirrup to stirrup with harmonic dissonance and discord in the melodic line ... the meter began to appear something like this: 1 & 2 & 3 4 1 & 2 & 3 4 ...
> A broken meter in the treble, played over an insistently regular beat in the left hand, with gradually increasing rapidity almost to the point of frenzy ... is capable of producing the identical disintegrating and almost hysterical effect on an organism.[72]

Man is, of course, essentially a rhythmical being. Respiration, heartbeat, speech, gait and so forth: all form a part of the unified set of rhythms, great and small, which is man. Even the cerebral hemispheres are in a constant state of rhythmical activity. Alice

Monsarrat therefore points out that it:

> ... is precisely at this point that rock 'n roll and much of the
> modern music becomes potentially dangerous. This is because, to
> maintain a sense of well-being and integration, it is essential that
> man is not subjected too much to any rhythms not in accord with
> his natural bodily rhythms.[72]

With the coming of jazz, pulsation and syncopation became
pronounced in music as never before. Syncopation places the accent
on the off-beat in 4/4 time. It is a deliberate attempt on the part of
the musician to disrupt the even character of his rhythm. The effect
of jazz syncopation is primarily sexual: the beat somehow ties in
with the rhythm of sexuality in man and woman. In fact, hard, loud,
relentless pulsation also has a similar effect. When pulsation and
syncopation are the rhythmic foundations of the music at a dance
hall, the movements of the dancers can invariably be seen to become
very sensual and oriented around the loins. Such rhythms actually
possess the capacity to force the subtle energies of the body
downward into this region of the anatomy, therefore increasing the
outpouring into the bloodstream of sexual hormones.

Once such biochemical and more subtle forces have become concentrated in the loins, they must find some manner of expression.
This may come through sexual activity shortly afterwards; or
through a more general tendency during everyday life and during
the ensuing days for the person to lack control over the sexual
impulses. It is not unknown for those who are the chief producers of
these rhythms, the drummers of modern music, to actually have
music-induced orgasms after several hours of non-stop drumming.[39]
Today's drummer differs but little from the shaman in his incessant
beating out of a rhythm, and likewise often enters into a form of
trance while performing.

Earlier in this book we commented on music as a communicator
and multiplier of states of consciousness. These comments throw
considerable significance upon the rise of virtuosoship and of an
increased degree of solo-improvisation in jazz. From the 1920s
onwards jazz audiences, whether in bars or by the side of a record
player, were exposed to a more exact and insistent rendition of the
inner state of the performer than ever before. The long, improvised
solo presented a highly precise and detailed stream of consciousness.
Denying all higher laws of art or of submission to a higher Will
than his own self-will, the jazz soloist roamed as the 'mood' took

him through the fog-bound and sociologically-treacherous valleys of melancholy and anarchy. To the sensitized mind, every such solo – without exception – displays one or more of the following undesirable traits: sensuality, physical over-excitement, despair, human moodiness, lethargy, selfishness, narrow-mindedness, mental disintegration, pride, egocentricity, self-assertion and rebellion. That some will consider the list controversial is in itself symbolic of the sad dilemma which the music poses to our society. For to the unspoiled and pristine mind, the truth of the list will be self-evident; yet the individual who has succumbed to this music will already have forsaken, though he will know it not, his capacity to view the issue objectively.

OFFSPRINGS OF THE JAZZ RHYTHM: INTO THE ERA OF PROTO-ROCK

On the commercial front the music now reached a stage which, in retrospect, can be seen to have been the stepping-stone between black music and the rock and roll which was to come. This stage was the flourishing of rhythm and blues, a music form which resulted from largely economic constraints. In order to be audible in clubs and bars, the blues singers had been going electric, amplifying their music; while the decline in the popularity of large 'swing' jazz bands had forced them to reduce themselves in size. Rhythm and blues emerged as a hybrid of the two.[73] At first only blacks listened to it. It became their most popular form of music. Again the subject matter was infidelity, perversion, drink and crime; again the mood was one of bewilderment and depression; again the tones were dissonant, and sometimes of a quite frenzied tempo.

The new genre brought forth its own stars: Johnny Otis, Nat King Cole, Julia Lee, B. B. King and innumerable others. Julia Lee 'sang salacious blues in sleezy gin mills', while Wynonie Harris was 'a lord of excess' who 'lived a life of complete mayhem ... shouting the blues with a wild and hard-driving boastfulness'. Muddy Waters, the Chicago bluesman, and John Lee Hooker of Detroit (one is reminded of the ancient concept of the name being the keynote of the inner man ...!) each 'cut ominous figures onstage, full of menace and prowling malevolence'. Cecil Grant, who came from Nashville, went over the airwaves with a sex message still not comprehended by the white broadcasters when he made the 1950 hit 'We're Gonna Rock' (promptly to die a few months later).[73]

Gradually, rhythm and blues began finding a white market. Simultaneously, several other strands came together which were destined to result in the rock revolution. The most significant of these was the popularization of American country music. By retaining only the more decadent subject matter of country music, and by fusing this with the more racy, black-style of beat, country music became country-boogie, which in turn led to rockabilly.

Popularized country music's most prominent exponent was Hank Williams. The tonal side of Williams' music was relatively simple and relaxed, yet his lyrics once more reflected that same mortal, pessimistic outlook that we have already encountered, and which was soon to take root in rock. So familiar are we today with the incessant playing in the background of songs about crying, desolation, betrayal and loneliness that it is almost difficult to re-focus our perspective into a more objective viewpoint. Yet only from such a viewpoint can it be realized that the communication of such states of consciousness to millions of young listeners must without doubt be to the detriment of future society.

Among Williams' hits were 'I'm So Lonesome I Could Cry', 'Rambling Man', 'Cold Cold Heart', 'Take These Chains From My Heart' and 'Weary Blues'. But the string of hits was not to continue. Almost as though the Power which guides the destiny of man had a symbolic message to communicate to us all, Williams never reached the age of 30. On 1 January, 1953, he died of a heart attack in the back of his chauffeur-driven Cadillac. His latest Number 1 hit was still in the charts: 'I'll Never Get Out of This World Alive'.

The scene, however, was now set.

Combining the rhythmic structures of rhythm and blues with elements of country and western music, Bill Haley and the Comets were the first to realize the enormous tonal power and commercial possibilities of what was to become known as rock 'n' roll. 'Rock Around the Clock' was released in 1954, and soon became incorporated into the film *Blackboard Jungle* (which dealt with the subject of juvenile delinquency). The song went on to sell over 20 million discs. The rest is history.

THE MODERN ERA

Jazz, in the meantime, did not attempt to compete with the sudden popularity of the new rock music. On the contrary: the genre retreated increasingly into a stance of ultra-intellectualism and exaggerated introspection which was by no means dissimilar to the 'new music' of the 'serious' musical stream. From the viewpoint of the materialist, non-idealist audiences, the prospect of the intellectualization of jazz as introduced by Miles Davis and others was an intriguing one. Yet from the higher perspective, the resultant music was really no less questionable than its predecessors.

Since this was now 'jazz for the thinking man' so to speak, the opportunities for cross-fertilization between jazz and other materialistically intellectualized genres were broader. Many of the new jazz musicians had at least a working familiarity with the theories and sounds of the 'new music'. And for their part, the contemporary avant-garde became yet more interested in the musical elements of jazz. Later, during the late sixties and early seventies, when rock also reached a stage of 'intellectualization', a similar cross-fertilization became apparent between jazz and rock.

Jazz itself, however, was to discover that increased introspection meant a decreased market. As had earlier been the case among the 'new musicians', the more intellectual jazz artists had trouble in combining their subjectivity with an objective perspective of what was or was not valid as art. Soon enough, jazz arrived at its 'modern' stage. Now, just as in the case of a few unplanned splashes of paint on a canvas, any random buzz of a saxophone or odd whine of a trumpet was immediately scoured for its meaning by an avid but dwindling body of devotees, then invariably to be hailed as an expression of genius. The saxophonist, Ornette Coleman, proclaimed his theory that the performer should be free to create any sound at any given time, and went on to perform accordingly, as was only too evident from the result. As Benny Green, the writer on jazz, aptly put it: 'Coleman's dialectics would be more to the point if he and his followers were each satisfied to play alone in a room.'[19]

We have noted in earlier chapters that the ancients sought to tread an artistic path which combined elements of individual freedom with certain definite restraints. Plato was only one of the earliest of the many commentators who have pointed out, down through the centuries, that the only freedom which is aesthetically viable in art is a freedom married to self-discipline. Otherwise freedom becomes a recipe for anarchy. And it is in search of ever-greater excesses of the latter that most jazz musicians have directed themselves over the last thirty years.

The author is strongly reminded of an essay on music therapy written by Howard Hanson in the 1940s, in which Hanson displayed an acute prophetic insight into what the music he heard around him would mean for the future. Hanson wrote:

I hesitate to think ... of what the effect of music upon the next generation will be if the present school of 'hot jazz' continues to develop unabated. Much of it is crass, raucous and commonplace and could be dismissed without comment if it were not for the radio whereby, hour after hour, night after night, American homes are flooded with vast quantities of this material, to which accompaniment our youngsters dance, play and even study. Perhaps they have developed an immunity to its effect — but if they have not, and if the mass production of this aural drug is not curtailed, we may find ourselves a nation of neurotics which even the skill of the psychiatrist may be hard pressed to cure.[65]

As with our comparison of the 'new music' with the music of ancient China, a comparison between jazz and the classical music of India reveals the same totally opposite natures and spiritual directions of the two. *Should* it be the case that music has no effect upon man, then music of the downward direction would be all well and good — but our discourse thus far seems to indicate strongly that this is not the case.

What is more, the statements of the wise of long ago regarding the ability of music to influence life patterns was only a part of their belief about the power of music. Music and sound, they stated, could also affect matter itself. Audible sound, as an earthly vessel for the universal OM, wielded a great energy. An energy which, according to the kind of music played, could create, preserve or destroy even material, inanimate conditions. It is a long-standing belief of the esoteric schools that in the distant past there once existed former advanced civilizations not dissimilar to our own, but which are lost to historical record. These are said to have been destroyed by physical cataclysms which were caused, in each case, largely through the continued misuse of sound and rhythm. Is there any truth behind such beliefs, and does music actually contain such a power to affect matter? If so, then the phenomena of jazz, rock, and other such musics — including, perhaps, the very allowance of their presence in our midst — would most urgently need to be looked at afresh.

ABOUT ROCK

In this book we have touched upon rock here and there only in passing, one reason being that the subject of this music and its societary effects is so vast as would require a volume in itself. In addition, it has been useful to deal with jazz since jazz, a parent of rock, displays its voodoo origins more blatantly; and it has been useful to discuss the 'new music' since its proponents are willing

and able to proclaim their inner philosophies and aesthetic stand-
points more clearly and intellectually than can the average rock
artist. Yet suffice it to say that all that we have commented on the
'new music' or on jazz is at least doubly true of all rock music.

Rock, properly understood, is music warfare waged upon an
unsuspecting society by guitar-gunners who are frequently fully
aware of what they are about.

More than any other form of the misuse of sound, it is rock with
which we must deal today. There is no question but that rock is
intimately related to the kind of state of consciousness found in vast
numbers of young people – young people who are to be the
'mature' adults of the future world. Rock has unquestionably
affected the philosophy and lifestyle of millions. It is a global
phenomenon; a pounding, pounding, destructive beat which is heard
from America and Western Europe to Africa and Asia. Its effect
upon the soul is to make nigh-impossible the true inner silence and
peace necessary for the contemplation of eternal verities. Its 'fans'
are addicted, though they know it not, to the 'feelgood',
egocentricity-enhancing, para-hypnotic effects of its insistent beat.
How necessary it is in this age for *some* to have the courage to be the
ones who are 'different', and to separate themselves out from the
pack who long ago sold their lives and personalities to this sound
and the anti-Aquarian culture which has sprung up around it!

I adamantly believe that rock in *all* of its forms is a critical
problem which our civilization *must* get to grips with in some
genuinely effective way, and without delay, it if wishes long to
survive.

Note

*The use of veiled lyrics so that only certain sectors of society and
not others realize what the songs are about, is also a widespread
practice in modern rock. In rock music both drug and sexual symbolism are frequently to be heard.

6.
Assessment:
The Physics of the OM

In the beginning was Brahman, with whom was the Word. And the Word is Brahman. – Vedas

In the beginning was the Word, and the Word was with God, and the Word was God. – Gospel according to St John.

As the religions of East and West so strikingly agree: in the beginning was the Word. But exactly what *was* – or, to use the *present tense* of the Vedic quotation, *is* – the Word? The above scriptures describe it as being a part of God, or Brahman. Further, the quotation from the opening of the gospel of St John continues, pregnant with meaning:

The same (the Word) was in the beginning with God. All things were made by him; and without him was not any thing made that was made.

We have, in these famous, deeply mystical lines from St John, then, yet another example of the universal ancient belief that God, or a Divine Being, created the universe, and did so by means of a vibratory emanation. This sacred vibration is usually referred to in early Christian texts as the Word (this meaning of the term having been forgotten or overlooked by most Christians today). In Hinduism the divine vibration is, as we have seen, more usually referred to as OM. Nevertheless, the Word and the OM are one and the same thing. Moreover, a great variety of other terms stemming from the different cultures of ancient times also refer to this same universal, eternal phenomenon. Cosmic Sound, infused with the essence of Consciousness, has been known variously as AUM, AMN, AMEN, AMEEN, OMEN, OMON, I AM, HU, YAHUVAH, the Logos, the Lost Word, and by other names besides.

In our previous 'assessment' chapter, 'Music, Man and Society', we looked at one half of the ancients' claims regarding the power of music — that music affects physical health, character, and society at large — and found that the ancients' claims seemed fully justified. Yet the power of music and of sound extended also to inanimate matter. In fact, the OM was the origin and cause of all matter in the universe. Granted, the concept of the OM seems far removed from our everyday life and experience; and at first sight it appears to bear no relation whatever to what modern science has to tell us about the origin and nature of matter. But is this really the case? Perhaps we need to examine the subject of the OM in more detail.

OM AND THE UNITY OF CREATION MYTHS

Music is the harmonious voice of creation; an echo of the invisible world; one note of a divine concord which the entire universe is destined one day to sound. — Mazzini

Of one thing we can be certain from the outset. The idea of a divine vibration being behind the cause of everything was no arbitrary, idiosyncratic concept of only one people. The same theory of cosmogenesis is discovered in pre-modern cultures with surprising regularity. Often the idea is clothed in the trappings of over-simplification or of superstition; but always the basic similarity remains. Sometimes reference is to the general creation of all substance and all life by the One Sound. At other times there are more precise references to the creator-god forming each object and each living creature by means of a succession of diversified 'words'.

The Sumerians believed the gods to have created the universe with their 'mighty, commands'. Similarly, life and matter was created through a sacred word or words spoken by the first god or gods in the myths of the Hebrews, the Celts, the Chinese, the Egyptians, the American Indians and the Quechua Maya. Described in more analytical terms, the same idea appears again in the Pythagorean concept of the Harmony of the Spheres, which concept retained considerable influence through the early Christian and Medieval eras. (Though first taught in Greece by Pythagoras, the concept of the Harmony of the Spheres seems to have stemmed originally from Pythagoras' own many years of travel and discipleship in Egypt and other Middle Eastern regions.)

In the *Popol-Vuh,* containing the creation accounts of the Quechua Maya, the gods Tepeu and Gucumatz form the earth by their commands:

Thus let it be done! Let the emptiness be filled! Let the water recede and make a void, let the earth appear and become solid; let it be done. Thus they spoke ... Then the earth was created by them. So it was, in truth, that they created the earth. Earth! they said, and instantly it was made.

Of the creation of the first human beings we are told that, 'They were not born of woman ... Only by a miracle, by means of incantation were they created and made by the Creator, the Maker, the Forefathers, Tepeu and Gucumatz.'

'AND GOD SAID ...'

Our very familiarity with the account of the Creation present within the dominant religion of our own culture can blind us to the realization that in Genesis too the Creation is manifested through the agency of sound. God is described as accomplishing each successive phase of the Creation *with his spoken words*. The *words themselves* seem to enact the Creation:

And God said, Let there be light: and there was light.

... And God said, Let the waters under the heaven be gathered together unto one place, and let the dry land appear: and it was so.

... And God said, Let the earth bring forth grass, the herb yielding seed, and the fruit-tree yielding fruit after his kind, whose seed is in itself, upon the earth: and it was so.

In the same manner, according to Genesis, were created heaven and earth, the sun, the moon and the stars, fish, fowl and every living creature. God is not described as creating these with his silent thoughts or desires alone; neither does he fashion the universe with mighty hands from on high. No, he *speaks*, describing what should manifest, and manifest it does. There seems to be a strong hint to us here that the text contains a deeper and more than merely literal meaning.

Indeed, much of Genesis must be taken allegorically to be correctly understood. The written wording of the account can be taken as merely a means of rendering the process and the act of the Creation intelligible to the reader. But the essential ingredient of the account is that of the use of some form of sound-emanation from higher dimensions of reality, these sounds being referred to symbolically as words of a mortal language.

There can be no doubt but that, much as the contemporary fundamentalist Christian would like to believe the Creation account of
Genesis to be a simple, literal record of events, this is not in fact the
case. Only from the fifth century AD did the Creation stories of
Genesis begin to be taken as literal historical records; this occurring
as knowledge of the ancient wisdom within the Christian movement
deteriorated or was forced underground. Before this, we find
Gregory of Nyssa (c. AD390) describing the Genesis Creation as
'ideas in the form of a story'. The other prominent churchmen of the
time also accepted the Creation stories as being allegorical.

The book is known to be a conglomeration of a number of
allegorical Creation stories which themselves were derived at least in
part from the Middle and Near East. Other writings which have
survived from these regions also hint at a general knowledge among
the mystics and priests that the Creation was linked with a form of
utterance or sound. The Hindu concept of the OM we have already
looked at. In the Babylonian account of the Creation, the original
state of the universe, before matter had been pulled together and
solidified, is, as in Genesis, referred to as 'waters', or as an 'ocean'.
(In all the Creation myths of antiquity, the concept of primeval
waters preceding the formation of the earth can be taken as
references to a primeval, flux-like, pre-solidified state of matter.) The
earth, we are told, still bore no *name,* and did not exist 'when no
name had been named'. The Creation only came forth when it was
'called into being'.*

From the cosmology of the Jews, in Psalm 19 we read the
following beautifully poetic lines:

> The heavens declare the glory of God ... Day unto day uttereth
> speech ... There is no speech nor language, where their voice is
> not heard. Their line is gone out through all the earth, and their
> words to the end of the world. In them hath he set a tabernacle
> for the sun...

Still more poetic is that supremely evocative question in Job 38:
'Where wast thou when the morning stars sang together?' – which
might have been written by Pythagoras himself.

The science of the archetypal cosmic Tones, as known to the
Hindus and early Chinese, we would not normally equate with
Christian doctrine and dogma. Yet elements of the science were
apparently known to the more mystically-minded among the
Christian movement, and were retained for some centuries after

Christ. The early Church Father, Hippolytus, stated that Marcus received the revelation that:

> the *seven heavens* ... sounded each one vowel, which, all combined together, formed a complete doxology ... the *Sound* whereof being carried down to earth, became the creator and parent of all things that be on earth.

The philosophy of the early Christians was in many ways indistinguishable from the ancient wisdom teachings of other lands. In fact, *Pistis Sophia,* a Gnostic gospel and an earlier work than the Book of Revelation, reveals Jesus himself as having mentioned the seven major Tones, and also the seven sub-tones of each the seven major Tones:

> Do ye seek after the mysteries? No mystery is more excellent ... *saving only* THE MYSTERY *of the seven vowels and their* FORTY AND NINE POWERS, and their number thereof; and no name is more excellent *than all these vowels* [text's italics]. A name wherein be contained all names, all Lights, and all powers, knowing it, if a man quit this body of matter no smoke, no darkness, nor Ruler of the Sphere, or of Fate shall be able to hold back the soul that knoweth that name ... If he shall utter that unto the fire, the darkness shall flee away ...

EGYPTIAN GENESIS

Turning to Egypt, we discover a science of mysticism and a mythology of the Creation as complex as those of India and China. And again we encounter the concept of the creative force of sacred sound. The Egyptian *Book of the Dead* and other sources declare quite unambiguously that God, or his lesser, servant-gods, created everything that is by combining visualization with utterances. First the god would visualize the thing that was to be formed; then he would pronounce its name: and it would be.

From as late as the reign of Alexander II, a text dating from about 310BC still has the god of the Creation declaring: 'Numerous are the forms from that which proceedeth from my mouth.' The god Ra was also called Amen-Ra, with the prefix 'Amen'. The term, Amen, or AMN, was well understood by the Egyptian priesthood, and equated with the Hindu OM. (The word is still used today of course, for the closing of the prayers of Christians.) One papyrus states: 'Ra spake at the beginning of

Creation and bade the earth and heavens to rise out of the waste of water.'

That the archetypal, primeval ocean of Creation, mentioned in so many myths around the world, is not to be taken literally as having been water is nowhere made plainer than in Egyptian Creation accounts. In these it is specifically stated that before there existed any forms of living beings there existed Nu, a vast mass of Celestial Waters. In this existed the germs of all living things that were later to take form, both gods of the heavens and creatures of the earth; but they existed 'in a state of inertness and helplessness'. From out of these Celestial Waters the first god, Khepera, or Ra, emerged into being by pronouncing his own name. Thereafter he began to create other forms and other gods by the combined process of visualizing them and uttering their names. The gods which had then been created by him were also able to create through a similar process, engaging in what we might call a 'stepping down of the frequency' of the One Vibration.

The Egyptian accounts of the Creation point to the primeval 'Waters' as having been an undifferentiated mass of energy. Into these 'Waters' were poured the vibrations of the Word, thus sending forth radiating currents, as when a stone is thrown into a pond. When in a pond the original waves are reflected back from the banks, a criss-crossing of the ripples results, and a much more complex pattern of geometrical forms emerges. As waves cross each other at angles, squares, triangles and other forms can be seen. These and more complex shapes, on the cosmic level, were to the ancient viewpoint the matrices for the precipitation of matter. The key to creation in matter was considered to be the *stress* resulting from 'opposing' waves of vibration.

Not only the Egyptian Creator-God, but also the lesser gods were accredited with the knowledge and the use of words of power, their mouths being 'skilled in uttering them'. With these words of power the hierarchy of gods could create and destroy form, heal the diseased and give life to the dead. The God of gods, Ra, 'spake creating words' in order to bring into being all the lesser gods of the celestial hierarchy. According to the Egyptians, Ra also gave the secret of certain words of power even to the earthly priesthood; words whereby reptiles, diseases and other evils could be overcome.

This shows that the idea of the creative power of speech was not limited to the mythical creation of the universe. It was believed that material conditions could be changed at any time by the utterances of the gods. Mortals, too, knowing how to wield the words of

power, could themselves invoke and direct the energies of the
heavens. One text has Ra saying:

> Hear me now! My command is that all my children be brought
> nigh to me [raised in consciousness] so that they may pronounce
> words of power which shall be felt upon earth and in the
> heavens.

In precisely the same way that the gods created by combining
visualization with speech, so too did the priests believe it possible for
man to work change within the physical world. Visualization
combined with certain mantras and invocations was considered to
be the vital key to success in most acts of white magic.

The Egyptians also had an identical concept to that of the Hindu
bija mantra. Everything in the universe, having been created by a
certain vibratory pattern or combination of patterns, could also be
mastered or influenced by the uttering of its corresponding sound-
pattern. Everything and everybody possessed a certain key-note
name, sometimes called the 'secret name' — secret because for a
person to reveal his secret name would enable others to gain power
over him. Ra, too, possessed a secret name, the most powerful of all
the words of power. We therefore find Ra declaring in one text:

> I am a god and the son of a god; I AM the Mighty One, Son of
> the Mighty One. Nu, my father, conceived my secret name
> which giveth me power, and he concealed it in my heart so that
> no magician might ever know it, and, knowing it, be given
> power to work evil against me.

The *bija* mantra or 'secret name' concept was widespread in the
ancient world, and is still present in some parts of the world today.
Every human being is believed to possess his own personal melody.
And by imitating the sounds of nature, many cultures have believed
that power was gained over the particular species of creature or
phenomenon of nature which was imitated. No living creature could
reproduce as many different sounds as could man, due to man's ver-
satile vocal apparatus and his ability to construct musical instruments. This gave man enormous power, for if he knew the particular
keynote-sound of an object he could reproduce it and thereby gain
possession of the energy with which the object was charged. To be
able to wield this in-dwelling force (*orenda, kami, manitu, sila, mana,*
and so on) was the key to all magic. The magician or shaman

regarded this energy to be an impersonal force which man, if he knew how, could control and direct.

As in China and India, Egyptian music was deeply associated with mysticism and cosmology. We have seen in previous chapters that many cultures believed the pentatonic musical scale, with its two auxiliary semitones (constituting what today is called the diatonic scale), to mirror the seven major Tones of Cosmic Sound. So too in Egypt. And again, even as other peoples believed each of the Tones to be produced by one particular divine being (such as the Elohim of the Hebrews) – so too the Egyptians. We may take, for example, one particularly jovial Creation account. A Gnostic Egyptian text of unknown date and unknown origin states allegorically that in the beginning God 'laughed' seven times:

Ha–Ha–Ha–Ha–Ha–Ha–Ha. God laughed, and from these seven laughs seven Gods sprang up which embraced the whole universe: these were the first Gods.

Many of the world's religions agree with the idea that there are seven 'first Gods' which are the living embodiment of the first differentiation of the One Tone into seven. The Hebrews called these Gods the Elohim. (And it is worth pointing out that in a number of passages in Genesis, when God is described enacting the Creation, the English Bible phrase 'Lord God' is actually a very poor translation of this *plural* Hebrew word, Elohim. That is, the original Hebrew version has it that the Creation was due to the Gods of the seven Tones.) These same first Gods, which emanate from the principle of the Trinity, are also a part of Hindu teachings; but here, in Hinduism, we also have the interesting distinction between five of them and two others, which surely relates to the fact that two of the seven notes of the diatonic scale are semitones. 'Seven are the great Gods below the Trimurti,' we are told. 'Five only are working and two concealed. They are Indra, Vayu, Agni, Varuna, Kshiti.'

Egyptian hieroglyphs, wherever they show – as they often do – the descending rays of the sun, are actually illustrating the descending Tones or 'rays' of the first Gods as these rays come forth from the One. Invariably the rays are depicted as radiating and descending lines; often with hands attached to their lower ends, indicating that their purpose is to create and fashion things. They are always shown in numbers indicative of the Cosmic Tones: seven, twelve or, occasionally, thirteen.

The Egyptian priesthood used sound as a means of invoking the power of the Amen, or OM. Both the music of instruments and the human voice, as in the giving of mantras, invocations and fiats, could be used for this purpose. The very word for sound itself (*heru*, literally 'voice') indicated that earthly sound was associated with the Word.

Single, sustained notes were intoned in exactly the same way that the Hindu intones the OM, this being for the purpose of achieving inner harmony and union with the Godhead. But probably more than anywhere else throughout the civilized historical world, the Egyptian mysteries involved the deliberate, scientific use of specific verbal formulas.

Maspero recorded with regard to the Egyptian magical ceremony:

> The human voice is the instrument *par excellence* of the priest and enchanter. It is the voice that seeks afar the Invisibles summoned, and makes the necessary objects into reality. Every one of the sounds it emits has a peculiar power which escapes the notice of the common run of mortals, but which is known to and made use of by the adepts ... But as every one [of the pronunciations and their pitches] has its peculiar force, great care must be taken not to change their order or to substitute one for the other.[74]

The power of the voice extended not only to the magical ceremony, but also to everyday speech. All utterances, it was believed, released a certain energy; good or bad, according to the inner state of the speaker and his use of rhythm, melody and syntax. The average man, ignorant as to the power of the spoken word, constantly created his own limitations of character, his own ill-health, and his own undesirable conditions of life, through his idle, thoughtless and malicious utterances. But a part of the training of the priesthood involved the correct and guarded use of speech at all times. The sixteenth-century cabbalist, Giulio Camillo, recorded that according to his information the Egyptian priesthood, in their perfect and scientifically proportional use of everyday speech, caused the words, when pronounced, to be 'animated by a harmony'.

Much that concerns the Egyptian mysteries is now cloaked in the mists of time. We can be sure that little if any of its innermost teachings were written down and have survived. Especially during the early dynasties, the Land of the Nile's system of mysticism and magical science was probably as highly-developed as that of any people. For example, there are indications that the use of tone may have been regulated, as in China and elsewhere, according to the cycles of time and astrology. The precentor of the temple regularly chanted the hours,[13] giving forth a release of sound for each new time-cycle. Dio Cassius of the second century AD gives the fascinating titbit of information that the Egyptians practised in their music *a sidereal scale*, from A to G, connected to the movements of the planets. (This again points to the crucial role of Egypt as the real birthplace of Pythagoras' teachings on the Harmony of the Spheres.)

THE WORD MADE FLESH

And the Word was made flesh, and dwelt among us, (and we beheld his glory, the glory as of the only begotten of the Father,) full of grace and truth. – John 1:14

In many religions the Second Person of the Trinity is equated with the Word of God. This we find in the New Testament, where Christ is a number of times referred to as the Word. The mystery of the incarnation of the Word is that the imperfection of man and the perfection of God are able to inhabit one and the same form; and that the former can become the latter. Thus, though the person, Jesus, was born of woman, the Word entered into and was with him. Gnostic Christians believed that this same Word could enter into any man who had sufficiently prepared, purged, and perfected himself. There may be something in the fact that the Latin word *sonus* became both the English word, son, or Son, and also the French word, *son*, meaning sound. This dual meaning of 'the Word' – that it was both Sound and the Son; both Vibration and Consciousness – is nowhere more apparent than in the apocryphal 'Poem of the Gospel of St John'. This work is almost word-for-word the same as the opening of the Biblical Gospel of St John – except that the term 'the Word' is in each case replaced by 'Mind': 'In the beginning was Mind ...'

As we have noted already, in China the dual Son-Sound concept is evident in the fact that the emperor was said to embody the *huang chung* or 'yellow bell' tone. In Hindu scriptures Vishnu, the Second Person of the Trinity, is called 'the Voice' or the 'great Singer', for he is said to have created the universe with his song. Incarnate within the personage of Krishna, Vishnu enchanted a multitude of maidens (allegorically representing human souls) by the playing of his flute. Closely paralleling this are the early apocryphal texts of

Christianity in which Christ is described as 'the player of the flute' or 'the leader of the dance'.

In Persia the name of the fabulous huma bird is derived from the root, *Hum,* which is related to OM. And tradition has it that should the huma bird alight for a moment upon the head of any person, then it is a sign that the person is destined to become a 'king'. Incidentally, the root, *Hu,* is a direct reference to the Word of God; and this is most interesting, for this same root is also a part of the word *human.* In 'human', the *man* portion comes from the Sanskrit *Mana,* or 'mind of the ordinary man'. So the term 'human' is therefore an eternal reminder of the ancient doctrine: that God is even now in all men, and can be more fully realized by all. Even as Jesus was also the Christ, demonstrating the unification of the principles of earth and heaven as both the Son of Man and the Son of God, so are all men *hu-man*; God-man.

Thoth is the most common Egyptian name by which the god basically corresponding to an Egyptian Second Person of the Trinity was known. Thoth himself is described as God's deputy whom God (in the form of Ra) brought into being by his word. Thence, as the Word of God, Thoth steps down the vibratory frequencies of the One fully to the level of material density, creating the earth with his word or words. But, like the Christ or the *huang chung* principle, the spiritual essence of Thoth could also incarnate within the extremely righteous and purified man. A number of accounts speak of Thoth as having lived and walked among men. According to Clement of Alexandria and other sources, Thoth was another name for Hermes Trismegistus, who was the 'inventor of music' and the author of books of Egyptian chants to the gods.

GENESIS NOW

It is usual to think of the Creation account in Genesis as being a depiction of events which transpired (whether literally or allegorically) aeons ago. Yet what emerges from a study of all other myths and doctrines which speak of Cosmic Sound is that this modern conception of Genesis is quite erroneous. The description of the Creation is not only meant to be the story of the original formation of the earth; it is also an account, couched in symbology and veiled allusions, of the eternal process of the creation *and preservation* of all atoms and all worlds.

According to the ancient wisdom, this process is ever-present and on-going. Matter is not only created, but also preserved – by means of Cosmic Sound, and by no other. Indeed, matter *is* Cosmic Sound

in densified form; matter *is* the Harmony of the Spheres —
crystallized! Putting it the other way around: Cosmic Sound is
matter in solution. As the ancients believed: take away the Word,
and matter instantly reverts into the invisible energy of the void.
The universe, the earth, and ourselves upon it only exist and continue
to exist because the Word still comes forth. To the yogi, the OM is
as immediate as the air around him, sounding out in the eternal
present. It beats the rhythm of all hearts, and speaks to the soul
having ears to hear. The great mystics of all time have felt the Word
to be imminent in and around themselves; have known that it was
the elixir of life; that the Creation was not done, neither fulfilled;
that the morning stars still sing together.

THE WORK OF ERNST CHLADNI AND HANS JENNY

Nothing brings a point home better than a graphical, physical
demonstration; and the formative power of sound has been
illustrated by none more clearly than by Ernst Chladni and Hans
Jenny.

Ernst Chladni, a German physicist, developed what became
known as Chladni plates around 1800. These violin-shaped metal
plates are able to render visible the kind of vibrations which are
natural to violins. The plates are evenly covered with sand, and a
bow then drawn across certain points on the edge of the plate. The
result is that the sand moves quickly into the pattern of the waves of
vibration produced on the plate. Plates of other shapes, and constructed of other materials, give the same effect; and anything from
sand to maple syrup, or from iron filings to paste, can be used to
render the vibratory waves visible. The study of this phenomenon is
called cymatics.

The patterns produced are wonderful to see in their poetic
regularity. They are also dynamic, changing quickly with changes in
pitch and resonance. In this manner it is possible to make visible the
vibrations produced by specific moments in the music of particular
works, such as from a Beethoven symphony or a Bach toccata.

Lyall Watson, the biologist well-known for his book *Supernature*
and other works, has commented with interest that Chladni's figures
often adopt familiar organic forms:

> Concentric circles, such as the annual rings in a tree trunk;
> alternating lines, such as the stripes on a zebra's back; hexagonal
> grids, such as the cells in a honeycomb; radiating wheel spokes,
> such as the canals in a jellyfish; vanishing spirals, such as the
> turrets of shellfish — all these commonly occur.[75]

These resemblances between archetypal sound-forms and life-forms may not be without their significance.

The Swiss doctor and scientist, Hans Jenny, has recently undertaken Chladni-like experimentation with a more sophisticated apparatus, the 'tonoscope'. The vibrating surface of the tonoscope can have the volume and pitch of its vibrations controlled at the touch of a dial. Again, it is possible to use various substances upon it, according to which best illustrates the patterns of the sounds in question. The shapes and effects produced are then captured on film. Some of the results are strongly reminiscent of various phenomena present in nature. Vibrated paste, for example, as pictured in one series of photographic plates, suggests the appearance of early stages of cell division.

Other photographs have been taken of liquids such as water, by means of a stroboscope. They capture intricate yet beautifully symmetrical interactions of various amplitudes of waves passing through the substances. The viewer has the impression of seeing the Creation itself as when the Word went forth into the Celestial Waters. The figures produced are in a constant state of flow. Rotary waves often emerge and set the pattern turning. One experiment resulted in the perfect and dynamic shape of the *T'ai chi*, which symbolizes the interplay of cosmic forces, or the *yang-yin* polarities underlying all manifestation.

This and much more work by Hans Jenny is described in detail by Jenny himself in *Cymatics I* and *II*.[76] Nothing could be more clearly illustrative of the power of sound to shape otherwise disorganized substances. Through Jenny's apparatus it is possible literally to *see* what one is hearing.

Complex and meaningful patterns are even more apparent in Jenny's sound-affected substances when viewed at the *microscopic* level. Then are revealed beautiful and mathematically-precise mandala-structures looking like groupings of microscopically-viewed snowflakes. The stress-interactions created in substances by their exposure to sound frequencies always result in formations replete with meaningful numerological, proportional and symmetrical qualities.

THE SONG OF THE ATOM

Atoms are called Vibrations in Occultism. – H. P. Blavatsky

How are we to take the widespread conviction that there exists a universal, super-physical vibration, and that it is the cause and core of all matter and all sound? Is the concept of the OM in fact nothing but primitive, irrational superstition? Or does it agree with what modern science has to tell us about the nature of matter?

Of course, the authors of the Upanishads and the twentieth-century physicists work within the frameworks of two very different systems of terminology. The two also exhibit radically distinct approaches to the gaining of knowledge. And what all this means is that while a brief glance may give the appearance that the two paint diametrically opposite pictures of reality, such appearances may be deceptive. The physicist may have arrived at the very same truths that were known to the early Hindus, but without his realizing it.

Let us ask ourselves: *If the concept of the OM is valid, how, in modern scientific terms, would the OM show itself?* We must recall: the ancients were adamant that the OM was not audible sound at all. Therefore we are not looking for 'sound' as such; not sound as we usually think of it.

But there are further leads. The OM is said to be a high-frequency vibration which not only shapes, but *is,* all material substance. To examine the possible validity of this in an unbiased and scientific manner, it is necessary to ask ourselves: *Is there any evidence that atoms or their constituent subatomic particles are formed by, or are related to, any physical energies or activities which are of a vibratory nature?*

It needs also to be taken into consideration that by 'vibrational activity' is also meant any activity or energy which is cyclic, wave-like or oscillatory in nature. Then it is realized that atoms and sub-atomic particles not only contain such energies: they are themselves composed of *nothing else but* energy in a state of oscillation. Many years ago H. P. Blavatsky, in *The Secret Doctrine,* wrote with disarming candour: 'Atoms are called Vibrations in Occultism.' To the scientifically-minded nineteenth-century reader Blavatsky's statement must have seemed confusingly contradictory to the 'known facts'. Only since then have physicists themselves proved that atoms are indeed vibrations, being almost alarmingly insubstantial, and not at all the tiny grains of matter which the mechanistic nineteenth-century physicist would have had us believe.

In short, there is to the open-minded person a quite amazing similarity between the discoveries and theories of modern physics and the philosophies of the ancients. These similarities have been admirably listed and examined in Fritjof Capra's *The Tao of Physics,*[77] which, since its publication, has become something of a minor classic. The deeper particle physicists explore into the nature of matter, the closer they find themselves to the teachings of antiquity. Let it suffice to remind ourselves that the apparent 'solidity' of matter is an illusion, since all substances are formed out of incredibly minute atoms; these being separated by distances which — relative to their own sizes — are vast. And that, what is more, atoms themselves are not in the least bit solid, but consist of energy in motion. In *cyclic* motion; which is to say, in vibration.

Scientists Douglas Vogt and Gary Sultan postulate in their book *Reality Revealed* that all of the physical elements manifest within the visible, physical plane of existence by means of the interaction of cyclic waveforms — these waveforms not in themselves being limited to the physical plane at all, but extending through into the physical from higher levels of reality. This is surely as close to rubber-stamping the ancient viewpoint on matter as contemporary science could get.

Or is it? The scientist, Andrew Gladzewski, did considerable research into the correlations between such phenomena as atomic patterns, plants, crystals and harmonics in music, upon which one of his conclusions was that 'Atoms are harmonic resonators.'[78] When we compare this statement to that of Blavatsky — 'Atoms are called Vibrations in Occultism' — we see how true it is that the barriers between science and esotericism are now crumbling.

It is actually a well-established principle now in atomic physics that atoms react and behave as though they had resonance. This resonance principle effectively disintegrates the barriers between physics and music, and promises to prove one of the most fertile fields of research for the theoretical atomic physicist of the near future. The principle is rapidly establishing the concept that not only the atom, but all subatomic particles, can be theoretically considered as being nodes of resonance. *In other words, some scientists are beginning to regard the atom as a kind of tiny musical note.* To venture a horrible pun, does this not ring a bell? Where now, the dichotomy between the ancient wisdom's conception of matter and that of the contemporary physicist?

Far removed from the knowledge or awareness of the average man in the street, academic journals on particle physics have for some years been postulating that the basic nature of subatomic particles, right down to the quark, is a harmonic one. More recently, papers have been published in such journals on the subject of what is known as 'exotic resonance', which goes even further, and which in the opinion of many atomic physicists is the most promising lead we have to the discovery and understanding of the quintessential nature of matter.[79]

A book which has been greeted with much interest by aware and esoterically-minded Germans is Wilfried Krüger's *Das Universum Singt*[80] which, as the title suggests, is more than a little Pythagorean in its contents. Krüger has combined a knowledge of musical theory with that of atomic physics, and has brought each of these to bear in an intriguing investigation into the heart of the atom. On the face of it, Krüger seems literally to have demonstrated that the structure of the atom contains ratios and numbers which resemble to a degree impossible to account for by chance the harmonic principles of music. His findings are supported in the volume by a wealth of detailed and painstakingly-prepared notes and diagrams. Among his conclusions are: 'With the harmonic minor scale we face a synthesis between the vertically-oriented forces of the inner atom and the horizontally-oriented forces binding the molecule together.'

Perhaps the most thought-provoking of Krüger's findings concerns the secret Pythagorean teaching, the Tetraktys. The Tetraktys linked the four musical intervals of the octave, fifth, fourth and second with ratios and proportions which, according to the Pythagoreans, governed the creation of the world and of all life. Krüger's research uncovered an unmistakable association between these intervals and the structure of the nucleic acids – which are the fundamental physical ingredients of organic life.

Donald Andrews is another researcher to have explored along such lines. His complex theory of the universe sees each atom as emanating one key-note 'sound', as a minute resonator, and conceives of collections of atoms (or notes) as forming the chords which are known to the physicist as molecules. Continuing the expansion outward in size, molecules combine to form the various objects and forms of the world, each object and living being therefore being composed of a large number of molecules, or chords, which give to the object or being its own individual and complex 'sound'. Hence the title of Andrews' book, *The Symphony of Life*.[81]

THE VOCAL RANGE OF THE ONE SINGER

Not only supposedly 'solid' matter, but all forms of energy, are composed of waves; which is to say, vibrations. All of the different kinds of electromagnetic energy – including radio waves, heat, X-rays, cosmic rays, visible light, infra-red and ultraviolet -- are composed of a wave-like or vibratory activity, these vibrations travelling through the universe at 186,000 miles per second. The only difference between each of these phenomena is their frequency of vibration or wavelength. Each merges into the other at a certain wavelength; which obviously means, when one gets down to it, that *they are each one and the same thing.*

When this vibratory activity occurs at a frequency of around 600,000 billion waves per second it becomes particularly interesting and accessible to us in everyday life, for this is the frequency at which our eyes have been designed to sense the vibrations and transmit them to our brains in the form of the visual perception of light and colour. Slight differences in wavelength give rise to the perception of different colours. That light should be scientifically described as a wave-frequency once again aligns modern science side-by-side with the ancients. The authors of the Upanishads, as we have recounted, knew that light was a form of vibration, being a fine or rarefied form of 'sound'.

Nature herself also indicates the close link between sound and light, the solar-spectrum of colours displaying a number of the properties of tones. The resemblance is just as though the one phenomenon – light – were a higher state of the other. Just as audible tone organizes itself naturally into the seven notes of the diatonic scale, so too does the visible solar-spectrum form the seven colours of the rainbow.

It will be recalled that the significance of the number seven has traditionally held to be associated with the fact that all of the universe is formed by, and therefore mirrors in nature, the seven major (and five minor) cosmic Tones. In fact, *all* of the mystical numbers of the Creation have their counterparts in the visible properties of light. One, the number of unity and of the Supreme, is mirrored on earth in the pure, undifferentiated white light. Two, the principle of opposing opposites, is present in the relationship between white and black, and all of their intermediary shades of grey. Three, or the Trinity, manifests visibly in the form of the three primary colours. Then, by mixing the light of these three colours as in Figure 1, seven colours including white are produced in all; these being the visible frequencies of the seven Tones.

THE MYSTICISM OF COLOUR

Figure 1 illustrates what happens when three spotlights of different colours – red, green and purple – are beamed onto a wall in such a way that they overlap. The result: one witnesses a symbol of the very process of the Creation itself. The green and red spotlights combine to produce yellow; green and purple produce blue; and so on. Where all three overlap, white is the result. This, in effect, is to work backward, moving from the point of the manifest Creation back to the Source. The descent of the creative energies really works in the opposite direction: from the One Light springs forth the three-in-one, the Trinity: blue, yellow and pink. (These colours containing the respective qualities of Father, Son and Holy Ghost; or Will, Wisdom and Love.) Thence, a further differentiation of the Trinity produces the three other colours, giving a total of seven light-frequencies; each corresponding to one of the seven cosmic Tones and to one of the seven notes of the diatonic scale.

Figure I: Colour Addition

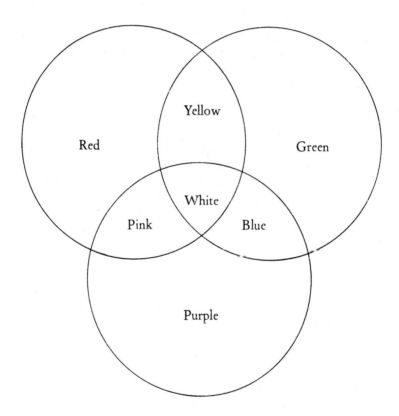

So similar are the properties of tone and of colour that during the 1920s and '30s a number of musicians branched off into an entirely independent artistic movement of colour-music. For example, keyboards were constructed which played, not musical notes, but beams of colour projected onto a screen in front of the audience. Colour-harmony, colour-counterpoint, etc. were all possible. Some colour-musicians preferred to play the classics, transposing them into the colour medium; others composed special works particularly designed for the light medium. Some artists, not wishing to make too complete a break from tonal art, constructed keyboards which emanated tones and colour-projections simultaneously. (As an artistic medium in its own right, colour-music cannot have been altogether successful, though, for it cannot really be said to have survived into the post-war era.)

Now, besides the seven colours named above, there exists a slightly different series of seven colours which can also be taken as representing the seven Tones. These are the colours of the rainbow, Nature's own gift of chromatic beauty. The seven colours of the rainbow are violet, indigo, blue, green, yellow, orange and red. These, and the entire span of the spectrum, are usually depicted in a straight line, one colour blending into the other from violet at one end to red at the other. Yet it is more revealing, and closer to the truth behind all things, to position the colours around the circumference of a circle. It is then possible to see how the solar-spectrum relates to the circle of the zodiac, which in itself is expressive of the total number of twelve Tones.

If the spectrum is placed around only about two-thirds of the overall circumference of the circle, we find that these must indeed be the correct positions for each of the colours, for the different shades are positioned in such a way as to be exactly opposite their complementary colours. This is a fact which has long been known, but its significance overlooked. When two colours are complementary, it means that when they are combined they have the effect of cancelling each other out, the result of the mixture being grey. In other words, any pair of complementary colours are the *yang* and the *yin* aspects which radiate forth from the centre on their particular axis of the circle. In astrology this has its direct parallel in the principle of opposing signs, which face each other across the six axes of the zodiac.

The fact that the solar-spectrum only encompasses about two-thirds of the circle is also thought-provoking, and may link with the fact that the seven major cosmic Tones are said to be more exoteric and tangible in their effects throughout the universe than the five minor Tones. These five minor Tones (sometimes called 'inner' or 'secret' Tones), as represented in colour, would account for the remaining third of the circumference. And since whichever colours

take up this remaining portion of the circle would still be complementary colours to the solar-spectral colours opposite them, it is
therefore possible to know which colours they are. Opposite the
solar-spectral colour of green, for instance, is a purplish-red, and
opposite to yellow-green comes a bluish-purple.

The total 360° circumference could accurately be called an
'octave' of colour. But to put our conception of this colour-zodiac
into a larger perspective, we should note that it is not a closed circle
at all, but rather, one 360° turn of a *spiral* as seen from above. That
is, the arc of the circle continues around once more, and again and
again, both anti-clockwise and clockwise, but at a lower and a
higher plane. The spiral of light-frequencies passes upward into the
ultra-violet spectrum and downward into the infra-red, passing in
each case beyond the range of our visual senses. Thus, the visible
octave of colour is but a note within a larger Octave, which is in
itself only a tiny portion of the entire range of frequencies of the
Word.

This entire range of vibrations is that known in physics as the
spectrum of electromagnetic waves. In Figure 2 it can be seen that
the known range of this spectrum extends from the point of zero
cycles or vibrations per second to a little beyond 10^{24} or a trillion
trillion cycles per second. Beyond that point of very high frequencies our instruments are not yet able to measure. The lower frequencies to the left include the broad range of inductive heat, and
the frequency used to convey electricity along power lines. Beyond
this come radio waves, and then the infra-red range. Beyond the
range of visible light are the vibrations modern science has termed
ultraviolet light, X-rays and Gamma rays. Finally come the cosmic
rays which are the highest frequency yet known along the
electromagnetic spectrum.

This spectrum of electromagnetism is referred to even in modern
physics in terms of its 'octaves', for it is by nature a range of
vibratory octaves, the entire known range encompassing about 70
octaves. It can be seen from Figure 2 that the range of visible light
takes up only a tiny portion of the entire spectrum. Curiously
enough, and as though by grand design, of the total 70 octaves,
visible light accounts for just about exactly one octave.

THE IMMINENCE OF THE WORD

In much the same way that the range of visible colour can be placed
upon one 360° turn of the electromagnetic spiral, so too can an
octave of audible sound be placed around the circumference of a

circle. Again, this 'circle' is actually only one revolution of a spiral. Around the 360° circuit, the seven major and five minor notes of the musical octave take up their twelve positions as co-ordinates of the twelve zodiacal signs and their Tones. Following the spiral down, we descend into lower octaves and eventually into the inaudible subsonic range of vibration. Above the audible range we enter into the supersonic range. Strictly speaking, the sonic frequency spiral cannot be said to be a part of the electromagnetic frequency spiral: the latter consists of electromagnetic vibrations, whereas sound vibrations are literally physical in that they vibrate the air. However, all can be seen to be derived from vibration at one level or another. Therefore all that there is – all matter, all energy – is indeed composed of nothing more and nothing less than – vibration.

The illumined sage has always known this to be true. More: he perceives in all of nature its essentially rhythmic foundations. The budding and withering of the flower; the rising and setting of the sun; the biorhythms of body, emotions and mind; the waxing and waning of the moon; the ebb and flow of the tide; the cycles of the seasons; and the movements of the planets and the stars – to the mystic these all testify of the Word and of the Music of the Spheres. Moreover, since all matter is but the warp and woof of vibration,

Figure 2: The Electromagnetic Wave Spectrum

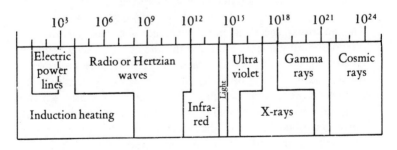

FREQUENCY   (waves per second)

the mystically-minded man considers everything his eyes can see as being, quite literally, the Word revealing itself.

The mystic considers his very own body and consciousness to be a manifestation of the Word. He considers the purified man to be a clear, sonorous note in the symphony of life. And such a man therefore has the ability — even the sacred responsibility — to invoke and send forth the energy of the Word to all life. This he is accomplishing even in silent meditation and in quiet prayer. But it is implemented with an additional force when audible sound itself is enrolled for the task. *Wherever* harmonious tones are sounding out, there is the door opened to higher dimensions of reality; there do the invigorating, resurrecting energies pour into the physical world and radiate forth like a divine electricity of life. In this is found the original meaning and significance behind the bells of churches, which so truly sound out the OM itself, along with dozens of beautiful overtones. Bells and gongs in the various temples and shrines of the world were originally for the same purpose. And for the same reason do Sufi dervishes play the *Nai* or *Algoza* (a double flute). So too do yogis blow the *Singh* (a horn) or the *Shankha* (a shell): to attune themselves to, and to flood forth, the spiritual qualities of the One Tone.[82]

Long ago the Aztecs used to blow their conch-shell trumpets to invoke the OM at dawn (specifically, at the rise of Venus). Even today, the music of Tibet is very strongly founded upon the principle of the One Tone. In the Western sense Tibetan music might scarcely be considered music at all, but to dismiss its worth for this reason would be to grossly mistake its actual significance and purposes. Lama Anagarika Govinda explains:

Tibetan ritual music is not concerned with the emotions of temporal individuality, but with the ever-present, timeless qualities of universal life, in which our personal joys and sorrows do not exist ... To bring us in touch with this realm is the purpose of meditation as well as of Tibetan ritual music, which is built upon the deepest vibrations that an instrument or a human voice can produce: sounds that seem to come from the womb of the earth or from the depth of space like rolling thunder, the *mantric* sound of nature, which symbolize the creative vibrations of the universe, the origin of all things.[83]

Few Westerners have learned the full import behind each aspect of Tibetan chanting and instrumental music; but even so, something of its deep mystery is obvious to all open-minded listeners. In the words of the music critic of the *Süddeutsche Zeitung:*

> Even if one has no idea of the former Gyoto lamasery, no inkling of the mystical concepts underlying the ceremonial chanting, no understanding of the text, this music radiates more than mere exotic charm. With only slight, occasional variations, the chant centres around one single note – but what a note! ...
> What is fascinating about this chanting is not merely its resonant depth, but a special voice technique that accentuates certain overtones so strongly as to give the impression that the monks are singing in harmony. But the deeper, mystic links between the proportions of the cosmos, of the human body and of the harmonic series (each perceptible pitch is connected with a particular part of the body – between solar plexus and forehead – which is its seat) are not, admittedly something that can be grasped at the drop of a hat.[84]

One particularly interesting aspect of the music, which has a great bearing upon its nature and purpose as an earthly reflection of the OM, is described by Peter Hamel:

> One peculiarity, which is also found in old Arabic traditions, concerns the breathing technique used in playing the instruments. The performer breathes in through his nose without any break in his playing – a feat which is made possible by the use of the mouth as a wind-reservoir. Apart from a slight darkening of the tone, the sound can be prolonged without interruption more or less indefinitely.[70]

HARMONIC RATIOS AND PROPORTIONS IN NATURE

See deep enough, and you see musically; the heart of nature being every-where music, if you can only reach it. – Thomas Carlyle

Fascinatingly enough, a number of the most basic of all the facts and phenomena of nature display the very same ratios that are found in tonal harmonics. Hans Kayser is the author of several books which prove in rigid scientific fashion that the whole-number ratios of musical harmonics – such as the octave, the third, fifth and fourth – correspond to an underlying numerical framework existing in chemistry, atomic physics, crystallography, astronomy, architecture, spectroanalysis, botany, etc.[85]

More recently, the quite well-known musician, Gary Peacock, interrupted his career to delve into the same area, undertaking a four-year study of molecular biology and organ physiology. Among his findings was that the relationships in the periodic table of elements, from which all matter is formed, resemble the overtone structure in music. Peacock says, 'It becomes clearer and clearer to me that the actual structure of tone in music and the actual structure of matter are the same.' In other words: matter is music. Other researchers have found a relationship between sound frequencies and various physical – even *notational* – shapes. For example, 540 vs. 300 frequency cycles per second displayed on an oscilloscope produces a minor seventh shape.

In his book, *The Power of Limits*,[86] Gyorgy Doczi has traced in detail the exact similarities between the proportions and ratios found in the various branches of science. Throughout the book these proportions and ratios are not specifically pointed out to be the same as those present in music, but on an early page Doczi himself explains why. Quite simply, *all* of the data in his book, which links physics with biology with astronomy with architecture and so forth, can be explained in terms of music, but this would open up too vast a subject in itself. Nevertheless, his book is inherently associated with the principles of music from cover to cover. The ratios which in music are known as the fifth and fourth intervals occur again and again throughout nature. One highly specific parallel between music and botany demonstrated by Doczi involves the arrangement of the veins of leaves on either side of the central stem. Some leaves, analysed in detailed diagrams, reveal nothing less than a perfect occurrence of counterpoint in the ratios and proportions to which the veins are arranged to the left and to the right of the stem.

There are in particular a number of fundamental occurrences in nature of the number seven. There are seven rows in the periodic table of elements (hydrogen, helium to flourine, neon to chlorine, argon to bromine, krypton to iodine, xenon to astatine, and radon to element 117). A slightly different way of ordering the elements is to give the two rare-earth series basically their own rows in the table, but still we find that this gives us seven rows of *stable* elements, these rows beginning respectively with hydrogen, lithium, sodium, potassium, rubidium, cesium and hafnium. The seven rows of the periodic table of elements arise out of the fact that a number of different elements tend to display similar physical properties, and are therefore listed together. (To give an example: helium, neon, argon and krypton are all inert gases, and tend not to engage in chemical reactions.) All this is highly suggestive of the possibility that the seven rows of elements represent the categories of elements which embody the frequencies and properties of each of the seven major Tones. (The number seven also occurs within the human anatomy, in such things as the seven major hormonal glands and the seven ventricles or cavities of the skull.)

Progressing upward in scale from atomic elements to the world of crystals, we find that crystals too are formally categorized according to seven different types or crystal systems. The seven crystal systems arise out of the fact that crystals tend to belong to one out of seven basic geometrical forms: cubic, rhombohedral, hexagonal, triclinic, monoclinic, trigonal and orthorhombic. Thus there are seven basic forms of crystal, rock and mineral. This again points to the seven types as being literally the respective crystallizations, within the mineral world, of the seven major frequencies of the Word. *Is* the Word truly so far removed from our sensory capacities and everyday life, then, or is it simply that we refuse to *see*?

On the subject of crystals, modern esotericists have often recommended crystals, pictures of crystals, and models of the molecular structure of crystals as a subject for meditation. Contemplation upon their geometry is said to provide a route by which the consciousness of man can attune itself to the various qualities of the Consciousness of the Supreme.

HARMONIC PRINCIPLES IN THE NATURAL PSYCHOLOGY OF MAN

I begin to understand more deeply the essence of our art (music) and its elemental power over the human soul. Man, being a creature of nature and subject to the cosmic influences that inform all earthly beings, must needs have been under the sway of that music from his earliest days; his organism reverberated with its vibration and received its rhythmic impulses. – Bruno Walter

The intervals and harmonics of music, mirroring the geometry of the heavens, may also be present in some mysterious way within not only the physical form of man, but also within the patterns of his psychology. It has often been pointed out, and even entire books written on the subject, that the architecture of previous times often displayed ratios and proportions such as are found in the intervals of music. From the constructions of ancient Greece to those of the more recent medieval and Gothic periods, there exist many examples of buildings based almost entirely upon the intervals of octave, fifth, fourth and so on. The same ratios are also found in the works of the grand master painters. At times these ratios in art and architecture occur with a frequency and precision that can only be conscious and deliberate; at other times it seems likely that the ratios were included unconsciously, because they 'seemed right'. Yet of the conscious and unconscious occurrence of such harmonic ratios, it is difficult to say which is the more astounding and ridden with deep implications.

That such ratios can occur unconsciously seems to be supported by the phenomenon known as Ur-song. This phenomenon takes us deeper still into the natural framework of the human mind. For Ur-song is the name given to a fundamental type of melody that infants everywhere in the world seem to sing quite spontaneously, without having learned it from their parents or the culture around them. On the face of it, there is no obvious reason why children, if they produce melodies spontaneously, should not begin with any of the infinite variety and number of different tones and tone-relationships. The notes of the Western diatonic scale are, after all, but a few points on a spectrum of tone-frequencies that actually includes an infinite number of points or minutely-different pitches. Yet in all lands, children from the age of eighteen months to two and a half years have been found to spontaneously sing melodic fragments with the intervals of second, minor third, and major third. Thence, in their second and third years, while systematically exploring the use of these intervals in what may be a very important developmental psychological process, children then go on to include fourths and fifths. (A descending third is a pitch difference or interval such as that between 'this' and 'old' in the tune 'This old man . . .'. An example of a fourth is the interval between 'Don-' and '-ald' in 'Old MacDonald had a farm'.) Only at the age of three does the particular musical style of their own culture begin to influence them, thus putting an end to their spontaneous and independent expressions of the Ur-song. (Ur is a German prefix for original, primeval.)

In 1973 the composer and conductor Leonard Bernstein, in his Charles Eliot Norton lectures at Harvard, described the Ur-song of the world's children as an archetypal pattern. He said that the song consists of a repetitive, descending minor third, often accompanied by another descending step to a fourth. In his opinion, Ur-song is the joint product of the physical laws of harmony, and of the innate, genetic pattern of all human beings.[87]

The concept of the diatonic scale being written into the genetic pattern of man is in itself full of implications. Yet we should not always immediately assume that all such innate abilities are *primarily* linked to genes, chromosomes, etc. for to do so is to fall into the trap of materialism. Ur-song may be demonstrating to us that the thought processes and the natural flow of consciousness (which is so uninhibited and spontaneous in infants) are themselves somehow linked to the harmonic principles which the ancients believed to be the foundations of the universe.

TOWARDS A GRAND UNIFIED FIELD THEORY OF PHYSICS

Our data thus far suggests that the entire universe may, then, be based upon vibration; that vibration may be the fundamental nature of each and every energy form known to science. Yet this opens up a possibility more astounding and mind-stretching than any we have yet touched upon: the potential of bringing forth a 'grand unified field theory'.

We have already seen that, though using their own terminology, both the authors of the Upanishads and the ancient Chinese were certain that a form of sacred vibration was the source and real nature of all the forces in the universe, including light (which would also include the entire electromagnetic spectrum, since light is but one narrow waveband within it). Let us note in this respect the interesting fact that ultrasonic sound vibrating a glass rod causes the rod to emanate both heat and light. In other words, this is a demonstrable example of sound energy becoming the energies of both heat and light.

Physicists are today searching for Einstein's dream, a unified field theory that could, in one go, explain all the forces of nature. There is even the hope of finding a grand unified field theory that would combine in one theoretical explanation and one basic underlying force all the dynamic qualities of the smallest and most fundamental particles yet known to science. Such a discovery would totally revolutionize all of science and all of life, opening up unbelievable technological possibilities.

According to the data we have discussed so far, the physicists involved in this search may do worse than to look to *vibration* as being the key to such a discovery. In their search for the ultimate power behind all manifestation, they should, perhaps, not lightly bypass the statement of St John:

In the beginning was the Word, and the Word was with God, and the Word was God ... All things were made by him; and without him was not any thing made that was made.

The last great unification within physics took place over a century ago when Maxwell revealed that magnetism and electricity were really different apsects of the same force. It is literally the result of this unification that today we have television sets, microwave ovens, and thousands of other inventions. If we were to tap the source of an even more fundamental unification of forces, the possibilities would be almost boundless. No matter how mind-wrenching these possibilities may be, the potential to realize them follows by straight-forward and uncomplex logic once it becomes possible to convert all forms of energy into any other. The potential for technological advancement that a grand unified field theory would open up would actually be no more magical or miraculous than that opened up by Maxwell. After all, a television set or digital watch would have *seemed* miraculous to the nineteenth-century man, just as the potentials stemming from a new, wider theory sound just as startling to us at first. For instance, electricity, light and heat would all be interchangeable *with gravity.* This would make it possible to develop machines for levitation, to convert gravity into light or heat, or even to *make* gravity from electricity. Energy could be transferred (probably in the form of what modern physics calls 'gluons') from higher planes of existence into the physical plane and vice-versa. Thus, instant materialization and dematerialization should be possible as a matter of course.

Opening the door for waves of force to enter freely into the material world would also enable man to tap infinite sources of omnipresent energy. Such supplies of infinite, omnipresent energy would expose as false the very concept that energy is 'limited' or that its available supply is 'dwindling'. There are really no limits to what might become possible if ever a grand unification theory were brought forth. In effect, it would be the 'theory' of the Word itself; and as the Bible adamantly reminds us, 'With God all things are possible'. All the evidence seems to tell us that all of nature does indeed function by virtue of one fundamental force. The theory, then, can be said to be already there, just waiting to be plucked from the tree of abundance.

Relevant to all of this are the teachings of modern esoteric schools: that though the universe and its many diverse phenomena and forms of energy may appear complex, the Creation is in essence extremely simple. Only two force principles are at work in everything: matter and dynamic energy. Here, 'matter' equates with the primeval Celestial Waters of the ancient Egyptians. By 'dynamic force' is meant God made manifest; meaning the descent of the Word into the Celestial Waters. The descent of this vibratory force gives rise, at its different frequency-levels, to all the supposedly different forms of energy. But the important thing is: that all the known energies represent *only the descent* of the Word from Spirit into matter. These energies represent only the progressive densification of the vibration – from cosmic rays through such waves as magnetism, electricity, light and heat, and into audible sound and tangible, material vibrations.

The realization of the implication of this may provide the key to unlock the scientific discovery of the age. For certain old esoteric schools which are said to have preserved intact elements of the original ancient wisdom have this to say: that the vibratory force does not move in 'straight lines' – but, in a sense, in circles. In other words, the Word does not forever become progressively denser in vibration. Like the reflection of a ripple off the bank of a pond, the vibratory force reaches a point in its 'arc of descent' at which extremes meet, after which the vibrations begin *ascending in frequency back to the planes of Spirit*. The point of the return is arrived at between cathodicity and magnetism. From here on, just as vibration brought substance into being, even so does it once more carry it out of being. Thus there exists, it is said, a 'Night Side of Nature' – a realm of nature and of force which it is possible for man to tap, and in which all the known forces have their opposites. Here, positive polarity becomes negative, cold becomes heat, and gravity becomes gravity-repulsion. Between these two extremes, a neutral point can be reached, and this provides the key to the practical application of anti-gravity as well as numerous other developments.

ASTROLOGY AS THE MUSIC OF THE SPHERES

There's not the smallest orb which thou beholdest,
But in his motion like an angel sings,
Still quiring to the young-eyed cherubims;
Such harmony is in immortal souls,
But whilst this muddy vesture of decay
Doth grossly close it in, we cannot hear it.

– Shakespeare

The reader will recall that the vibrations of the Word were said to change according to the movements of the sun, the moon and the planets. The study of the effects of these changes in vibration was the science of astrology. According to the ancients, the astrological harmonics change in such a way as to affect all of matter and life.

This idea is widely held. Though it receives its most famous exposition in Pythagoras' Harmony of the Spheres, a similar concept can be traced to a number of ancient cultures. In the above quotation we find the notion emerging even as comparatively recently as Shakespeare. (Here, Shakespeare also agrees with the traditional esoteric concept that the divine man can 'tune in' to, and be aware of, the heavenly harmony, but that the ordinary dense mortal is too far out of alignment with this harmony even to be aware of it. This much is clear from the last three lines of the quotation.)

What evidence is there for the science of astrology being valid, and for the concept that it is based upon vibrations from the heavens?

Whatever its *modus operandi* may be, astrology itself is rapidly emerging from the misty realms of superstition, newspaper columns and ignorant laughter, to establish itself as a valid science. It accomplishes this the more freely and painlessly when it enters the halls of science in disguise, under another name: there exists a growing body of information culled from physics, statistics, astronomy, chemistry, psychology and, in particular, biology, which indicates all manner of influences which the sun, the moon and the planets exert over life on earth. Astrology by any other name smells just as sweet!

A number of marine creatures such as oysters have been found to be sensitive to the position of the moon irrespective of whether or not they are in water and can feel the tide.[88,89] Other creatures respond to the moon's 28-day cycle. One of them, the worm *Platynereis drumerilii*, swarms to the surface of the sea every time the moon reaches its last quarter.[90] It has been discovered that potato tubers react to the position of the moon: they display changes such as in their metabolic rate according to whether or not the moon is above the horizon, is at its zenith, or whether it is setting.[91]

As for the influence of the sun, it is now commonly known that all manner of events — political, social, military, seismological, atmospheric and biological — occur in cycles of about eleven years, apparently following the regular eleven-year cycles of sunspot activity. By altering the earth's magnetic field, sunspot activity has been found to affect the internal processes of human beings. This influence simultaneously affects people living in different regions of the world, and has been found to continue even in experimental subjects placed six hundred feet underground.[92,93]

The moon also affects geomagnetic activity on earth, and this may account for at least some of its documented influences over life. It was reported by Harold L. Stolov and A. G. W. Cameron in 1964 that their analysis of 31 years of data revealed an average of a four per cent decrease in geomagnetic activity during the seven days preceding the full moon, and a four per cent average increase during the seven days following the full moon. Though these four per cent figures may not seem large, a statistical analysis shows that they have a less than five per cent probability of having occurred by chance alone.[94]

The planets are much farther away from earth than the moon, and some are at a far greater distance from us than even the sun. Yet there is strong evidence that they too exert an influence over events on earth. J. H. Nelson demonstrated over 30 years ago that by the position of the planets it is possible to predict changes in the sun, which in turn affect the earth's magnetic field, thus spoiling radio receptions.[95] The alterations in earth's magnetic field also affect living creatures. Nerve activity, for example, is known to be subtly influenced by all such changes. Also, as the planets move around in their orbits, corresponding variations have been found to take place in the electrical potential of trees.[96]

Regarding human beings – and approaching closer to the subject of astrology proper – Michael Gauquelin has conducted a series of statistical surveys over a number of decades into the correlations between character and the astrological conditions at birth. His findings have been widely reported, and the reader may well be familiar with them already. The most important of them are summarized in his book, *The Cosmic Clocks*.[97] Briefly, Gauquelin found there to be strong statistical correlations between the astrological factors present at birth and the type of profession later taken up by individuals. For example, physicians and medical doctors tended to have been born when Mars or Saturn had either just risen or had attained to their highest position in the sky. On the other hand, the artistic professions, including musicians, painters and writers, tended not to furnish individuals who had been born at such times. A rising Jupiter in the birth sign tended to be found in the birth-charts of politicians and soldiers, but rarely in those of scientists.

THE PLANETS SUITE

All this may mean that there is, after all, something to astrology. But is there any evidence that the astrological influences of the heavenly bodies work in some way that is related to vibration, or to a sort of celestial music?   Perhaps there is. From the study of our own planetary body we do know that it is possible for planets to 'chime' like a gigantic musical instrument. Seismographs first revealed that the earth 'rings' with deep vibrations when the powerful Chilean earthquake of 1960 was noticed to have sent oscillations throughout the sphere, the 'chime' being reduced in 'volume' by a half every two days. Of course, these vibrations were far deeper than could be heard as audible sound, having a wave-frequency of 53.1 and also 54.7 minutes. Since 1960 many other chimes, more subtle in volume, have been recorded on these same two pitches. (Interestingly enough, these pitches of the earth are twenty octaves below the audible range of man, whereas the tone of the atom is twenty octaves above it; thus the hearing of man is placed mid-way between the worlds of the macrocosm and those of the microcosm.)[79]

If other planets also chime in this fashion, it would be quite conceivable for them to radiate electromagnetic vibrations of extremely low frequency across the void, thus inducing resonance and harmonics in each other. Certainly the planets are 'in contact' with one another in the higher ranges of the electromagnetic spectrum, since each send out powerful radiations of radio and other waves. Yet there are even indications that incredibly deep vibrations in the frequency range of only one wave per forty seconds (meaning that the waves are each seven million miles long) travel through the flux of space.[98] As yet, these waves are still cloaked in mystery.

The sun itself has been described as a 'great musical instrument' by Dr Martin Pomerantz of the Bartol Research Foundation, Newark, Delaware. Dr Pomerantz and others have detected oscillations on the sun's surface which they believe originate from acoustic or vibratory waves inside the fiery sphere. Eighty overtones or different kinds of vibration have been observed, with periods of from two to eight minutes.

These oscillations, as well as the radio waves of space, have been transposed into audible sound. The results, though interesting, cannot really be said to correspond with music as we know it. However, Saturn's magnetosphere produces waves which, when transposed into sound, have been described as 'a slow, dreamy melody'. When *Voyager 2* drew close to the ringed world it picked up the whines and hisses of the magnetosphere and beamed them back to earth. These were then speeded up and played through a music synthesizer, and the waves were indeed found to consist of a kind of melody. Of the waves, Dr Hunt, a British scientist who worked with NASA on the *Voyager* project muses that, 'Perhaps they will reach Top of the Pops in years to come.'

If the planets *do* radiate tones across the void to each other, then factors such as their relative orbits, orbital speed, and distance from one another could be expected to be very important factors in determining the harmonic results. This sets one's mind immediately to thinking of Bode's Law.

Bode's Law is one of the most clear-cut astronomical messages that the universe has to offer us in order to convince man of the inherent order and meaning within the Creation. It was Johann D. Titius, in 1766, who first discovered the Law, but six years later Johann Bode did a better job of drawing attention to it, so that it afterwards became known as Bode's Law. Titius had noticed that all of the planets known to astronomers in his day possessed mean orbital distances from the innermost planet, Mercury, these orbits becoming progressively greater by the ratio of 2:1 as the planets increased in distance from the sun. That is, Earth was twice as far from Mercury's orbit as was Venus, Mars was twice as far from Mercury as was Earth, and so on. The ratio 2:1 is, of course, the ratio of the octave itself, and so it was as if the planets formed a chain of octaves, each next planet representing one octave. The distances involved were not *exactly* of the ratio 2:1, but were near enough to suggest to early European astronomers that a definite law of some sort might be involved.

However, there was a gap in the chain of octaves: there existed no known planet between Mars and Jupiter where, according to Bode's Law, there should have been one. Then, in 1801, Giuseppe Piazzi discovered Ceres, a planetoid with a diameter of 480 miles which orbited almost exactly where Bode's Law had predicted that a planet should. Not only did this discovery fulfil for Bode's Law the standard supporting factor necessary for any scientific law: that it should be able to *predict* further discoveries; but Piazzi had not had the Law in mind at all when he discovered Ceres. He had simply been making routine observations for a catalogue of star positions. Later, hundreds of other planetoids were also discovered within the same orbit, and the orbit became known as the asteroid belt. The asteroids appear to be the remains of a planet which once followed this orbit, but was somehow mysteriously destroyed. This former planet has by some been posthumously called Maldek.

More discoveries were to follow in the fulfilment of Bode's Law. For since 1772 there have come the discoveries of Uranus, Neptune and Pluto. Of these three, Uranus and Pluto have mean orbits extremely close to the exact distances necessary to complete two further octaves. Neptune has sometimes been cited by reductionist materialists as evidence that the Law is no law at all, since the planet does not fall upon an octave position. Yet in fact it *is* located almost exactly *half-way* between Uranus and Pluto, as though to fill in the half-octave position. Table 3 shows the exact distances of the octaves going out from Mercury, taking Earth's orbit to be two units out, and shows too the actual distances of the planetary orbits themselves.

Table 3 : Bode's Law

Planet	Perfect Octaves: units of distance from Mercury	Mean Orbits: actual units of distance from Mercury
Mercury	0	0
Venus	1	1.1
Earth	2	2
Mars	4	3.7
Asteroids	8	Approx 8
Jupiter	16	16
Saturn	32	30.5
Uranus	64	62.6
Neptune	$(64 \times 1\frac{1}{2} = 96)$	98.9
Pluto	128	130.1

Could there be further planets yet to be discovered, also keeping to the predicted orbits of the Law? If so, the nearest would be twice as far out as Pluto, and therefore not an easy body to locate.

What do contemporary astronomers themselves say of the Law? Smaller astronomical texts refer to the Law merely as 'a curious numerical relationship', without even mentioning the essential fact that it completes a series of octaves. More detailed texts content themselves with the observation that, 'It is probably a mere coincidence'! In fact, a science based upon materialism can say nothing else, no matter how many more planets might yet be discovered in accordance with the Law. (The day upon which the 'X factor' of God is finally admitted and reincorporated back into the scientific outlook of man will be a significant day indeed. Perhaps no event more than this will signal the formal arrival of the Aquarian Age, in which religion is to be more scientific, and science more religious, for the perfect wedding of the two.)

Bode's Law concerns itself with the distances out from Mercury of the orbits of the planets; but there may also exist other harmonic laws, unnoticed by astronomers, which concern the speeds of the planets' movements around in their orbits. Literally, these speeds, on the harmonic level, would represent the planets' pitch-frequencies. It may therefore be the case that when planets come into conjunction with one another (i.e. become arranged in a more-or-less straight line going out from the sun) that 'chords' are produced. What is interesting in this respect is that a number of regular planetary conjunctions occur over particular periods of time which, in their ratios to each other, reflect with considerable accuracy the ratios of length which are necessary to produce the *diatonic* notes of an octave.

This is best illustrated in diagrammatic form. Figure 3 shows a line representing an octave, divided into seven intervals by eight notes.

Figure 3 : Planetary Conjunctions as 'Chords'

	DO	RE	MI	FA	SOL	LA	SI	DO
Saturn			29					
Jupiter	22				33			44
Asteroids		21			28		35	
Mars				14			21	
Venus	15			20		25		30
Mercury	75			100		125		150
Years	24	27	30	32	36	40	45	48

The line could as well, for instance, be the string of a one-stringed musical instrument. Planetary conjunctions take place over time according to these same ratios that divide up the length of the string.

In the diagram, the numbers below the line, beginning with 24 on the left, show the numbers of years involved; while above the line are indicated the conjunctions of each planet with the sun and the earth; the planets involved being represented as circles. The numbers within these circles indicate the number of conjunctions which the planet has made with the sun and the earth within that time period. (Since these would always be bound to occur as the two planets continue in their orbits, they are not statistically important.)

To take Jupiter as an example then, it encounters a conjunction with the sun and the earth every 398 days. This being a little more than a year, it means that Jupiter comes into conjunction eleven times every twelve earth-years. As it happens, each eleventh conjunction takes place virtually exactly every twelve years, and so we can see that Jupiter appears on the diagram at the 24th-year, 36th-year and 48th-year points. What is more, every 24 years it comes into conjunction not only with the earth, but also with Mercury and Venus, making a four-planet line-up. Twelve years later, on the 36th-year point, Jupiter encounters a conjunction not only with the earth, but also with the main portion of the asteroid belt. Then, finally, as shown in the right of the diagram, the 48th year sees the repetition of its conjunction with Mercury and Venus, and the completion of the octave.

Only further statistical evaluation could determine whether or not this table of data is open to criticism on two points which occur to one in looking at it. Firstly, the data would need to be examined statistically in some detail before its real worth or significance could be known, since possibly such conjunctions would always be expected to occur, through chance. Secondly, the data used is from the standard astrological tables. However, such data is earth-oriented, including only conjunctions with the earth, whereas there seems no obvious reason why significant conjunctions excluding earth, such as could be gleaned (at length) from astronomical sources, should not also be included in the scheme. Yet, nevertheless, the alignments are at the very least thought-provoking, being most suggestive of a series of cosmic chords.

Experiments such as those with Chladni plates or with Hans Jenny's tonoscope leave us in no doubt as to the potential which sound vibrations possess to take undifferentiated substances and instantly organize them into regular forms. From there it only requires one step of the imagination to understand how vibrations of a much lower frequency (such as the seven million miles long electromagnetic waves mentioned above) or of a much higher frequency (such as cosmic rays and beyond) could create — and sustain to the present moment — atoms and worlds.

One or more kinds of wave-forms, travelling between the planets, could also account for many astrological effects. In fact, the planets may interact much more continuously and intimately than is usually suspected. A report by Gerald Atkinson in the *Transactions of the American Geophysical Union* (December 1964) stated that statistical evidence had indicated a relationship between magnetic activity on earth and the positions not only of the moon, but also of Mercury and Venus. But, what was more, the study found that interplanetary waves may have been the cause; specifically, the action of shock and bow waves in the supersonically streaming plasma coming out from the sun. It is therefore only possible, though, for this particular inter-planetary effect to be exerted from a more inward-orbiting planet upon one further out from the sun. Thus, while Mercury and Venus affect our own geomagnetic field, we might at least have the satisfaction of knowing that our planet likewise disrupts whatever radio reception there may be on Mars! In fact, Atkinson did find that the position of the earth influenced the frequency of the surface features known as Martian blue clearings.

That high frequency waves from space could significantly affect conditions on earth would tend to be indicated by experiments into the effects of known vibrations produced in the laboratory. For example, it has been found that music is capable under laboratory conditions of changing the chemical structure and the strength of crystals. This effect is particularly marked when ultrasonic music is used in the presence of heat.[79] And since we have suggested that wave-frequencies from the heavens equate with the ancient science of astrology, this confronts us with the distinct possibility that astrological conditions themselves might even be able to influence measurable physical and chemical processes.

Amazingly enough, this does seem to be the case. We have already briefly reviewed some of the effects of the heavenly bodies and their positions upon organic life, and upon the atmosphere of the earth. The sunspot cycle and other conditions have been statistically linked with the occurrence of earthquakes and other phenomena. And, in view of the effect of music on crystals, the most interesting discovery of all is that in crystal growth, the physical shapes of the crystals have been found to be slightly influenced according to the positions of the zodiac and the planets. This discovery creates quite a link between astrological influences and the idea that they may be based on vibration. (It also throws into doubt the entire concept of the perfect scientific experiment, with its controls and laboratory conditions. Should the finding come to be independently replicated, we will then have to live with the knowledge that the ever-changing influences of astrology cannot be excluded from the test-tube!)

INFRASONICS, ULTRASONICS AND ACOUSTIC ODDITIES

Acoustic oddities and phenomena related to sound-vibrations beyond the range of human hearing are reported from time to time in scientific journals and newspapers as though they were strange, misbegotten misfits of the aural world. But it becomes increasingly apparent that many 'strange' acoustic phenomena may not be quite so 'strange' or 'odd' at all. They may simply constitute those rare instances when the vast universe of acoustics which exists beyond our own range of hearing at times overlaps and enters into our perceptible range.

It may be that the interplanetary flux itself is sometimes audible to the listener upon earth, and without any need of a music synthesizer ...

We have seen that astronomical/astrological events do influence earth's magnetic field. What is more, this field in turn has much to do with the production of the Northern Lights, the auroral phenomenon visible from Norway, Canada, and other northern lands. And numerous reports attest that the aurora at times appears along with an audible sound. Since the aurora is related to the supersonically streaming plasma from the sun, it may then be that the aurora is occasionally able to render these solar vibrations at an acoustic frequency suitable for the human ear.

One of the most thorough investigations into the aurora sound was undertaken by the dedicated researcher of the northern spectacle, Sophus Trumholt, and was reported in the *Nature* of 24 September, 1885. Earlier that year he sent out about a thousand questionnaires to all parts of Norway, asking if the recipients had ever heard the aurora sound, and if so, what did it sound like? Of the 144 replies he received, 92 (64 per cent) believed in the sound — 53 (or 36 per cent) because they had personally heard it, and the others because they knew people who had heard it. Of the scores of descriptions of the aurora-sound which Trumholt received, we can list a sampling:

Quiet whizzing, hissing;
Soft crackling, sizzling;

A kind of sound as when you tear silk;
Rush, as from a stream;
Flapping, as a flag before the wind;
Cutting, hissing, as from flames;
Roaring, as from a storm;
Whispering and glistering.

Two things are noticeable from these descriptions. First, their similarity with each other, which suggests that the phenomenon is objective, and not a figment of the imagination. Second, the similarity of these descriptions with the kind of sound that results when electromagnetic waves in space are picked up and converted into sound through a synthesizer! Perhaps in some strange way the aurora makes it possible to hear the eternal whispering and roaring of space. It is not at all impossible for electromagnetism somehow to become naturally converted into audible air vibrations. For example, a number of reported sightings of meteors and meteorites are on record where the observer first had his attention drawn to the spectacle by a rushing or roaring sound from the burning body. Yet meteors are usually seen at such a great distance that it would be impossible for ordinary sound-waves to arrive at the observer's position at the same time as the visible light ... unless the observer were hearing electromagnetic waves which had somehow been translated into air vibrations in his locality.

A lengthy scientific paper by Charles R. Wilson in the *Journal of Geophysical Research* of April 1969 provides support for the idea that the aurora is related to frequencies of sound which man cannot normally hear. Recording and analysing infrasonic waves at College, Alaska, Wilson found their structure to be related to the time and space distribution of the supersonic auroral motions during polar magnetic substorms. Rapid auroral motions accompany the break-up phase of magnetic substorms, and it was then that the infrasonic waves were observed to occur. Wilson was able to verify that auroral electrojets generate the infrasonic shock waves.[99] The aurora, then, seems to be associated with acoustic frequencies within, below and above the range of the human ear.

A planet pervaded by ultrasonic and infrasonic waves, some of them being related to the cycles of the sun and the planets ...

The occasional translation into audibility of acoustic and vibratory events normally beyond the range of human hearing may also be responsible for the large number of other strange sounds in the air which are reported from time to time. Such reports are ignored as yet by most scientists, yet they have been faithfully collected and published for a number of years by writers and journals specializing in strange phenomena. The two most common forms of strange aerial sounds are those known as 'barisal guns' and the 'Big Hum'. The latter of these is a low-pitched, intermittent hum reported by people from many parts of the world. Writing in *Fate*, Lucille C. Hieber has offered her own description of the Hum:

> For about a year and a half I have been hearing a humming of this same nature. While there is a low humming sound connected with it, there also seems to be a more pronounced overtone in the middle range. It is continuous now, and sometimes loud and sometimes faint, but always there.
>
> ... the hum does not seem to be so much something heard as something felt, possibly a form of radar; for one woman stated she hears it even when she closes her ears.[100]

The possibility that the Big Hum might be purely physiological and internal seems discounted due to the fact that it is heard by many people together, and within definite space-time localizations, when for a period of weeks or longer complaints pour in about it to the local authorities. One famous 'outbreak', for instance, was in England in 1960, when the majority of reports came from East Kent. At that time the phenomenon was taken very seriously: it was discussed in Parliament and in military circles. The Ministries of Science, Supply and Aviation, the General Post Office and the Electricity Board all disclaimed responsibility.

Some have thought the Big Hum to be the emission of secret radar bases, but it seems more likely to be related to geophysical or other factors to do with vibrations normally beyond the audible range. (Or somebody somewhere doing a loud OM?!)

The picture we are arriving at is one of a world permeated with sounds and waves of all kinds of different frequencies, and which at times are linked to extra-terrestrial factors. In an early chapter we looked at the various very potent ways in which *audible* sound affects man's mind, body and emotions – and not all of these effects depended upon the sound needing to be consciously heard. What, then, of the effects upon man of infrasonics and ultrasonics, not to mention electromagnetics?

To take infrasonic waves, for instance, these have been found to cause disequilibrium, disorientation, blurring of vision, nausea and lassitude. (Identical symptoms to those which have sometimes been felt by people some minutes before the physical onset of earthquakes.) Researcher R. W. B. Stephens further states that:

> Internal damage may occur due to the fact that infrasonic waves easily penetrate deeply and may induce resonant effects on organs ... Accidents, absenteeism, and other factors indicating degradation of human performance can be correlated with infrasonic waves arriving from storms 200 miles away.[101]

Such statements expand our conception of just what sound is, and what the effects of even inaudible vibrations can add up to. This brings us to two implications. Firstly, that natural wave-forms such as those that might originate from beyond the earth could indeed affect us. These waves would relate at least partially to the ancient conception of the OM, the seven Tones, and astrology. Secondly, since we are apparently so ignorant as yet about the long-term effects on human beings of inaudible *man-made* wave-forms, should we really use them so lightly and frequently, without a great deal more research being undertaken first? As the reader reads this sentence, he is being bombarded by hundreds of different frequencies of radio, and perhaps even radar, waves. Though we cannot hear them, does this really mean that they cannot affect us?

The ancient philosophers had only the live performances of wrong music to contend with. Make of it what we will, but the possibility is there that wrong music, travelling through the air by means of inaudible vibrations, may be as dangerous as audible wrong music. Several modern esoteric authorities have stated just this to be so: that the penetration of the planet and its people by the radio waves themselves from hundred of radio stations broadcasting discordant music is at least as destructive in the long run as the misuse of ordinary sound-waves.

Of course, it is unnecessary to add that as level-headed citizens of the enlightened modern era we must discount such wild ideas. And along with them, therefore, we had better also discount the experiments conducted by A. H. Frey, as reported by Mary and Donald Romig:

> He found that some human subjects exposed to beams of low-power radar sets perceived sensations of sound described as buzzing, clicking, hissing, or knocking, depending on the transmitter characteristics. Care was taken to exclude possible

rectification (by loose tooth fillings and the like) of the pulse-modulated signal. A peak of electromagnetic power density of as low as 400 microwatts per square centimetre at the observer could be perceived as sound ... We shall not discuss here the possible mechanisms for electrophonic hearing, but *perhaps the electromagnetic waves act directly on the brain* [my italics].[102]

Would not such signals also act upon the brains of those who could not hear them? Perhaps it is time for the invention of a portable anti-radio-wave body shield. But in the meantime we are going to have to live with thirty or forty simultaneous transmissions of pop and punk coursing through our blood, bones and brain. Which brings us directly back to the subject of music and its power ...

CONCLUSION

We have seen that wave-forms, whether audible or otherwise, are a far more important phenomenon than is usually recognized. The information we have looked at also strongly suggests the objective reality of the OM, its link with astrology, and its actual ability to affect matter on earth. All this has enormous implications for the musician and music-lover. This very same power of the OM is that which was said to be contained within all audible sound. Chladni plates and tonoscopes demonstrate most graphically the power of music to organize and re-organize substances according to the tones produced. All this leaves us not very far at all from the idea that some music is *objectively* good and some music *objectively* bad or evil. (Once, passing by a crowded dance hall where rock was being played, I could not help perceiving the floor of the hall in terms of a Chladni plate, and the dancers appeared for all the world like the jumping, helplessly manipulated grains of sand.)

Considering that Western man only emerged a few decades ago from the nineteenth-century style 'little granules' or 'tiny coiled springs' theories of the atom, the fact that the earliest recorded civilizations were already aware of the insubstantial, vibratory nature of matter can only leave us awe-struck. Whence came this knowledge? Where, and how long ago did it first arise?

Whatever the answer, that the ancients possessed such knowledge makes one thing clear: that it would be most unwise for us to dismiss other aspects of the ancient wisdom such as those appertaining to the inner power of music. It might be said that our current understanding of the real nature and ability of sound is as yet in the same kindergarten stage as was the physics of the nineteenth century. Who can say what scientific discoveries are yet to come?

Modern man needs to treat music with a greater respect. Music is vibration, and vibration is the energy of the Supreme. Like nuclear energy, which can be used to destroy an entire city, or to furnish all the energy requirements of that same city, music too is a neutral force — and its ultimate effects, for good or evil, may not be at all dissimilar in their potency to those of nuclear energy. Only man can decide how music is to be used; and thus, perhaps, decide also what his own fate is to be. As we treat the energy of the atom, with great care and caution, so too do we need to handle music. In the final analysis, we should strive to realize more fully, it seems, that when we deal with sound we are dealing not merely with the energies of science, nor only with the art of mortal minds, but with God.

> *My soul counselled me and charged me to listen for voices that rise neither from the tongue nor the throat.*
> *Before that day I heard but dully, and nought save clamour and loud cries came to my ears;*
> *But now I have learned to listen to silence,*
> *To hear its choirs singing the song of ages,*
> *Chanting the hymns of space, and disclosing the secrets of eternity.*

— Kahlil Gibran

Notes

*It was the particular hallmark of the god, Marduk's, power that he could cause objects to vanish and to be created by his words. This power the other gods asked him to demonstrate as they spread out a garment in front of him. Then, 'As Marduk uttered the word, the garment disappeared; and again he spoke, and, behold, the garment was there.'

Appendix to
6.
The Mystery of Pythagoras' Comma

One of the greatest of the mysteries of the science of sound is the strange phenomenon known as Pythagoras' comma, which since time immemorial has been to man a symbol of his fallen state of imperfection.

Given that different pitches of tone arrange themselves into octaves (which have the ratio of 2:1), man from the earliest times needed to find a method whereby the notes *within* each octave could be calculated. This could be done, it was discovered, by using the next most fundamental and harmonious tonal ratio, that of 3:2, or the interval known in music as a pure fifth. If one pictures the octave as a circle, then the interval of a fifth represents a seven-twelfths circuit of the circle, from 12 o'clock, moving clockwise, to 7 o'clock. This gives one pitch. By continuing around clockwise again, another pitch is produced, but not at 2 o'clock on the same circle, for the 'circle' is actually not a circle at all, but a section of a spiral which spirals upward into higher octaves. By going around clockwise in a series of perfect fifths, a series of twelve notes can be produced, related by the vibratory ratios of the series 1, 3:2, $(3:2)^2$, and so on to $(3:2)^{11}$. Try this out for yourself: by advancing twelve times around a clock face in jumps of seven hours at a time, you will end up back at 12 o'clock, having landed once on each hour.

However, these twelve notes could not practically be used as the scale of a system of music, since they extend over several octaves with wide gaps in between each note. Therefore the ancient philosopher-musicians devised schemes whereby intervals of a fifth could be used to calculate twelve notes within only one octave. For instance, the Chinese went up in pitch by the ratio of 1:3, then down by 3:1, up by 1:3, and so one. Such a practice was capable of producing twelve approximate notes all within one octave, as shown in Figure 4.[6]

Figure 4

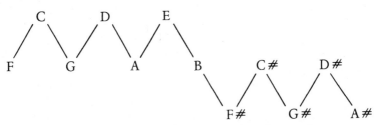

However, given these twelve notes, if a thirteenth note was attempted, in order to complete the octave with a series of twelve intervals of a fifth, it was found that *the octave could not be perfectly completed!* This is a universal law of the physics of tone and, indeed, of mathematics: a cycle of twelve fifths completes seven octaves (note the mystical numbers: twelve and seven) *plus* a little more. Expressed mathematically: $(3:2)^{12} > (2:1)^7$ by a slight excess interval. This interval, since Pythagoras was one who noted it, has become known as Pythagoras' comma. The difference is a ratio of about 80:81, the extra 1 being the comma.

The comma produces huge cosmological, as well as practical, implications and results. Since this system of calculating twelve notes does not perfectly complete the octave, the specific twelve pitches it produces are imperfect for use together in harmony. They do not perfectly harmonize since they do not divide the octave into perfectly accurate divisions of twelve as, say, the hours of a clock do perfectly divide a clock face. Yet to adjust their slight pitch-discrepancies in order to produce perfect harmony would render each note imperfect as an interval of a fifth, or as a ratio of 3:2. The perfecting of their musical system was paramount to the ancients, for their music had to harmonize with the eternal laws of the universe. Therefore the perfect ratio of 3:2 and its interval of a perfect fifth were regarded as sacred and inviolable. If the system resulted, as it did, in the harmony of mortal music being imperfect, then this had to be borne as a manifest symbol of man's fall from grace, and of the inherent imperfection of the non-heavenly realm of time and space. Indeed, perhaps the ancients were correct in this, for the comma is a strange and wide-ranging phenomenon, being literally 'written into' the physical and mathematical laws of the universe. We are entering here into regions of thought difficult for the Western mind to grasp, but the possibility seems to be that it is by the phenomenon of Pythagoras' comma that the very nature of our lives within the realm of mortality is arranged.

Though the comma may be a symbol of the imperfection of man's mortal state, the very same comma simultaneously provides the way back to the original state of perfection. For the comma is not a slight interval *less* than seven octaves, but *in excess* of them. In the ancient world this fact was widely conceived as a symbol of *renewal*. The cycle of twelve perfect fifths did not *close* and finish a cycle of seven octaves, but exceeded it, and thus, as it were, spiralled *upward*. There is evidence that this upward spiral of renewal was mystically associated with the widespread ancient myth of the phoenix, the archetypal 'bird' which is resurrected from its own ashes. Pythagoras' comma, then, can be seen as being God's own engram written into the very laws of the universe and of physics. And it is by the nature of this engram that man is heir to the promise of eventual resurrection and ascension out of the dim caverns of mortality.

Through the ages civilizations have often wrestled with the dilemma of whether to put up with imperfect musical pitches while retaining pure idealism in their system of pitch-calculation, or else to depart a little from alignment with the heavenly ideal by taking the practical path of slightly adjusting their notes in order to harmonize them. Though there were individual figures who dissented, the ancient cultures generally opted, in their idealism, for heavenly alignment at the expense of having slightly imperfect relationships between their notes. However, by the seventeenth century AD the Western world had begun its entry into the present era of science and logic. This era was marked not only by an attitude of over-materialism, but also by a most useful pragmatism. This pragmatism entered into the debate on tuning, and the controversy heightened: should man opt for heavenly perfection and musical inharmony, or for a departure from abstract idealism for the sake of expanding music's harmonic possibilities? (Also, on the very down-to-earth level, the construction of instruments such as keyboards according to the precepts of idealism was proving insuperably problematic in some aspects: a great many more keys were necessary in order to incorporate the many 'extra' notes created by a cycle of perfect fifths.)

The idea of man's imperfect state being related to a tonal misalignment with the Above was widespread in the poetry of the seventeenth century. Clement Paman wrote:

> Screw thee high My heart: up to The Angels' key.
> What if thy strings all crack and flye?
> On such a Ground, Musick 'twill be to dy.[103]

George Herbert actually went so far as to associate man's tonal imperfection with the Crucifixion:

The Cross taught all wood to resound his Name,
    Who bore the same.
His stretched Sinews taught all strings, what key
Is best to celebrate this most high Day.
Consort both heart and lute, and twist a song
    Pleasant and long:
Or, since all musick is but three parts vied
    And multiplied,
O let Thy blessed Spirit bear a part
And make up our defects with His sweet Art.[103]

J. S. Bach became the first major musician to depart from the idealism of tradition, opting for the pragmatic approach of equal temperament, or octaves divided into twelve 'equal' divisions. This opened up vast new avenues of harmonic possibility, and led the way into the towering musical developments of the eighteenth and nineteenth centuries. The intensely religious Bach was as good as saying, 'Well, since we do find ourselves in this fallen state of mortal imperfection, we had better be practical about it, harmonize our music, and by this very process begin composing a new and better art form. An art of enhanced sublimity can in itself lead us back to the heavens.'

This, in essence, is a summary of man's relationship and dealings with the phenomenon of Pythagoras' comma. But it is not the end of the entire story, for the heavenly bodies themselves have a final tale to add.

We have noted a number of times that the months of the year were associated in antiquity with the total twelve notes of the musical octave. But there are, of course, two slightly different kinds of months: the solar or calendar month which averages 30.44 days, making a total of 365.256 days per year, and the synodic lunar month of 29.5306 days. The solar month is exactly one twelfth of the time it takes for the earth to orbit once around the sun. The synodic lunar month is the time which the moon takes to pass through all of its phases — say, from new moon to new moon. Though the lunar month is not exactly the same as a solar month, it comes remarkably close, with the curious result that there are approximately twelve lunar months (yes, that number twelve again!) per calendar year. Indeed, since solar months offer less obvious signs of their coming and going than do those of the moon, it has frequently been by the phases of the moon that cultures have measured the passing of time.

The reader will probably not have missed the noteworthy fact that this phenomenon of two different divisions of the year into two slightly different lengths of months strikes a very close parallel with Pythagoras' comma, with its two slightly different sets of twelve notes around the circle of an octave. That the parallel may be more than academic is suggested by the fact that according to the ancient wisdom the year *does* represent the passage of the earth through an octave of twelve notes, or Cosmic Tones. Taking the parallel to its logical conclusion, the solar year, which totals the exact and accurate length of 365.256 days, equates with a cosmic form of equal temperament: by measuring time by the solar year rather than by the lunar year, man not only displays an obvious practicality, but also opens for himself the possibility of renewal and self-evolution.

The two ratios — between the two years (solar and lunar) and the two types of musical scale (of perfect fifths and of equal temperament) — are astonishingly close to each other. The ratio of Pythagoras' comma is 531441 to 524288, the former figure being larger than the latter by the factor of 1.01364. The ratio between the two years is 365.256 days to 354.3672, the former being the larger by a factor of 1.03073. To express the closeness of the two ratios in a more graphic way, we can translate the ratio of the comma into calendar terms. That is, 531441 is to the solar year of 365.256 days as 524288 is to the time period of 360.340 days — which is only six days out from the precise lunar year of $354\frac{1}{3}$ days.

As might be expected, the cultures of antiquity seem not to have missed this phenomenon of a 'cosmic comma'. Traditionally, the measurement of the year by means of solar months was considered holy and righteous; whereas to keep time by the moon was both incorrect and evil. This was one of the chief differences of opinion between the Pharisees and the Sadducees. Whereas the Sadducees marked time by the *sun*, the Pharisees marked time by the *lunar* year. Interestingly, however, this lunar year was not stated as being $354\frac{1}{3}$ days long, which it is, and which the Pharisees must easily have been able to observe that it was. Rather, it was dogmatically stated to be *360* days in length. This figure was a direct but coded reference to the cosmic Pythagoras' comma since, as we have calculated above, 360 is the nearest whole number of days to what an absolutely perfect incidence of the comma would turn out to be, at 360.340 days.

The cosmological and moral significance of the two different years is an important theme in the famous apocalyptic text, *The Book of Enoch*. Certain sections of *Enoch*, and especially chapters LXXII to LXXXII, sometimes called *The Book of the Courses of Heavenly Luminaries*, take this as their central subject. In fact, though establishment scholars have called this particular section 'uninteresting in the extreme',[104] they have missed the point that it is actually, along with the following sections, a mystical text on the subject of *astrology* (which is taught to Enoch, according to the book, by the heavenly being Uriel). In *Enoch* LXXXII we are informed that the reason for it being evil and dangerous to reckon time by the moon is that due to the moon's inaccuracy the entire civilization would become out of alignment with the cycles and seasons of the heavens. Verses 4 and 5 read:

> Blessed are the righteous, blessed are all those who walk in the way of righteousness and sin not as the sinners in the reckoning of all their days in which the sun traverses the heaven ... Owing to them men shall be at fault and not reckon them in the whole reckoning of the year: yea, men shall be at fault, and not recognize them accurately.[105]

Running right through the astrological sections of *Enoch* one finds the widespread concept in antiquity that the sun embodied righteousness and perfection, whereas the moon represented mortality and error. The author of the work sought to ensure that his readers would align themselves to the cycles of the sun. But this alignment had both an outer, astronomical, and an inner, spiritual character. The exhortation for man to follow the solar year was imbued with deeper implications of heavenly attunement and spiritual renewal. And the very name, Enoch, became associated with these implications, as is evident from Genesis 5:23-4, in which we are allegorically told: 'And all the days of Enoch were three hundred and sixty and five years [i.e. the number of whole days in the solar year]: and Enoch walked with God: and he was not; for God took him.' That is, by attuning himself spiritually to the cycles and vibrations of the sun, and to the God behind the manifested sun, Enoch is said to have ascended into immortality. The number 365 is therefore an esoteric reference to the fact that by 'walking with (being close in consciousness to) God', any man can 'be not' (being no longer found in time and space), for God will take him (in the process and ritual of the ascension).

Pythagoras' comma is an eternal reminder to us of the ancient mystical concept that there exist two fundamental states or frequencies of being: the dense and physical state of mortality, and the state of immortality as attained by Enoch, Jesus Christ, and other great masters of East and West. And that it is the goal and destiny of all men to so purify and perfect themselves that they can be translated from the lower state to the higher. If the Word was made flesh in one man, the Word can be made flesh in all.

Coda:
The Ancient Wisdom Revisited:
The Modern Esoteric Viewpoint

'Oh, please, Master, will you tell us all about the Rays?'

An ironically naive question if ever there was one! Yet the Master smiled benevolently at the chela (disciple), only a humorous twinkle of the eye betraying his inner reflections.

'Well, I cannot tell you *all* about them,' he carefully replied, 'until you have reached a very high Initiation. Will you have what I *can* tell you, which will be partial and inevitably misleading, or will you wait until you can be told the whole thing?'[106]

THE GNOSIS RETURNS

The chela and his two companions decided that anything would be preferable to nothing, and so the Master proceeded to talk for some time upon the subject of the seven rays. The chelas, taking notes as the Master spoke, understood portions of his information but, as he had foretold, found much of it incomprehensible. However, the Master's discourse marked only the beginning of what was to come. Thereafter, stage by stage, an abundant wealth of fascinating data was released to mankind on the subject of the seven major rays or Tones. Much was to be told about the individual nature of the rays, their relationship to each other, and, above all, how they each influence the material, psychological and spiritual patterns of life upon earth.

Yet the above conversation did not take place in ancient India, nor in the China or Egypt of the long-passed golden ages of those lands. The talk is recorded by Charles W. Leadbeater, who was present, to have taken place in the late nineteenth century. The chela who asked the question was the author, Mr Cooper-Oakley, and the Master was Djwal Kul, one of the brotherhood of Adepts known as the Great White Brotherhood. The incident took place in India during the early days of the Theosophical Society.[106]

The fact is that the wilder excesses of gross materialism in science, and in the general outlook of Western man, in many ways peaked around the late 1800s, and have since been steadily on the wane. True, present Western civilization can hardly be said to display the same extent of a mystical outlook as prevailed in antiquity. Yet there is present in the West today what is almost a hidden force at work; an underground network of individuals who cannot ever be specifically pinned down, defined or counted, since there is as yet no one organization – no esoteric *Solidarność* – to which they belong.

Meditation, astrology, human aura studies, reincarnation, acupuncture – one could compile a lengthy list of such subjects which are now captivating a considerable interest in a large minority of people. The gnosis is returning. Clothed in somewhat different raiment perhaps, and with more of an emphasis upon scientific documentation, but what is essentially the same system of beliefs as that of the ancient wisdom is again finding quite a number of adherents. And this time it has more than ever to tell us about the power of sound.

Esotericism in the form of myths and religious texts can be read and spoken about fairly comfortably by all – it is sufficiently removed in time so as not to disturb us and force us to think. But when we find that same esotericism confronting us, with all of its claims, face-to-face in our own time, we have then the inevitable dividing of the way between the acceptors and the sceptics.

How objective and valid *are* the tenets of modern esotericism? It would not be possible in this book to debate the question at sufficient length as would have worth. I would simply say, on the personal level, that a number of experiences in life have taught me, for one, that no truer statement was ever uttered than that *truth is stranger than fiction.* At times science fiction and even the most fanciful of fantasies have absolutely paled, appearing inexpressibly unimaginative, in comparison with some of the secrets which reality has elected to offer glimpses of. This being said, it must be left to the reader to make up his own mind as we now discuss some of the things which modern esotericists have to tell us about the inner powers of sound.

Since the conversation between Cooper-Oakley, Leadbeater and Djwal Kul on the roof of the Theosophical Society's headquarters, the great brotherhood of Adepts to which Djwal Kul belonged has given out more information on the seven frequencies of the Word known as the seven rays. From this information, it is possible to construct a table to show the main attributes of each of the rays. Table 4 shows which chakra, colour, God-qualities and perversions of the God-qualities relate to each ray. Not only music, of course, but all the activities of life – every thought, word and deed – amplify one or more of the seven rays or their perversions. Nevertheless, the use of tone is a major means by which the seven rays or their perversions become amplified. The column indicating the God-qualities shows which psychological and spiritual qualities are expanded throughout self and society wherever beautiful and harmonious music is played. Wrong music amplifies within the performer, the audience, and the community at large the various listed perversions of the rays. From this table there may be gained an understanding of many of society's present ills, as well as the understanding of how these ills may be dissolved by the promulgation of correct music such as Eastern and Western classical music. Looking at the table, I am struck by how *immediately* and *noticeably* these traits appear in people whenever music is played, good or bad.

MUSICIANS REDISCOVER THE INNER WORLDS

As the gnosis has gradually re-emerged in recent decades, composers have lost no time in incorporating its precepts once more into their art. Or then again, did they ever fail to do so? From the very beginnings of the Western classical tradition and throughout its history, strong elements of mysticism have been incorporated into numerous musical pieces. As we noted in an early chapter, many of the works of J. S. Bach, Beethoven and other great composers are deeply mystical. Yet this kind of mysticism is of a general nature. The spiritual outlook of these great men, having come naturally to them, was not for the most part related to any particular esoteric school. (The obvious exception to this being Mozart, who to a large extent based his operas and his instrumental works upon the metaphysical and numerological principles of Freemasonry.)

From the late 1800s, however, and particularly within our own century, the stream of serious composers of music has been connected to a background of esotericism to a degree rarely realized even by most musicologists. *This esoteric background can be seen in retrospect to have been the prime factor behind the composers' choices of style and subject matter.*

One might ask, how did there come to be this marked association of recent composers with the esoteric? Perhaps the musical mind finds itself being directed naturally by music into the realms of mysticism and metaphysics. Or is it, on the other hand, that the

Table 4: The Seven Rays

Ray no.	Chakra or centre which sustains the frequency of the ray in the anatomy of man	Corresponding colour	God-qualities of the ray	Perversions of the God-qualities of the ray	Chohan or Lord focusing the Christ-consciousness of the ray at this time; location of their retreats*
1	Throat	Blue	DIVINE WILL: Omnipotence, perfection, protection, faith	Human will, absence of energy, imperfection, state of unprotection, doubt	El Morya: Darjeeling, India
2	Crown	Yellow	DIVINE WISDOM: Omniscience, illumination, understanding, discrimination	Human folly, human logic, witchcraft, lack of comprehension, narrow-mindedness	Lanto: Grand Teton, Teton Range, Wyoming, USA
3	Heart	Pink	DIVINE LOVE: Omnipresence, compassion, charity, creativity	Human love, selfishness, human sympathy, sensuality, disunity	Paul the Venetian: Southern France
4	Base of spine	White	DIVINE PURITY: Wholeness, self-discipline, morality, spiritual bliss	Impurity, lack of self-control, immorality, lust, loneliness	Serapis Bey: Luxor, Egypt

5	Third eye	Green	DIVINE SCIENCE: Truth, healing, divine vision, abundance	Superstition, error, disease, absence of manifest works, lack ???	Hilarion: Crete, Greece
6	Solar plexus	Purple and Gold	DIVINE PEACE: Ministration, service, desirelessness, harmlessness	Emotional turbulence, egocentricity, social cliques, gangs, war, free love, disruption of family and community life	Nada: Saudi Arabia
7	Seat of the soul	Violet	DIVINE FREEDOM: Ritual, transmutation, justice, mercy	Servitude, rote, disorderliness, dogma, injustice, hardness of heart	Saint Germain: Transylvania, Romania, and Table Mountain in Teton Range, Wyoming, USA

*The positions or offices of the rays are positions in the hierarchy of the Great White Brotherhood which have existed since time immemorial. The names of some of the great souls whose attainment has qualified them to embody these positions at this time are well known to students of the Mysteries. The retreats of the seven Chohans are largely focused on the etheric plane of being, but they also include concealed physical aspects. It is the responsibility and sacred calling of the Chohans to oversee and direct the activities occurring on each ray at all levels of being throughout the planetary body.

Table compiled from information in *Climb the Highest Mountain* Book 1.[109]

mystical mind turns naturally to the art of music? Whatever the answer, there is no doubt that music and mysticism go together like the proverbial horse and carriage. Each of the two fields of endeavour illumine and add to one's strivings and attainments with the other. The sage of old would have said that the two are so closely connected because mysticism *is* music, and music *is* mysticism.

The conscious use of esoteric principles in music can be traced back even to the period before and during the Middle Ages when the original ancient wisdom teachings disappeared from public view. Peter Hamel states: 'A tradition of musical esotericism, manifesting through Rosicrucian and other cabbalistic, Pythagorean and alchemistic groups, runs right through the Middle Ages and up to our own times.'[70]

The modern phase of musical esotericism has been one of mixed blessings, however. Though many major composers have worked from an esoteric background, by no means all of them were the purified chalices into which the perfect *Logos* could be poured, as demanded of all musicians by the ancient philosophers. Sometimes their motives and characters were impure; at other times the esoteric teachings which they tapped were themselves faulty, or else were imperfectly understood. Alexander Scriabin (1872-1915), after early years as an admirer and follower of the works of Chopin, elected to delve so deeply into metaphysical musical systems that, in the view of many commentators, his actual music became as much hindered as helped. Scriabin's aim was to translate 'the essence of soul and spirit' into musical notation, to which end he utilized a complex theoretical background of Theosophy and colour-tone correspondences. However, the end result is well-described by his follower, Sayaneyev, as 'the ecstasy of hyper-aesthetic emotions, of nameless nightmares, of love and suffering'. The chief characteristics of his style were often those of morbidity and sorrow; and whether these are truly 'the essence of soul and spirit' is open to question. In England at around the same time, several lesser composers also based their style upon a system of what they believed to be the accurate correspondences between musical notes and visual colours. The resultant music was not, however, highly memorable.

Some of the more successful esoterically-inclined composers were briefly discussed in Chapter 2: Debussy and his leadership of the weird secret group, the Priory of Sion, as well as his fascination with the occult works of Edgar Allen Poe; Maurice Ravel, who was intrigued by many aspects of occultism. Another prominent figure,

Erik Satie, was a member of the French Rosicrucian Order. Arnold Schoenberg delved deeply into the Old Testament and into the spiritist teachings of Swedenborg. What influence this had upon his development of the revolutionary technique of serialism we can only conjecture, but it must have been considerable. It is an almost universal feature of students of the esoteric, and understandably so, that their studies assume prime importance over almost anything else in their life, and certainly in their inner life of intuition and intellect. (The standard kind of biography which is written about composers, as well as other great figures such as politicians, writers and scientists, continually neglects to note this vital factor. Whenever the record shows that a musician studied esoteric matters (and sometimes when the record does not show it!) we can in fact be sure that these studies were of at least equal importance to him as his music. And therefore esotericism will have lent itself greatly to the shaping of his personality and his artistic style.)

Following in the footsteps of Schoenberg, the other serialists were also esotericists. Webern studied, among other things, cabbalistic numerology. Josef Hauer (1883-1959) was a Rosicrucian initiate who saw each note of the scale as having its own particular spiritual effect, and thus devised his note-series in order to group these effects into particular sequences. Other well-known musicians have also reflected various esoteric doctrines or aspects of occultism in their works, among these being Olivier Messiaen and Carl Orff, and even, in certain pieces, Sergei Prokofiev and Paul Hindemith.[70] As for the contemporary avant-garde, they draw more than ever upon esotericism as the foundation for their works, though their own particular brand of 'esotericism' has little in common with the genuine article. The output of John Cage is very largely oriented around his beat-Zen philosophies (evolved after attending the lectures of the Zen Master, D. T. Suzuki, for several months during the 1940s). The most recent major work by Karlheinz Stockhausen, entitled *Sirius,* was released in an LP format (with a cover very much of the rock music style) accompanied by page after page of metaphysical gibberish written by the composer, attesting to how his latest production reflects the Music of the Spheres and the sacred tones released by the astronomical body of the title.

These many distortions of the genuine principles of esotercism are most unfortunate for, as Mozart, Beethoven and others have demonstrated, metaphysics and mysticism are capable of providing a tremendous fount of creativity. But this is true only for those who are humbly willing to adjust and shape *themselves* into conformity *to the esoteric principles.* The opposite results when there is an absence of humility and listening grace: the result being that the composer seeks *to shape and adapt the timeless truths of the Spirit to his own will.* In the purer of these two paths Gustav Holst, for one, possessed the humility to succeed excellently. His deep studies of astrology resulted in his popular and timeless *The Planets* Suite, while his knowledge of Sanskrit and of Christian Gnosticism likewise resulted in highly original and accomplished spiritual works.

In the United States a quite unique composer, Norman Thomas Miller, has brought forth several tone poems which truly deserve to be called New Age music. Working from a background of the teachings of the Great White Brotherhood, N. T. Miller has evolved a style which, while in many ways being entirely novel, also seeks to return the tonal arts to the traditional principles of aesthetics. His music deliberately avoids the trap of over-intellectualism, and can be understood and enjoyed by any spiritually-minded person. It is tonal except where dramatic development specifically requires a deliberate discord. N. T. Miller's most important work to date is *The Call of Camelot*,[108] a thirty minute tone poem of unique and scorching spirituality. Miller is actually an accomplished multi-media artist, being not only a musician, but also a painter, poet, photographer and art director. Yet in *The Call of Camelot* he seems somehow to have combined all of these talents into the medium of music, for there could hardly be a composition more picturesque — and even photographic — in the clarity of the visions which it offers to the attuned listener. The Call of Camelot is the voice of the indwelling God, the inner Grail — calling us to be all that we truly are, all that God is. The work utilizes an orchestra, other more subtle instruments and sound-effects, and indescribably moving vocals to transport the listener — with Merlin through an enchanted forest; riding with Arthur into the thick of an archetypal spiritual-physical battle; in procession by twilight to a torchlit cathedral. Besides being deeply mystical, Miller's work also constitutes a most potent call to action. If this is the spiritual direction of the music of the future, then the years ahead hold much of promise in store for us. Including lyrics by none other than El Morya, the famous Adept and Chohan of the Great White Brotherhood (adapted from his writings), the work peaks musically and spiritually with a transcendent vocal meditation, 'The Revelation of the Holy Grail'.

CYRIL SCOTT, 'THE FATHER OF BRITISH MODERN MUSIC'

Cyril Scott, whose writings we have had occasion to quote from several times in earlier pages, was another multi-talented composer who may have drawn his inspiration from the great body of Adepts known as the Great White Brotherhood. Certainly Scott himself believed that he did. His 1933 publication, *The Influence of Music on History and Morals*,[109] was an important and pioneering venture in its study of the inner power of music and was one of the first books in modern times to renew people's thinking and awareness on the subject. Yet what is perhaps even more fascinating than the book itself is the background and life out of which it was written. For the life-story of Cyril Scott serves well to show us just to what great a degree esoteric sources have influenced the art and artists of our day.

Cyril Scott was born at Oxton in Cheshire on 27 September, 1879. We are told that by the age of two and a half he was able to pick up tunes by ear and perform them on piano, and could also improvise. Not, however, until he arrived at the ripe old age of seven did he receive instruction in how to read and write musical notation. Perhaps not surprisingly, by the time he had matured Scott had developed into a virtuoso pianist. A. Eaglefield Hull, the musicologist and general editor of the Waverley Music Lover's Library, once wrote of him:

> Last night I was spellbound at the nonchalant ease with which he played through his superb *Piano Concerto* from the full score MS., rippling along (as I flung the pages over almost continuously) with truly astonishing gifts of technique, touch and reading; whistling the while flute and violin melodies, and vocalizing horn parts in a peculiar nasal tone, like horn notes forced through mutes. Where and how did he attain such tremendous powers?[110]

More than for his playing, however, it was as a composer that Cyril Scott gained a wide reputation in Great Britain and on the Continent during the early twentieth century. His works included symphonies and other orchestral pieces, choral compositions, a number of pieces of chamber music, and a very large number of songs and works for solo piano. Strangely though, his music is little known today – strangely so, since during his day he was mentioned in the same breath as artists such as Vaughan Williams, Arnold Bax, Percy Grainger and Claude Debussy. A. Eaglefield Hull said

around 1920 that Cyril Scott was, 'undoubtedly the richest har-
monist we [the British] possess'.[110] In Debussy's estimate, Scott
was, 'one of the rarest artists of the present generation'.

Besides possessing the aforementioned talents, Cyril Scott was also
an accomplished conductor, a lecturer, a translator, and a writer on
music. In addition to this, at the age of 21 he began writing verse,
and became well known thereafter as a poet. His first published
collection of verse, *The Shadows of Silence and the Songs of Yesterday*,[111] came out during his early twenties, and reflected what was
then his rather pessimistic outlook of agnosticism. The second, *The
Grave of Eros and the Book of Mournful Melodies*,[112] was written
during what he later called, not altogether seriously, his 'decadent'
phase. However, he went through this phase only half-heartedly,
and without conviction. This phase was to end abruptly upon his
discovery of Theosophy and Indian philosophy. Indeed, it would be
difficult to conceive of a more graphic example than the life of Cyril
Scott following his finding of the ancient wisdom in order to
demonstrate the close relationship that has often prevailed in
modern times between esotericism and music.

According to Scott himself, he was eventually contacted directly
by the Great White Brotherhood, and intimately sponsored and
guided by them in the production of much of his mature musical and
literary works. Already hailed by Eugene Goosens as the 'father of
British modern music', Scott now turned also to the writing of
books; books on esotericism and alternative medicine. He was, too,
the author of the series of three 'Initiate' books, which are still very
well-known among esoteric circles. These were penned anonymously by Scott, using autobiographical material given to him by an
unnamed poet. The first of the three, *The Initiate, Some Impressions
of a Great Soul*[113], describes the poet's encounters in England
with a high initiate of the Brotherhood who accepted the poet as his
disciple. The second book, *The Initiate in the New World*[114],
follows the spiritual career and teachings of the initiate in the
United States, and in the third volume this initiate of the Great
White Brotherhood again returns to the British Isles, after many
years of absence.

Some have doubted the veracity of these three immensely
readable and steadily popular books, considering them to be fiction.
But certainly Scott himself maintained that the books are factual
accounts of episodes in the life and teachings of the great soul about
whom they were written. Before continuing, what attitude should
we take in regard to Scott's belief that he received direct contacts

from the Great White Brotherhood? Though the original material
upon which the 'Initiate' books were based was not Scott's, nevertheless he revealed later in life, when the anonymity of the books
had been seen through, that he too had been a disciple of the
initiate; indeed, that he was also a protagonist in the second and
third books. And, he said, after the events described in the books he
still continued to receive contacts from Masters of the Brotherhood.
Did it, then, all happen just as Scott said that it did?

Ultimately, each of us must decide for ourselves on that point. It
does seem impossible to believe that Scott would have been
deliberately untruthful: throughout his life, his absolute sincerity and
needle-sharp sanity were plainly evident. It is on the question of
whether or not he was ever misled that we must at this point
suspend judgement either way. On the one hand, it is not unknown
for individuals who have received *some* contact from the Masters to
later get carried away or misled by others into believing that these
contacts are continuing when they are not. Yet on the other hand,
there is no doubt but that at least some of Cyril Scott's beliefs were
founded on solid ground. (And I do not say that they all were not.)
For example, several of the disguised characters portrayed within
the 'Initiate' books now stand revealed, and all recounted by Scott
concerning them has proved genuine. 'David Anrias', for one, an
astrologer and Theosophist in the books, was Brian Ross, who at
one time worked for Annie Besant in India during her time as Presi-
dent of the Theosophical Society.

But to return to Scott's experiences themselves. The initiate,
according to Scott's account, was as impressive an individual as one
could imagine. Even as Voltaire described Saint Germain, the
'wonderman of Europe', the initiate of Scott's books also seemed
to be 'a man who never dies, and who knows everything'. Though
he rarely demonstrated them, his spiritual powers by which he could
influence the material world around himself are said to have been
quite superhuman.

But the most important aspect of the Initiate books from the
point of view of our present line of investigation is that in the States
this individual – called Justin Moreward Haig, or "JMH", in the
books – was conducting regular meetings of his chelas, many of
whom were prominent people in their various lines of work, *and
who included among their ranks, musicians, poets, artists and writers.*
The point being that most among mankind are unable or unwilling
to accept the reality and existence of the Brotherhood, and are in
any case not infrequently incapable of absorbing the Masters' pure

teachings in the form that they are given out. Therefore, besides the giving forth of their pure and undiluted words, the Masters have often taken the course of training disciples to step-down their message and vibration. In the broadest sense, this is literally a stage in the stepping-down of the frequencies of the Word. The disciples then promulgate through their line of service the principles of ethics, morality and spirituality, as well as any more specific concepts which the times might demand for the betterment of the race. But they do so without usually ever revealing the Source of their initial inspiration. In this way, many chelas of the Brotherhood have worked throughout history – in the arts, the sciences, and also as politicians and as the great, moral leaders of men. Many a famous and important episode of history – such as the American Revolution, which we discussed earlier, to name but one – has an entirely different and unrevealed story behind it if the truth were but known: the story of the causes behind the effects; the story of the Adepts of the Great White Brotherhood and those historical figures who were, unbeknownst to the world, their chelas. This has a most important bearing upon our study of the secret power of music. For the story of the great music of ancient times, and also that of the Western classical tradition – of what actually inspired it and of where much of it really came from – *is one which goes completely unsuspected by all but the few.*

And yet, a hint of this story of the ages can perhaps be gathered from the life and writings of Cyril Scott.

Following his encounter with esotericism, Scott was never the same person again. Oriental philosophy, Theosophy and the practice of yoga and meditation became his absorbing interest in life. Immediately, from this moment on, succeeding compositions entered into the realms of mysticism and Orientalism. From his pen there now came musical works such as the Hindu-style *Jungle Book,* the darkly magical *Sphinx, Lotus-land,* the *Chinese Songs,* and many more. His third volume of verse, *The Voice of the Ancient,*[117] displayed a radical change in subject matter and emotional effect, as did succeeding volumes. Scott's *raison d'être* as an artist in any medium was now absolutely goal-oriented towards the highest purpose and aim in life – the spiritual path.

Where would Scott have taken his stand in relation to the subjects we have discussed in this book, about the use and misuse of the power of music? With regard to the artistic directions of the fellow-composers of his generation, Scott made his position quite clear. In a hard-hitting but well-argued criticism of the avant-garde,

The Philosophy of Modernism in its Connection with Music,[115] Cyril Scott compared the Modernists to a man who sets out on a walking tour with the intention of never, under any circumstances, setting foot upon an established road. In keeping to such a rigid doctrine, the Modernist thereby finds not freedom, but the ultimate bondage, since he is not free to retain those well-tried and proved principles which are the very foundation of beauty and sublimity in music. (The Modernists Scott often, in fact, preferred to call 'Monsterists'!) True freedom, Cyril Scott argued, lies with the composer of the Romantic class, who is able to keep to the established paths, or not, as he chooses.

Now it is evident from the second Initiate book that 'JMH''s circle of chelas included literary and other artists of world repute. The individual who supplied his own autobiographical material to Scott as a foundation for the books, is himself described as both a poet and a composer. (In the books this is the first-person narrator, disguised under the name of 'Charles Broadbent'.) Then, at least two other composers are referred to, one of whom we now know to have been Cyril Scott. This fact, that Scott himself was one of the circle of chelas in America for a time, is confirmed in an addendum on the subject of the Initiate books which is to be found in the 1935 edition of Scott's *An Outline of Modern Occultism*. It seems that Scott must have been the individual referred to as 'Lyall Herbert', since this is the only composer who turns up in both the second and the third Initiate chronicles; and according to Scott's own addendum referred to above, he himself does appear in these volumes.

The various artist-chelas of 'JMH' are said to have been under the guidance of the Brotherhood of Adepts of East and West, the role of the composers being to bring forth a God-aligned music for the furthering of the evolution of the race. It can be seen therefore, should we choose to accept the account, just how direct an influence on the music of the world the secret guiding hand of the Brotherhood can prove to be.

As for the individual named in the books as 'Lyall Herbert', probably identifiable as Scott himself, it is worth noting that at one point during the final volume, *The Initiate in the Dark Cycle,*[116] a Master says to him: 'And you, you will write a new kind of music – as well as a book on the subject – for which you will receive special preparatory training at a Master's hands.' This calls to remembrance Scott's path-breaking book, *Music, Its Secret Influences Throughout the Ages.*[5]

Yet regardless of who 'Lyall Herbert' really was, there is one
passage involving him which never ceases to fascinate. For at one
stage this well-known English composer is taken, as is 'Charles
Broadbent' the poet, to the abode of a Master in the English countryside. (And we should note that in his addendum Cyril Scott,
writing *as* Cyril Scott, refers to this Master and his estate in the
South West of England in such a way as to indicate first-hand
knowledge.) Here, 'Herbert' and 'Broadbent' are specially
prepared to clairaudiently hear a celestial music from superphysical
realms of existence. And then:

> From far away I heard the strains of an organ with which was
> mingled the sound of voices so pure and ethereal as to suggest
> the chanting of a celestial choir, wafted on a peaceful evening
> breeze. The music was unlike any music I had heard before; it
> was subtle, yet melodious, sweet, yet devoid of all sentimental
> lusciousness; at one moment powerful and awe-awakening, at
> another soft and tender as the caress of an angel's hand.
>
> 'My Brother Koot Hoomi playing on His organ ... and the
> voices you hear are those of the Gandharvas ... Listen well, and
> remember, for one day you shall give forth such music to the
> world ...'
>
> It was Sir Thomas who had spoken, and his words were
> addressed to Lyall.
>
> The music continued for a while, then gradually faded away,
> and there was another silence.[116]

This passage is by no means quoted here for the mere purpose
of recounting a thrilling or controversial tale. Rather, the account
serves well to indicate just how strongly guided many great
musicians may have been, though the world has not known it, and
how close to our everyday life these guiding powers have at times
approached. Though there would not be room to include them all
here, there exist quite a number of such accounts, in which mortals
appear to have been the beneficiaries of a parting of the veil, during
which they heard a celestial music of indescribable sublimity. Sometimes the individuals concerned have been spiritual seekers; sometimes they have been known composers of acknowledged stature.
To refer briefly to two of the more widely-quoted episodes: Robert
Schumann wrote music at a late stage in his life which he said was
dictated to him by angels, a claim which his wife believed, stating
after his death that, 'It is in the music of Robert Schumann that the

angels sing.' Though the critic could also point to Schumann's mental instability, the same can in no way be said of Handel, who felt that his *Messiah,* one of the greatest pieces of music ever written, had likewise been revealed to him. During its composition he felt the very gates of heaven had been opened to him, and he was able to see and hear the other-worldly chorusing of superphysical and divine beings. As he later declared: 'I think I did see all Heaven before me and the great God Himself.' It is recorded that the experience of penning the work moved him so greatly that tears flowed with and blotted the ink. Considering both the towering stature and timeless perfection of the work, as well as its length, weight is added to the claim that it was revealed to him, and that he did not have to strive painstakingly to put it together himself, by the startling fact that it was written in but three short weeks, and during one of the most trying periods of his life. The concept of 'revealed music' is not often given consideration during our present materialistic age, yet, whatever its explanation, it seems to be a very definite phenomenon, and one deserving of further study. In this respect, we must not forget either that in both traditional religious and modern esoteric literature there is also the concept of there being *two sides.* That is, the good and the evil. Suppressing a slight shudder, we can recall again those mysterious words of Stravinsky about *The Rite of Spring:* 'I heard, and I wrote what I heard. I was the vessel through which *Le Sacre du Printemps* passed.' As for our own day, more than one esoteric authority has claimed that virtually all of the lyrics of the more heavy rock bands are unconsciously received as dictations from malicious discarnate entities − a claim which becomes not quite so unbelievable when one pays close attention to these lyrics, to see just what exactly it is that is being said. For example:

Ugh.
Ahhh. [A poetic start! − D.T.]
Can't help feeling strange.
The moon is up I think I'm gonna change.
You're so *smooth and tender.*
A livin' breathin' dream.
I'm listen' for your *scream.*

I'm almost human; I'm almost a man,
I'm almost human.

'Almost Human' − Kiss

The male rock star, Alice Cooper, says that he took the name after contacting a discarnate called Alice Cooper during a seance, and that it is the discarnate who partly takes over his actions and singing on stage. All said for the sake of publicity? Our answer probably depends on just how real, or else how non-existent, we consider the non-physical dimensions to be. Certainly the idea of evil entities bringing forth new and disruptive forms of music through their human channels receives a number of mentions in early Christian literature. St Chrysostom, for one, said that: 'lest demons introducing lascivious songs should overthrow everything, God established the psalms'. Rarely, however, has the process of musical revelation (from one 'side' or the other) been so candidly described as in Scott's book.

Meanwhile, concurrent with the episode of the musical revelation, Cyril Scott was at work upon the book which was first released in 1933 under the title, *The Influence of Music on History and Morals*.[109] Unlike the Initiate books, this one was released under Cyril Scott's own name. In 1958 an updated edition came out, being the still-available *Music, Its Secret Influence Throughout the Ages*.[5] Only in this second edition did Scott reveal his belief that both editions of the book had been inspired upon him by numerous and detailed discussions with Koot Hoomi Lal Singh, one of the great Adepts who had also been behind the formation of the Theosophical Society in the last quarter of the nineteenth century.

After a long and fruitful life during which he truly pioneered the reawakening of man's awareness of the secret power inherent in all music, Cyril Scott passed from this world in 1971. And yet, after all, to quote his own lines:

What are the world's foolish toys, and death's ephemeral sorrows,
Seeming endless, yet by the Endless, fleeter than lightning's flashes.[117]

Needless to say, many among the mainstream of the music world looked askance at these 'eccentricities' of Scott's; his talk of 'Masters', his books on alternative medicine, esotericism and the like. Further, it has been suggested that his decline in popularity after the heady days of his young maturity, when some felt him to be the father of British modern music, must be directly related to this 'dissipation' of his talents.

But in an autobiography published at the age of ninety (*Bone of Contention*, Aquarian Press, 1969), Scott discounted this, and claimed that esotericism, and in particular the Masters who guided him, had been one of the major inspiring factors behind his creative output. Indeed, at the age of sixty-five he had made his own personal decision to bring his years of composing to an end; but the Masters, he says, had urged him to continue, which he did until the end of his life. (At the Masters' own request, Scott recounted, the first work he next completed was his third opera, *Maureen O'Mara*.)

Certainly it must be said that whatever the source of his inspiration, these revelations of Scott's are of major importance in again demonstrating the reality of the influence of esotericism upon music. Whatever our own standpoint with regard to Scott's unusual claims, that *he* believed them makes the great influence of esotericism upon his music undeniable. That a modern composer of such significance should have felt himself to be in rapport with the legendary Great White Brotherhood is a quite extraordinary fact. And who can say that among Cyril Scott's many compositions there are not those which are indeed his transcriptions, to the best of his ability, of the music inspired upon him by the Master Koot Hoomi, and which are the direct reflections of the music of the spheres?

It was once said of Scott that he was a hundred years in advance of his generation. Perhaps this gives a hint as to the meaning of the later decades of his life. For while the critics, music publishers and performers generally ignored both his early and later work, and while he more than once felt discouraged and ready to throw in the towel, he was prevailed upon by those he believed to be his Guides to continue composing up until the last. This, even though the works went largely unpublished and unperformed.

In the autobiography Scott states that from the Masters' point of view 'the first thing is to get the work written; the rest if needs be can wait — sometimes even as long as till after the composer's death'. True it is that many of the most famous works of today's concert hall repetoire were almost totally unknown during the lives of those who brought them forth. Take most of the works of J.S. Bach (revived in the 1800s) or the 'Unfinished' Symphony of Schubert (discovered as a discarded manuscript after his death) for example. If Scott's work was indeed, as it came forth from his pen, a hundred years in advance of his generation, it may therefore be most interesting to observe the course of events concerning it in years to come.

ESOTERICISTS REDISCOVER MUSIC

— Or then again, did they ever forget it? We have seen that there exists a certain horse-and-carriage relationship between esotericism and music. And this explains why it should be that recent decades have witnessed the gradual surfacing of a new, twentieth-century esoteric manner of studying the tonal arts. With the re-emergence of esotericism in general, a new and wider realization of the inner secrets of sound and music has naturally begun to follow.

In fact, the first esoteric study of the properties of sound to take place within comparatively recent times was that of Baron von Reichenbach (1788-1869) during the last century. Reichenbach's study was part of a more extensive study into a mysterious force or energy which he called Odic Force. Distinct from magnetism or electricity, yet related to each in certain ways, Odic Force seems to have been the same 'extra' and occult force, unknown as yet to science, which numerous modern investigators have come across, calling it everything from vital force or etheric energy to bioplasma and orgone energy. Reichenbach's many detailed experiments with this force, which could be seen and described by clairvoyant sensitives, were first published in serialized form in 1844, and are in print today as the book posthumously entitled *The Mysterious Odic Force*.[118] What distinguishes Reichenbach from most later researchers into this force is the particularly scientific manner in which he went about his work.

Within a completely darkened room, the sensitives were able to see Odic Force as 'light'. Discovering this, Reichenbach devised a number of experiments to see how various things affected this mysterious 'light'-force. Having conducted Odic experiments in relation to electricity, magnetism, psychology, colours, chemical reactions and crystals, he then had the brainwave of trying out the effect of sound. Standing in a darkened room with a Viennese sensitive, Reichenbach struck a bell. Immediately the sensitive reported that the bell had become visible and luminous to him. Apparently sound itself emitted a radiation of Odic Force. While this force was both invisible and inaudible to the average person, most clairvoyants could see it. Reichenbach tried striking other objects – a metal rod, a horseshoe magnet, a different bell, glass tumblers – and all were reported as having become luminous by a succession of sensitives. The degree of luminosity depended upon the strength of the blow, which is to say, the volume of the sound. The light was also brighter, the higher the pitch. It was further noted that as the tones audibly vibrated or oscillated, so too was the light seen to become brighter and dimmer. Upon a violin being played, not only the strings but also the whole resonance box became luminous to a number of observers. One bell, being continuously struck for quite a while, had the effect (to the sensitives) of lighting up the entire room. The obvious inference from all of this is that, whatever the unknown energy is, it radiates from all musical instruments and from all things which emit sound.

Our own century has witnessed the appearance of many occult groups and systems of esoteric thought. While many contain similar elements to each other, they also each possess their own distinct features; but a number of these groups, movements and New Age writers have had things to say about the esoteric side of music. Universally, they agree with the beliefs of the ancients. One such New Age writer, Corinne Heline, who was born into the prominent Duke family of America's Old South, wrote considerably on the subject. She considered there to be two distinct streams in the music of the world. Each releases a different tonal force into the planet. Consonances bring forth the constructive force and strengthen man's higher nature; dissonances bring forth the destructive force and strengthen man's desire nature. Jazz and modern popular music she believed to be responsible for many of society's present ills: 'Jazz and juvenile delinquency are twins. Where one flourishes the other will appear.'[13] On the optimistic side, besides extolling the artistic merits of Western and Eastern classical music, and writing considerably of their beneficial effects, Corinne Heline was also supremely confident that in the near future we are to witness the birth of a more advanced and even more sublime form of tonal art – a New Age music, the effects of which will radically transform all of civilization. After the tradition of Plato and Aristotle, Corinne Heline believed that music and man's degree of spirituality and other character traits are indissolubly linked; that in fact styles of music and man's degree of spirituality:

> stand apart only to our limited perception. In their essence they are inseparably united, and in higher realms of being it is recognized that musical understanding and spiritual realization are identical.[13]

Such writings seem definitely to foreshadow an imminent major resurgence of the Pythagorean and other ancient styles of thinking on the subjects of sound and tonal art. Yet for this return to ancient principles to be truly powerful and effective in its action, it is likely that it will need to combine not only a resurgence of former wisdom, but also something entirely new and revolutionary. Such a revolution in man's approach to the science of sound is believed by many esotericists to be provided today by the Great White Brotherhood through their outer organization, the Summit Lighthouse. While researching for this book I could not escape the dual conclusions that not only is this organization a prime moving force through which the theory and practice of the use of the inner powers of sound is re-emerging in this age, but also that nothing similar has appeared elsewhere. We will therefore need to look at the Summit Lighthouse in some detail.

THE SCIENCE OF THE SPOKEN WORD

In getting right down to the essence of things, one discovers that the Summit Lighthouse is purely and entirely about the Word – the Word as sound; as the Music of the Spheres; as invocation, fiat and dynamic degree; the Word as the inner nature of physics, as currents of light opposing miscreated darkness for supremacy in the heart of the atom and in the heart of man; the written word of wisdom in all of its aspects; – and the Word incarnate in the Guru-chela (Master-disciple) relationship.

Over a century ago, the Adept known to many in the world as El Morya helped to form the Theosophical Society through his chela, H. P. Blavatsky, who thereby became the living mouthpiece of his Word. She became what is known as a messenger of the Great White Brotherhood – an individual capable of fully representing and giving forth the Word and teachings of that great body of the Adepts of East and West. In a somewhat similar fashion, but as a part of the ongoing mission of the Brotherhood, El Morya chose for his messengers in our own day Mark and Elizabeth Prophet, each of them possessing a great momentum of service to the Brotherhood from the past. El Morya himself wrote in 1975 on the subject of the messengership:

> The Word is all and everything. The Word is the eternal Logos. It is the voice of the Ancient of Days thundering the Ten Commandments from Horeb's height, etching out of the living flame the markings of the law on tablets of stone. The Word is the will of the AUM and the ray of your divinity. The Word is life and love and truth. The Word is law and principle. The Word is individuality through and through.
>
> We send forth messengers of the Word whose souls, anointed by God himself, have knelt before the altar at the Court of the Sacred Fire and received the commission of the Four and Twenty Elders.[119] And their authority is that of the Great Central Sun

messengers. To be a messenger for hierarchy is a high and holy calling – one that is not lightly given, one that aught not to be lightly received...

In 1876, Helena Petrovna Blavatsky was ordered by the Master Kuthumi and me, then known as the Masters K. H. and M., to write *Isis Unveiled.* Later she was given the responsibility of imparting *The Secret Doctrine* to the world. Commissioned by Jesus the Christ, the Ascended Master Hilarion, and Mother Mary, Mary Baker Eddy was given certain revelations which she set forth in *Science and Health with Key to the Scriptures.* Though at times beset with their own preconceptions and the burden of the mass consciousness, these witnesses codified the truth and the law of East and West as the culmination of thousands of years of their souls' distillations of the Spirit.

Such messengers are not trained in a day or a year or a lifetime. Embodiment after embodiment, they sit at the feet of the masters and receive the emanations of their mantle in the power of their word and example. A number of others who were selected to perform a similar service for hierarchy failed in their initiations through the pride of the intellect and their unwillingness to submit identity totally unto the flame. They have become thereby totally self-deluded and they continue to draw innocent souls into the chaos of their delusion.

In the 1930s came the twin flames Guy W. Ballard and Edna Ballard imparting the sacred mystery of the law of the I AM, further knowledge of hierarchy, the invocation of the sacred fire, and the path of the ascension. Representatives tried and true of Saint Germain, they were commissioned to remain the only messengers of the hierarchy of the Aquarian age until mankind should redeem a certain portion of their karma.

When that cycle was fulfilled, Saint Germain, together with the Darjeeling Council, sponsored Mark and Elizabeth Prophet to carry on the work not only of the Ballards and the I AM movement, but also of Nicholas and Helena Roerich. The Roerichs set forth the word of Morya destined to reach both the Russian and the American people with the energy and the enlightenment that should deter the red dragon[120] of World Communism. And so the Mother flame of Russia and the Mother flame of America converge in spirals of freedom and victory for the sons and daughters of God in both nations and in every nation upon earth.[121]**

In this mission of messengership, Mark and Elizabeth Prophet have given forth in their lectures and books, through the Summit Light-house, a great wealth of teachings on a variety of New Age subjects. And among this system of thought and its practical application we find much of relevance to our study of the power of sound. In *The Science of Rhythm for the Mastery of the Sacred Energies of Life,*[122] a lecture released in recorded form, Elizabeth Clare Prophet relates which of the seven rays and seven chakras are par-ticularly associated with which class of musical instrument and which style of music. The lecture, which constitutes the Summit Lighthouse's fundamental release on the subject of music, encompasses a great deal of new information; but at least a little of it we can best summarize in the form of a table, as shown in Table 5.

Among the many other aspects of the science of the Word which the Summit Lighthouse has released is one of particular interest to us in this book. This is the practice of using the science of the spoken Word itself – *which so closely resembles the careful and conscious use made of the spoken Word by the ancients.*

We have reviewed in earlier chapters how the Chinese used gigantic musical ensembles out of the belief that they radiated forth an uplifting spiritual energy throughout the planet; how the Hindus have for millennia given mantras and bhajans for the sustainment of civilization and the physical equilibrium of the planet; how highly developed was the Egyptian priesthood's sophisticated system of invocation (as well as their training in how the spiritually advanced individual should use speech in everyday life). Researching for this book into the power of sound and the modern uses of the spoken word, I was struck by the peculiar absence today of such practices. The ancients believed the use of sound to be the most powerful key of all for the unlocking of the door to higher states of consciousness as well as for the effecting of practical changes in the world at large. In contrast to this, however, modern spiritual aspirants and world-servers concentrate almost exclusively upon silent techniques of meditation. At most, the modern devotee has known only how to pray, or to sing a hymn, or has uttered a few printed lines from a book. The giving of Eastern chants is, too, not an altogether vanished practice. Yet none of this bears any resemblance to, say, the extremely scientific use of consonants and vowels as practised in ancient Egypt in order to accomplish selfless, right-motivated, and highly specific acts of white magic. The head of the Summit Light-house, Elizabeth Clare Prophet, believes that this science of the spoken Word is the missing link in modern man's aspirations for

Table 5   *The association between the Seven Rays and Particular Musical Forms and Instruments*

Ray	Chakra (spiritual centre in man which both absorbs and emits energy)	Rhythm of the chakra	God-quality which the chakra is particularly intended to focus in the consciousness of man	Instruments which particularly influence the chakra	Examples of music which correctly energize the chakra by expressing the divine qualities of the ray	Musical styles which particularly pervert the correct functioning of the chakra
2	Crown	—	Divine Wisdom	Strings	Symphonies	Jazz
5	Third eye	2-4	Divine Science	Piano	Piano concertos	Computer music (The 'new music')
1	Throat	—	Divine Will or Power	Brass	Marches (e.g. 'Pomp and Circumstance' Nos 1 and 4)	Rock vocals; also folk-rock vocals
3	Heart	3-4 and 12-8	Divine Love	Harp	Waltzes. Also harp music.	Foxtrot, Tango and the 'jazz waltz'
6	Solar plexus	5-4	Divine Peace and Ministration	Organ	Indian *bbajans* and Western devotional music	Blues
7	Seat of the soul	6-8	Divine Freedom and Ritual	Woodwinds	The true and original 'soul' music in folk music such as 'Greensleeves'	That which is *called* 'soul' music
4	Base of the spine	4-4	Divine Purity	Drum, percussion	Early American patriotic pieces and the rhythms of Indian classical music	Voodoo and rock rhythm

From *The Science of Rhythm for the Mastery of the Sacred Energies of Life; Uses and Misuses of the Word in the Music of East and West*[122] self-evolution. Could it indeed be that the exclusively silent path is in some ways an unbalanced one, given the dire needs of our age for effective changes to take place swiftly on the world scene? Certainly it was believed of old that whereas meditation and prayer raise mankind's consciousness to God, only the scientific use of the throat chakra, applied with concentration and determination, can fully invoke the energies of God down into the world of form in which we live. And in a remarkably similar vein to this concept of antiquity, thousands of people today also believe the spoken Word to be capable of creating and sustaining a most potent and planet-wide revolution into higher consciousness.

The most usual form in which the Summit Lighthouse makes use of the power of sound is in the giving of what are called dynamic decrees. Dynamic decrees are specific worded formulas for the sublimating and perfecting of personal and planetary conditions. In the standard exposition of the subject, *The Science of the Spoken Word*, penned by Mark L. and Elizabeth Clare Prophet, we read:

> Various yogic systems of meditation offer methods whereby the mind of man can be stilled and a greater attunement with the Divine be achieved. Some of these methods become haphazard when applied by Western man, for they do require an advanced mental and spiritual discipline on the part of the one employing them. Decrees, on the other hand, are relatively simple to master once the basic principles are understood; and they are far more efficacious.
>
> It must be understood that decrees given without feeling and without thought will not produce the full perfection which they are intended to bring about; for man must have in his consciousness the correct patterns of thought and feeling which act as receptacles for the energies he invokes from the Godhead.
>
> Decrees which are set forth according to the science of the spoken Word begin with a preamble. These preambles direct the attention and the energies of the decreer to his own I AM Presence (the inner God Self) and to his Holy Christ Self (the Christ-identity), as well as to those cosmic beings who have made mighty progress in God's kingdom.
>
> These preambles are invocative of the highest Good — that is to say, they invoke the goodness of God by an appeal, made in the name of God and his Christ, to the hierarchies of heaven to anchor their energies and their love in order to amplify to levels of almost limitles comprehension the action of the decree as it is

fulfilled in the world of time and space.

The giving of each call with fervor and love automatically invokes the energies of the heavenly hosts on behalf of the decreer and all mankind. In addition, decrees are a definite statement of truth that the mind of the individual may follow to a logical conclusion. And in this case, it is the conclusion of the Logos, of the Word that is made flesh by the power of the spoken Word, that is, by the power of decrees. By cosmic law the worded ideas *must* eventuate in actuality when they are released in the name of God and by the authority of the Christ flame ...

Those who understand the power of the square in mathematics will realize that when groups of individuals are engaged in invoking the energies of God, they are not merely adding power by the number of people in the group on a one-plus-one basis, but they are entering into a very old covenant of the square which squares the release of power to accomplish the spoken Word by the number of individuals who are decreeing and by the number of times that each decree is given.

We heartily recommend individual decrees to accomplish untold blessings in the lives of those who will discipline themselves in this ritual of invoking light to a darkened world. But group decreeing, when accompanied by an intense visualization of the good desired, is more efficacious on a world scale than individual decreeing and will result in a speedy response to those engaged in it, not only to themselves but also on behalf of all mankind ...

Rhythm is also important in decrees. Proper rhythm creates a most penetrating projection of the spiritual vibrations that will magnetize all over the planet the qualities of God that are being invoked through the decrees. The momentum of these waves that form undulating circles over the planetary body creates an intensification of light wherever devotees come together to participate in a like endeavor.[123]†

These dynamic group-decree sessions of the Summit Lighthouse can be said to represent the very first genuine re-emergence, then, of a spiritual science and practice which was once basic among the ancient priesthoods. Only by looking very, very far back in time do we encounter records of anything similar. Such a practice is depicted taking place in the royal standard of Ur, the city of Abraham, for the purpose of driving a wave of gloom and pestilence away from the city. Priest-King Gudea and his musicians are accomplishing this by the power of music and vocalizations, given together. Corinne Heline commented on the depiction:

> Esotericists understood that it was by the magic of music that a cloud of evil and error which enveloped the city was being transmuted, and the city's vibratory rhythms correspondingly raised. This important function of music will someday be rediscovered and used.[13]

Of course, different individuals react in two very different ways to the idea of men and women acting as tonal transformers for sacred energy to enter into the earth from higher dimensions of being. The contemporary materialist viewpoint sees the universe in terms of matter – as atoms, planets and stars formed by coincidence – and in which the phenomenon of life is a mere accident of nature, being almost completely irrelevant in the total scheme of things. Yet to the spiritual idealist, life – and consciousness above all – *is what the universe is all about*: the very point and purpose of the material Creation of atoms and worlds was to provide a platform on which life could exist and evolve. These two diverse viewpoints are never more divergent than in their reactions to the idea of mystical chants by which the ancients believed the evils of the world could be dispelled. To the materialist, the idea is quite irrational. Yet to the mystical outlook nothing could be more sensible than that the most highly evolved phenomenon in the physical universe – man – should be able to act as an invoker and transmitter of the highest of all forms of force. For this force or spiritual energy, while as yet being unknown to science, is believed by the mystic to be the controlling and guiding force behind all the known physical forces.

From the mystical point of view, Priest-King Gudea and the musicians of his city were simply utilizing a known and tested means of dispelling plague and other evils. They would only have been guilty of irrationality and foolishness had they *failed* to do so.

THE SCIENCE OF THE WORD IN ANCIENT BRITAIN

A hint that the science of sound may have been used in ancient Britain is provided by the historian Diodorus of the first century BC. He wrote of 'an island in the ocean over against Gaul' wherein was found a city consecrated to Apollo, 'whose citizens are most of them harpers, who, playing on the harp, chant sacred hymns to Apollo in the temple, setting forth his glorious acts'. Diodorus' account may refer to the same chanters as a Welsh account brought to light recently by John Michell, the scholar and author. In his classic work, *City of Revelation*,[125] John Michell mentions one of the Welsh Triads, verses of great age which incorporate oral traditions from bardic historians of prehistoric times. From this account it would seem that the power of the Word was not only once used in Britain, but also, was evidently applied with a great deal of sophistication.

The Triad states that once, long ago, the British Isles possessed three perpetual choirs where saints maintained a ceaseless chant, twenty four hours a day. The three choirs of pure and illumined saints were located at Glastonbury, Stonehenge and Llan Illtud Vawr (near Llantwit Major in Glamorgan). (This was, we must remember, thousands of years *before* the first Christian community established at Glastonbury.) At each of the three locations 2,400 saints maintained the tag-chant, a hundred for each of the twenty four hours. The chanted verbal formulas of spiritual power are said to have varied with the hours, seasons, years and other cycles. John Michell states:

> The song that the elders sang at the perpetual choir was an astrological chant, pitched to the music of the spheres, celebrating the order of the heavens and guiding the ritual order of life on earth. The temple was the central power station of the whole country, transmitting throughout the nation the current of the divine word, generated through the ceaseless activity of its astrologers, priests and officials.[125]

The similarities between this and the huge Chinese orchestras are obvious. However, the sacred generation of power by the saints of ancient Britain was of a much greater significance, for almost always it is the enunciated Word, the sounds spoken by Man as the incarnate Christ, which is of a greater efficacy than the sounds of inanimate instruments.

Plotting the three sites on a map, John Michell found them to be spaced equally apart. From Llantwit to Glastonbury is about 38.9 miles, and Glastonbury to Stonehenge is the same distance again. The three sites are not located on a straight line, however, but on the arc of a circle that can be drawn through them all. Continuing this arc eastwards from Stonehenge to a point a further 38.9 miles from Stonehenge, Michell found himself pinpointing a further site at Goring-on-Thames. Upon investigating, it turned out that there once existed at Goring a temple near a river crossing of several prehistoric tracks. Were the circle to be completed, ten such sites in all would face each other around its circumference; and the centre of the circle is just south of a prehistoric city on Midsummer Hill in the Malvern Hills.[125]

An interesting adjunct to Michell's discoveries is the subsequent history of the middle site named by the Triad as one of the locations of the three perpetual choirs. For this is Glastonbury, strongly reputed to have been the very first site in Britain to which the Christian religion was brought. The Christian faith is said to have been anchored at Glastonbury a mere few years after the crucifixion and ascension of Christ. What is in any case certain is that Glastonbury became the first major centre of the new religion in these Isles, and held a prominent position as a scholastic, religious and mystical centre for over a thousand years. That Glastonbury was chosen for this role cannot have been accidental. A tradition of keeping the energy flowing from that established and purified point – energy as a spiritual 'power supply' for the sustainment and advancement of the nation – was seemingly not lost with the onset of the Christian era. Indeed, the monks of Glastonbury Abbey adhered during the Abbey's heyday to a regimen of prayer and chant more intense than any of which I have heard in the Christian world: amounting to at least several hours each and every day.

But finally an end came. It is a timeless esoteric law of the flow of energy that spiritual light always tends to attract the opposition of darkness. The effective service of individuals and movements which contain light is a threat to the very existence of planetary evil; thus evil in all its forms seeks to perpetuate itself by the extinguishing of the light. Outside of the present, civilized society provided by the West, in other parts of the globe and at other times in history, the opposition of evil has been able not merely to take the forms of gossip and slander, but also of physical violence. And in this way there eventually came the order by a military and totalitarian regime for the ransacking, dissolution and tearing down of Great Britain's Glastonbury Abbey.

And so the light that illumined a nation went out. The saints were scattered, and were no longer able to congregate to offer themselves as scientific, self-sacrificing transformers of the Word unto a nation and a people.

We have now only the ruins to look back upon. But even these have yet their secrets to reveal. We have John Michell to thank for the discovery that there exist certain clear associations between the account in the Welsh Triad and the deeply mystical text of Revelation revealed to St John on the Isle of Patmos. The angle formed between the lines linking Llantwit with Glastonbury and Glastonbury with Stonehenge is about 144°, a sacred number which occurs in Revelation both in the measurements of the New Jerusalem and in the archetypal number of saints – 'an hundred forty and four thousand, having his Father's name written in their foreheads' (purified third-eye chakras?). The total number of British saints in the three sacred choirs was 2,400 × 3 = 7,200: exactly one half of 14,400 (or one twentieth of the Biblical 144,000). This number surely did not occur by chance. Further, Michell indicates that the complete circle formed by the completion of the arc of the three sites has a radius of 504 furlongs and a circumference of 3,168 furlongs. These numbers are an essential ingredient of the proportions of the archetypal New Jerusalem of Revelation. They are also manifested in the traditional systems of metrology themselves, since the radius of the earth combined with the radius of the moon gives a total figure of 5,040 miles; and a circle of this radius would have a perimeter of 31,680 miles.

The number 144 also occurs in the Old Testament's account of Solomon's consecration of the Temple into which the Ark of the Covenant was placed. There is perhaps no more awesome a record than this of the power of specific tones to invoke sacred energy from heaven for the blessing and healing of the land.

Previously, King Solomon's father, David, in making preparations for the Temple, had divided his musicians according to their service into 24 categories consisting of twelve in each category, giving a total of 288.[126] Here, the 24 categories represent the dual *yin-yang* polarities of the twelve Tones of the zodiac, and the total number is therefore 144×2.

For the consecration of the Temple itself, King Solomon assembled together all of the Levitical priesthood, the elders, the heads of the tribes, and all the men of Israel. The account, in 2 Chronicles, conveys very tangibly the great hush and sense of expectation which envelops the gathering as the Ark is brought in. Then comes that penultimately powerful moment when the trained priest-musicians invoke the fiery Presence of the One:

And it came to pass, when the priests were come out of the holy place: (for all the priests that were present were sanctified, and did not then wait by course: also the Levites which were the singers, all of them of Asaph, of Heman, of Jeduthun, with their sons and their brethren, being arrayed in white linen, having cymbals and psalteries and harps, stood at the east end of the altar, and with them an hundred and twenty priests sounding with trumpets;) it came even to pass, as the trumpeters and singers were as one, to make one sound to be heard in praising and thanking the Lord; and when they lifted up their voice with the trumpets the cymbals and instruments of musick, and praised the Lord, saying, For he is good; for his mercy endureth forever: that then the house was filled with a cloud, even the house of the Lord; so that the priests could not stand to minister by reason of the cloud: for the glory of the Lord had filled the house of God. ...

Now, when Solomon had made an end of praying, the fire came down from heaven, and consumed the burnt offering and the sacrifices; and the glory of the Lord filled the house. And the preists could not enter into the house of the Lord, because the glory of the Lord had filled the Lord's house. ...

And the Lord appeared to Solomon by night, and said unto him, I have heard thy prayer, and have chosen this place to myself for an house of sacrifice. If I shut up heaven that there be no rain, or if I command the locusts to devour the land, or if I send pestilence among my people; if my people which are called by my name, shall humble themselves, and pray, and seek my face, and turn from their wicked ways; then will I hear from heaven, and will forgive their sin, and will heal their land. Now mine eyes shall be open, and mine ears attent unto the prayer that is made in this place. For now I have chosen and sanctified this house, that my name may be there for ever; and mine eyes and mine heart shall be there perpetually.[127]

The Temple of Solomon and its use, then, provides the universal, archetypal matrix for all peoples and all ages. Similar temples, where 'the Lord's eyes and His heart were there perpetually' were established in ancient Britain, and the same could be re-established today. In fact, there are a number of hints in the Bible that the science of the Word may indeed provide the essential key for the bringing in of a new golden age.

We can take, for example, the book of Revelation. Revelation is coming increasingly to be recognized as being, in part, an allegorical key to the events that are to accompany the transition of the earth from Pisces to Aquarius. If this is a correct assessment, and I believe it is, then the numerous references to the power of the spoken Word cannot be mere coincidence. The servants and saints of God are described repeatedly in Revelation as combating darkness with sound in a final conflagration of good and evil before the birth of a golden age of peace and enlightenment:

> For their power is in their mouth,[128] ... And if any man will hurt them, fire proceedeth out of their mouth,[129] ... And they overcame him [Satan] by the blood of the Lamb, [energy of the Christ] and by the word of their testimony.[130]

Finally, there is described the final coming of the incarnation of the Word:

> ... and his name is called The Word of God. And the armies which were in heaven followed him ... And out of his mouth goeth a sharp sword, that with it he should smite [all evil in] the nations.[131]

Even as the Chinese believed each new age to begin with a new Tone which sounds the age's key-note, so too does Revelation seem to imply that a new inundation of the earth with the Word will come forth, which will be stepped-down fully into the earth by the archetypal 144,000 saints, for the full manifestation of the Aquarian age:

> And I heard a voice from heaven, as the voice of many waters, and as the voice of a great thunder; and I heard the voice of harpers harping with their harps:
> And they sung as it were a new song ... and no man could learn that song but the hundred and forty and four thousand, which were redeemed from the earth. ... These were redeemed from among men, being the first-fruits unto God and to the Lamb.
> And in their mouth was found no guile: for they are without fault ...[132]

How saturated with the deepest of meanings is that line: 'And they sung *as it were* a new song' (my italics)! The 'new song' is the new use of sound in both New Age music and in enunciated, rhythmic invocations. One of the most important things about this new song is its relationship with the New Age as a fully manifested golden era of civilization. Of the new song and the New Age we must remind ourselves *which*, according to the tenets of the ancient mystery schools, will be the *parent*, and *which* the *offspring*. For the power of music and the enunciated Word rules everything, Vibration being the creative force of the universe. Therefore the New Age cannot come first, somehow arising spontaneously, and the new song appearing only as a result of it. Rather, it is always the new uses of sound which lead the way into the new era. The New Age can only ever come forth as a *result* and *offspring* of New Age music and the intense, devoted practice of the science of the spoken Word.

THE HALLOWED CIRCLE OF THE AUM

We approach now the conclusion of our study of the secret power of music and sound. And yet, before closing, one cannot help but wonder: what would be the effect — personal and planetary — were the sacred science of the Word, as practised in the three choirs of the saints of ancient Britain, *to be resumed today?* What magnificent resurrecting energies might not this bestow upon the British Isles, and upon every nation upon earth? In an age when so many potential catastrophes threaten with an imminent presence — terrestrial upheaval, world war, totalitarianism and starvation, to name but four — it may be of great significance that the ancients believed the power of the Word to be capable of averting all such occurrences. And even if any of these eventualities come to pass — a global economic collapse of large proportions appearing particularly likely for this decade as I write in early 1983 — what might not a rebirth of what John Michell called 'central power station(s) of the whole country, transmitting throughout the nation the current of the divine word' be able to accomplish for the swift resurrection and stabilization of a new era of peace, prosperity and brotherhood?

One of the final conclusions of our study must be that the secret power of music and sound should not be secret at all. As of old, when the correct, studied use of music and verbal formulas created and sustained great golden age cultures, so too can and should this power be used once more. That which was, and then was not, must be again.

In fact, the return of the science of the Word to the earth seems already to have begun. We have noted previously the importance with which the ancients regarded the two solstices and the two equinoxes of the year. And it is at these times that El Morya has called for conferences and gigantic decree sessions to take place in our age. These conferences and group-decree sessions, attended by thousands from all over the world, are now held at the four cardinal points of the year, as well as at other times, in the United States (where the largest and central gatherings are held) and also in other nations. Let us therefore close with the words of El Morya himself:‡

Of such import has been the coming-together of devotees of light down through the ages that when the Summit Lighthouse was founded, I set the pattern of the quarterly conferences for the anchoring of the cycles of the year. By coming together four times a year to give and receive, chelas of the ascended masters render an incomparable service to the Great White Brotherhood. If you could behold our quarterly conferences from the inner planes, you would observe how the chelas build the forcefield in the physical plane by their devotions and by their oneness and how hierarchy lowers a grid that is the mandala for that class in the etheric plane over the physical place where the class is held.

The mandala is like a snowflake – unique in its design, never seen before, never to appear again ... Each lecture that is scheduled and each dictation that is given fills in a portion of the mandala, and the application of the students intensifies the action of the sacred fire that can be released to the planet.

Our conferences are held for the turning of the cycles of the year – winter solstice, spring equinox, summer solstice, and autumn equinox. The physical changes occur prior to the conference and the light released from the hierarchies of the sun at the change of the season is then expanded by ascended and unascended beings serving together at the conferences for the fulfilment of a cosmic purpose on earth as it is in heaven.

Whenever possible, you should seize the opportunity to attend such a conference. What's more, you should make possible the impossible through the alchemy of invocation to your own God Being. Not only are these conferences the most important experience of a lifetime in terms of the expansion of consciousness and the transmutation of untold substance in your world, but your willingness to serve as a co-ordinate on earth for the hierarchies of light will earn for you a momentum of good karma that you can ill afford to be without.

God needs man and man needs God. This is the law of the hallowed circle of the AUM. And when you find yourself standing in that circle, ever-widening, that is formed for the final release of the Lord of the World to the devotees at the conclusion of a conference, you will know that all I have told you is indeed true; and by the thread of contact with hierarchy which you have established, your life will never be the same.[121]

Further Reading
(And Listening!)

This list is designed not simply to go over material which the preceding pages have already covered, but to expand into further related areas of music and esotericism.

On Beethoven

Why 'On Beethoven'? Though the subject of Beethoven – the man, the music and the mission to which he set himself – has not been a prominent part of this book, a study of Beethoven is actually an archetypal musical experience. For Beethoven himself was an archetypal spiritual artist. In studying the music and life of Beethoven we actually attune ourselves to much broader issues – the essential spiritual philosophy behind all good music; the necessity for altruistic motive; the struggle between purity and error in the personality of the artist himself; how music can be used to spiritualize the race, and what kind of music does this. Beethoven was quite aware of the power of music, and in his life story and works we see how supremely he put this knowledge into practice.

● *Beethoven, His Spiritual Development* by J. W. N. Sullivan (first pub. 1927, now in paperback edition, by George Allen & Unwin, London). The most authoritative book on the subject of its title. Highly readable and quite short (127 pages), yet full of penetrating insight into the spiritual aspects of Beethoven and music in general.

● *Beethoven and the Voice of God* by Wilfrid Mellers (Faber & Faber, London, 1983). This book is a companion volume to Mellers' *Bach and the Dance of God,* by which we can be certain of its quality. Sure to become a key text for a deeper understanding of the spiritual/emotional meanings behind the notes of Beethoven's main works. Mellers analyses the music in great detail, however, note-by-note, making this title more suitable for he who reads music than for the layman.

● *Beethoven* by Marion M. Scott (J. M. Dent & Sons, London,

1934). Quite possibly the best one-volume work available on Beethoven as man and musician. An intelligent introduction to the subject, but without being over-scholarly. Marion Scott sprinkles her pages with a good deal more heart than is often to be found in studies of composers.

● *Beethoven's Nine Symphonies Correlated with the Nine Spiritual Mysteries* by Corinne Heline (J. F. Rowny Press, Santa Barbara, 1971). New Age writer Corinne Heline examines the esoteric aspects of each of the Beethoven symphonies.

On Rock Music

● *The Marxist Minstrels. A Handbook on Communist Subversion of Music* by David A. Noebel (364pp, American Christian College Press, Tulsa, Oklahoma, 1974). This is actually the best critique there is on all aspects of rock, not just its politics. Clearly a book which involved a great deal of investigation over time; a labour of love by a dedicated moral researcher. Thirty-nine chapters and six appendices include: 'Communist Use of Hypnotism'; 'Distribution of Communist Records in the United States'; 'Rock, Drugs and the Beatles'; 'Rock and Revolution'; 'Communist Subversion of Folk Music'; 'The *Sing Out!* – *Broadside* Axis'; 'Spiritual Implications', and 'Guide to Action'. May be difficult to get hold of in Europe, though, in which case try writing to the publishers, or to Summit Youth Ministries Publications (an organization of which Noebel is the director), PO Box 207, Manitou Springs, CO 80829, USA.

● *The Day Music Died* by Bob Larson (Bob Larson Ministries, Box 26438, Denver, Colorado, 1973). Not far behind Noebel's book ·in quality, but less detail. Larson writes from knowledge, having been a rock guitarist himself. But again, difficult to obtain this side of the Atlantic so, if interested, try contacting the publisher. Chapters include: 'American Aura'; 'British Beats'; 'Sound Waves and the Psyche'; 'Body Blows'; 'Dangers of the Dance'; 'The View From the Microphone'; 'Spiritual Keynotes'.

From the Summit Lighthouse

Summit Lighthouse books and cassettes are available from: The Summit Lighthouse, Box A, Malibu, CA 90265, USA.

● *The Great White Brotherhood in the Culture, History and Religion of America* by Elizabeth Clare Prophet, 1976. This is actually a book of world-wide significance. An introduction *par excellence* to the subject of the Great White Brotherhood and their work, yet also much more than an introduction. Contains more than could be summarized here, including a chapter containing information nowhere else available on New Age astrology. Also an introduction to the science of the spoken Word. One of the most remarkable books I have ever read.

Prayer and Meditation by Jesus and Kuthumi, 1968. The latest edition also includes a sizeable section on the giving of dynamic decrees. A handbook, therefore, on the three major aspects of the *practice* of the spiritual life: prayer, meditation and dynamic decrees. Written by Masters of the Great White Brotherhood.

The Science of the Spoken Word, Mark and Elizabeth Prophet, 1983. The standard work on the science of invocation and the use of dynamic decrees. Includes much instruction on the violet transmuting flame, and essential key for the purification of self and society.

The Science of Rhythm for the Mastery of the Sacred Energies of Life; Uses and Misuses of the Word in the Music of East and West Elizabeth Clare Prophet, 1978. Boxed set of two cassettes (3 hours). Includes musical examples.

The Call of Camelot. The orchestrated tone poem composed by Norman Thomas Miller is distributed in cassette form by the Summit Lighthouse. Besides the title-piece mentioned in the Coda of this book there is also an hour of further music. Performed by Excelsior.

By Cyril Scott

Music, Its Secret Influence Throughout the Ages. First paperback edition by the Aquarian Press, Wellingborough, 1976. The Initiate books are published in Great Britain by Routledge & Kegan Paul; in the USA by Samuel Weiser: *The Initiate, Some Impressions of a Great Soul; The Initiate in the New World; The Initiate in the Dark Cycle.* All as mentioned in the Coda under the heading 'Cyril Scott, "the Father of British Modern Music".' (The Initiate books are still published anonymously, accredited to 'his pupil'.)

Other Useful Books

The Hidden Face of Music by Herbert Whone (Gollancz, London, 1974). Also: *The Simplicity of Playing the Violin.* Each a kind of 'Zen of musical performance'. Important reading for the spiritually-inclined practising musician, but also absorbing for the general reader. Herbert Whone has the ability to word the most esoteric of subjects in such a way as to make it appear sensible and obvious to even the most sceptically-minded.

The Golden Book of Life by Azelda. A beautifully poetic and deeply mystical treatise on the seven Tones and their 49 subdivisions. I *would* recommend it, except that although it was written in the 1920s, this 190,000-word manuscript, unlike anything else in world literature, has never been published! However, booklets of extracts are available from: MRG, Archers' Court, Hastings, Sussex, England.

● *Thought-Forms* by Annie Besant and C. W. Leadbeater (Theosophical Publishing House, 68 Great Russell Street, London WC1B 3BU). Several Theosophist clairvoyants have written about the non-physical structures which music creates on the inner planes. This book includes a section on these music-forms, and was the first such study to be written. Besant and Leadbeater say that music has two effects visible to the clairvoyant: a radiation of spiritual energy which goes forth in all directions, and a music-form which remains over the location concerned for some time afterwards, exerting an influence on all who happen to be there. 'Each class of music has its own type of form, and the style of the composer shows as clearly in the form which his music builds as a man's character shows in his handwriting. Other possibilities of variation are introduced by the kind of instrument upon which the music is performed, and also by the merits of the player.' Three particular music-forms are described in detail, with colour plates of each; these being from the music of Mendelssohn, Gounod and Wagner.

● *Fantasia.* For anybody who hasn't seen it, this 1940 Disney production is a must! A superb marriage between the visual and musical arts. Most of the sequences (not the Mussorgsky or Stravinsky) are what New Age cinema was intended to be!

● *Music Therapy, A New Anthology* compiled by Lionel Stebbing (New Knowledge Books, PO Box 9, Horsham, Sussex). Music therapy for specific illnesses, and for handicapped children and the elderly. Music in child education. Outline of a new music therapy.

Reference Notes

1. Menuhin, Yehudi *Theme and Variations* Heinemann, 1972
2. Joshua 6:1-20
3. Most of the major works written by both Aristotle and by Plato include at least several pages on the psychological and societary effects of music.
4. Portnoy, Julius *Music in the Life of Man* Holt, Rhinehart and Winston, 1963
5. Scott, Cyril *Music, Its Secret Influence Throughout the Ages* Aquarian Press, 1958
6. Blom, Eric (Ed.) *Grove's Dictionary of Music and Musicians* Macmillan London, 1954
7. Medhurst, W.H. (trans.) *The Shu King*
8. Martens, F.H. 'Music in Chinese Fairy Tale and Legend' *Music Quarterly VIII*, 4, October 1922
9. *New Era Community* Agni Yoga Society, 1926 (transcribed by Nicholas Roerich)
10. Rudhyar, Dane *The Rebirth of Hindu Music* Theosophical Publishing House, Adyar, India, 1928
11. Gulik, R.H. van *The Lore of the Chinese Lute* Tokyo, 1940
12. Wellesz, Egon (Ed.) *Ancient and Oriental Music* Vol. 1 of *The New Oxford History of Music* Oxford University Press, 1957
13. Heline, Corinne *Music: The Keynote of Human Evolution* New Age Press, Santa Monica (undated)
14. *Encyclopaedia Britannica* (15th edition) Encyclopaedia Britannica International
15. Aalst, J.A. van *Chinese Music* Shanghai, 1884
16. Sachs, Curt *The Rise of Music in the Ancient World, East and West* J.M. Dent & Sons, 1944
17. See for example the books on Beethoven listed in the Further Reading section of the present book.

18. Heline, Corinne *The Cosmic Harp* New Age Press, Santa Monica, 1969
19. Hindley, Geoffrey (Ed.) *The Larousse Encyclopedia of Music* Hamlyn Publishing Group, 1971
20. Láng, Paul Henry *Music in Western Civilization* J.M. Dent & Sons, 1941
21. Quoted in Machlis, J. *Introduction to Contemporary Music* J.M. Dent & Sons, 1980
22. Routh, Francis; *Contemporary Music, An Introduction* Hodder & Stoughton Educational, 1968
23. Yates, Peter *Twentieth Century Music* George Allen & Unwin, 1968
24. Griffiths, Paul *A Guide to Electronic Music* Thames and Hudson, 1979
25. Also quoted in Small, ref. no. 27
26. Quoted in *Bulletin of the American Composers' Alliance* June 1952, and thence in Routh, ref. no. 22
27. Small, Christopher *Music–Society–Education* John Calder, 1977
28. *Circus* February 1972, p. 41
29. Garr, Doug 'The Endless Scale' in *OMNI 3*, 6, 1981
30. Fielden, Thomas *Music and Character* Ivor Nicholson and Watson (undated–1932?)
31. Darwin, Charles *The Descent of Man, and Selection in Relation to Sex*
32. Kendig, Frank and Levitt, Richard G. 'Overture: Sex, Math and Music' in *Science Digest 90*, 1, January 1982
33. Kostelanetz, Richard (Ed.) *John Cage* Allen Lane 1971
34. Merrill, Sally 'Composing Computers' in *Science Digest 90*, 1, January 1982
35. 'Teaching Music by Computer' in *Music in Education*, quoted in Small, ref. no. 27
36. Skinner, B.F. *Beyond Freedom and Dignity* Alfred A. Knopf, New York, 1971
37. Podolsky *Music For Your Health* Bernard Ackerman, New York
38. Gilman and Paperte *Music and Your Emotions*
39. Larson, Bob *The Day Music Died* Bob Larson Ministries, Box 26438, Denver, Colorado, 1973
40. Ingber, Dina; Brody, Robert and Pearson, Cliff 'Music Therapy: Tune-Up For Mind and Body' in *Science Digest 90*, 1, January 1982

41. 'Mysterious Melody Malady' in *Science Digest 89*, 3, April 1981, p. 102
42. *Time 7* February, 1972, p. 45
43. *Time 7* August, 1968, p. 47
44. *Medical World News* 13 June, 1969, p. 13
45. *Time* 12 April, 1968
46. Curtis, T. Olga 'Music that Kills Plants' *Denver Post* 21 June 1970
47. Day, Langston and De La Warr, George *Matter in the Making* Vincent Stuart, 1966
48. Useful discussions on the subject are in Hilgard, Ernest R.; Atkinson, Richard C. and Atkinson, Rita L. *Introduction to Psychology* Harcourt Brace Jovanovich, USA (various editions), section on 'Genetic Basis of Intelligence'; and in Butcher, H.J. *Human Intelligence, Its Nature and Assessment* Methuen London, 1968
49. Bandura, A. and Huston, Aletha C. 'Identification as a Process of Incidental Learning' in *Journal of Abnormal Social Psychology* 63, 1961, pp. 311-18
50. *The Viewer and Listener* Summer 1982
51. Brown, Roger *Social Psychology* Collier Macmillan, 1965
52. Crosby, David in *The Rolling Stone Interviews* Arthur Barker, 1981
53. *American Journal of Psychiatry 99*, p. 317
54. 1 Samuel 16: 14-23
55. Heline, Corinne *Healing and Regeneration Through Music* New Age Press, Santa Monica
56. Pontvik, A. *Heilen durch Musik* Zürich, 1955
57. In Stebbing, Lionel (compiler) *Music Therapy, A New Anthology* New Knowledge Books, 1963
58. Kneutgen, Johannes *Neue Wege der Musiktherapie* Düsseldorf, 1974
59. Bailey, Philip *They Can Make Music* Oxford University Press, 1973
60. Peggie, Andrew 'Musical Adaptations' *The Times Educational Supplement* 12 June, 1981
61. Kennard, Daphne and Gilbertson, Moyna *The Music to Help Disabled Children Move* available from the Physiotherapy Dept, Bray's School, Bray's Road, Birmingham, England
62. Shepherd, John; Virden, Phil; Vulliamy, Grahem and Wishart, Trevor *Whose Music? A Sociology of Musical Languages* Latimer, 1977

63. Shepherd, John 'The "Meaning" of Music' in ref. no. 62

64. Shepherd, John 'The Musical Coding of Ideologies' in ref. no. 62

65. Noebel, David A. *The Marxist Minstrels, A Handbook on Communist Subversion of Music* American Christian College Press, Tulsa, Oklahoma, 1974

66. Lawrence, Vera Brodsky *Music For Patriots, Politicians and Presidents; Harmonies and Discords of the First Hundred Years* Macmillan, New York, 1975

67. Ouseley, Sir W. 'Anecdotes of Indian Music' in *The Oriental Collections 1* and in Tagore, Sourindro Mohun *Hindu Music From Various Authors* (2nd ed.) Calcutta, 1882, I, p. 166

68. Shankar, Ravi; *My Music, My Life* Jonathan Cape, 1969

69. Prophet, Elizabeth Clare 'Sound, Life's Integrating Phenomenon' in *The Coming Revolution 2*, 1, Spring 1981, Summit University Press, USA. This article is a condensation of a lecture given by Elizabeth Prophet in Philadelphia in 1980.

70. Hamel, Peter Michael *Through Music to the Self: How to appreciate and experience music anew* (trans. Peter Lemesurier) Compton Press, 1978

71. Tirro, Frank *Jazz, A History* J.M. Dent & Sons, 1979

72. Monsarrat, Alice English 'Music – Soothing, Sedative or Savage?' *American Mercury* September 1961, p. 47

73. Millar, Bill 'Rhythm and Blues' in *The History of Rock I, 2*, Orbis Publishing, 1982

74. Maspero *Études de Mythologie*

75. Watson, Lyall *Supernature,* Hodder & Stoughton, 1973

76. Jenny, Hans *Cymatics I and II,* Basilius Press AG., Switzerland

77. Capra, Fritjof *The Tao of Physics* Shambhala Publications (USA), Fontana (UK), 1975

78. Gladzewski, Andrew 'The Music of Crystals, Plants and Human Beings', reprinted from *Radio-Perception* September 1951

79. Murchie, Guy *The Seven Mysteries of Life: an Exploration in Science and Philosophy* Houghton Mifflin Company, Boston, 1978

80. Krüger, Wilfred *Das Universum Singt* Trier, 1974

81. Andrews, Donald *The Symphony of Life* Lee's Summit, Missouri; Unity Books, 1966

82. Khan, Inayat *The Mysticism of Sound* Sufi Movement, 1923
83. Govinda, Lama Anagarika *The Way of the White Clouds* Rider & Company (Hutchinson), 1966 (p/bk edition 1973)
84. Polaczek, D. in *Süddeutsche Zeitung* 15 October, 1974 (quoted and translated by Peter Hamel in ref. no. 70)
85. Kayser, Hans *Lehrbuch der Harmonik; Der hörende Mensch; Akroasis; Harmonia Planetarum* and *Orphikon*
86. Doczi, Gyorgy; *The Power of Limits,* Shambhala Publications USA, 1981
87. Gardner, Howard 'Do Babies Sing a Universal Song?' in *Psychology Today 15*, 12, December 1981
88. Brown, F.A. 'Persistent Activity Rhythms in the Oyster' *American Journal of Physiology* 178, 1954, p. 510
89. Carson, R. *The Sea Around Us* Staples Press 1951
90. Hauenschild, C. 'Neue experimentelle Untersuchungen zum Problem der Lunarperiodizität' *Naturwiss* 43, 1956, p. 361
91. Brown, F.A.; Park, Y.H. and Zeno, J.R. 'Diurnal Variation in Organismic Response to Very Weak Gamma Radiation' *Nature* 211, 1966, p. 830
92. Takata, M. 'Uber eine neue biologisch wirksame Komponente der Sonnenstrahlung' *Archiv Met. Geophys. Bioklimat.* 486, 1951
93. Takata, M. and Murasugi, T. 'Flockungszahlstörungen im gesunden menschlichen Serum, kosmoterrestrischer Sympathismus' *Bioklimat. Beibl. 8* 17, 1941
94. Stolov, Harold L. and Cameron, A.G.W. *Journal of Geophysical Research* 69, 1 December, 1964, pp. 4975-82
95. Nelson, J.H. 'Planetary Position Effect on Short Wave Signal Quality' *Electrical Engineering* 71, 1952, p. 421
96. Burr, H.S. 'Tree Potential and Sunspots' *Cycles* 234, October 1964
97. Gauquelin, M. *The Cosmic Clocks* Peter Owen, 1969
98. Heirtzler, J.R. 'The Longest Electromagnetic Waves' *Scientific American* April 1965
99. Wilson, Charles R. *Journal of Geophysical Research* 74, April 1969, pp. 1812-36
100. Hieber, Lucille C. *Fate* 14 March 1961, p. 122
101. Stephens, R.W.B. *Ultrasonics* 7, January 1969, pp. 30-35
102. Romig, Mary F. and Lamar, Donald L. *Sky and Telescope* 28, October 1964, pp. 214-15
103. Quoted in Mellers, Wilfred *Bach and the Dance of God* Faber & Faber, 1980

104. Oesterley, W.O.E.: Introduction to Charles, R.H. (trans.)
      The Book of Enoch S.P.C.K., 1917
105. Charles, R.H. (trans.) in ref. no. 104
106. Leadbeater, C.W.; *The Masters and the Path*, Theosophical
      Publishing House, Adyar, India, 1925
107. From information in Prophet, Mark and Elizabeth *Climb the
      Highest Mountain* Book 1, Summit University Press, USA,
      1972
108. Miller, Norman Thomas (composer) *The Call of Camelot*
      (see Further Reading (And Listening!) section of the present
      book)
109. Scott, Cyril *The Influence of Music on History and Morals*
      Rider & Company (Hutchinson), 1933 (updated edition:
      ref. no. 5)
110. Eaglefield Hull, A. *Cyril Scott: The Man and His Works*
      Waverly Book Company (undated)
111. Scott, Cyril *The Shadows of Silence and the Songs of Yesterday*
      Donald Fraser, Liverpool
112. Scott, Cyril *The Grave of Eros and The Book of Mournful
      Melodies with Dreams from the East* Donald Fraser,
      Liverpool
113. His Pupil *The Initiate, Some Impressions of a Great Soul*
      Routledge & Kegan Paul, 1920
114. His Pupil *The Initiate in the New World* Routledge &
      Kegan Paul, 1927
115. Scott, Cyril *The Philosophy of Modernism in its Connection
      with Music* Kegan Paul, Trench, Trubner & Company
116. His Pupil *The Initiate in the Dark Cycle,* Routledge & Kegan
      Paul, 1932
117. Scott, Cyril *The Voice of the Ancient* J.M. Watkins, 1910
118. Reichenbach, Baron Karl von *The Mysterious Odic Force*
      (orig. pub. 1844) Aquarian Press 1977
119. Revelation 4:4
120. Revelation 12:3
121. El Morya *The Chela and the Path* Summit University Press,
      USA, 1976
122. Prophet, Elizabeth Clare *The Science of Rhythm for the
      Mastery of the Sacred Energies of Life; Uses and Misuses of the
      Word in the Music of East and West* (see Further Reading
      (And Listening!) section of the present book)
123. Prophet, Mark and Elizabeth *The Science of the Spoken Word*
      (see Further Reading (And Listening!) section of the present
      book)

124.   Isaiah 45:11
125.   Michell, John *City of Revelation* Sphere Books, 1973
126.   1 Chronicles 25
127.   11 Chronicles 5:11-14; 7:1-2, 12-16
128.   Revelation 9:19
129.   Revelation 11:5
130.   Revelation 12:11
131.   Revelation 19:13-15
132.   Revelation 14:2-5

Index